The City of the Gods

A STUDY IN MYTH AND MORTALITY

THE CITY
OF THE
GODS

A Study in Myth and Mortality

JOHN S. DUNNE, C.S.C.

UNIVERSITY OF NOTRE DAME PRESS

Notre Dame, Indiana

University of Notre Dame Press Edition 1978
Copyright © 1965 by John S. Dunne, C.S.C.
Published by arrangement with The Macmillan Company

Library of Congress Cataloging in Publication Data

Dunne, John S.   1929–
   The city of the gods.

   Reprint of the ed. published by Macmillan, New York.
   Includes bibliographical references.
   1. Death—Comparative studies. I. Title.
[BL504.D8 1978]   291.2'3   78-2588
ISBN 0-268-00725-X
ISBN 0-268-00726-8 pbk.

Printed in the United States of America

Preface

The modern man, it has been said, is not any and every man who lives in the present epoch but only the man who lives on the leading edge of contemporary experience.[1] Every epoch will have its modern man according to this definition since the leading edge of experience will be constantly changing like a wave front. The standpoint of the modern man of one epoch, the wave front of experience in that period, will appear to have been merely the myth of that period to the modern man of another·epoch. What we call "myths" at the present time, for instance, are usually expressions of the experience of earlier times, and what we are willing to regard as myths current in our own time are for the most part what we recognize to be survivals or revivals of these earlier myths. It will not be the accessory elements of our own culture which will be regarded as myth in the future, though, but the most important element of it, the measure by which we judge earlier myths to be myths, the standpoint which makes the modern man modern. This thing about which we are most serious, the point of view which constitutes our enlightenment and our emancipation, will appear in coming ages to have been our myth.

There will be an existential truth in every myth, nevertheless, and in our myth too, the truth of the basic attitude toward life and death which the myth reflects, a truth which can be measured, I believe, by the power of the myth to solve what I shall call the "problem of death." In its most general form the problem of death would be this: "If I must some day die, what can I do to satisfy my desire to live?" On the one hand, the man who is not sufficiently conscious of his mortality to pose such a question will hardly be conscious enough to live on the leading edge of human experience. The man who is conscious of his mortality, on the other hand, will almost surely ask himself the equivalent of this question, will know that he must some day die and will be concerned about what he can do to satisfy his desire to live. The answer this second man finds, if he finds one, will then become his standpoint, his philosophy of life and death; this standpoint of his will become in permanent value a nodal point, as it were, in the standing wave of experience; and this philosophy of his, if his consciousness is normative, will become what will afterward be known as the myth of his epoch and his society.

What has suggested to me this method of resolving myths into solutions to the problem of death is the *Epic of Gilgamesh,* the epic of the man who went searching for the means of indefinitely prolonging life. The figure of Gilgamesh is more archaic and more archetypal than the well-known figures of literature associated with the idea of quest, Odysseus, Aeneas, Parsifal, Faust. One indication of this is that where the quest of each of these other figures was successful the quest of Gilamesh was a failure. It is as though the others were seeking only surrogates of what Gilgamesh was seeking, as though Gilgamesh openly sought what man really desires and without which he is dissatisfied until he attains it. Gilgamesh seems to be the image of man in his most ultimate concern, his concern over death, and in the reflection of this archetypal image Odysseus seems to become a more telling image of early classical man, Aeneas a more telling image of late classical man, Parsifal a more telling image of medieval man, and Faust a more telling image of modern man. Each of these figures is the image of what was or what is the modern man of an epoch, the man who lived or who lives on the leading edge of experience in an epoch, but Gilgamesh is the image not only of archaic man but of man himself because we can discern in his stark figure the reason why no standpoint has remained the leading edge of human experience for long.

That I see so much in the figure of Gilgamesh and in the problem of death is undoubtedly due in part to being influenced by contemporary existentialism and especially by Heidegger's ideas that human existence is reality concerned about its own reality, that the concern about reality is ultimately a concern over death, and that human existence is therefore fundamentally a "being towards death." Yet the approach I propose to take here is not equivalent to that of existentialism. On the contrary, the existentialist philosophy of life and death will prove to be a characteristic instance of what I am calling "myth" and defining as solution to the problem of death. Heidegger's interpretation of human existence as "being towards death" will prove to be a characteristically modern formulation of the problem of death, and his understanding of "authentic being towards death" as "freedom towards death" will prove to be a characteristically modern solution to the problem of death.[2] It is typical of the modern myth in its various versions, as we shall see, that the problem of death is conceived to be a problem of alienation, an alienation from life to death, and that the solution to the problem is envisioned to be some form of autonomy, an autonomy with respect to life and death.

In each society and in every epoch, we shall see, the problem of death takes a characteristic form and receives a characteristic solution. In the most ancient civilized societies it took the form of a separation of mortals from the company of the immortals or a separation of the dead from the company of the living which had to be remedied by some sort of intercourse between mortals and immortals or between the dead and the living. In the Greek and Roman republics it took the form of a lapsing of lives into oblivion or a passing of lives with time which had to be remedied by some sort of perpetuation of lives in memory or permanency of lives in deeds. In Roman imperial society it took the form of an untimely cessation of experience which had to be remedied by some sort of uniform and complete course of experience. In feudal society it took the form of an escheat or reversion of lands and titles and status which had to be remedied by some sort of continuance of lands and titles and status through hereditary or other succession. In our own society it takes the form of an alienation of the person from his life in virtue of his liability and subjection to death which has to be remedied by some sort of autonomy with respect to his life in virtue of which his death will become voluntary and free.

I invite the reader of this book to join me in tracing these various solutions to the problem of death, an investigation that will be similar in many respects to the quest of Gilgamesh himself. Our search will range over time instead of distance but we shall be seeking what Gilgamesh was seeking, to learn what ways have been found of circumventing death. Homer said of Odysseus that "he saw the cities of many men and learned their mind."[3] We shall be seeking in our fashion to do just this, to see the cities of many men and learn their mind, only to us the cities of men will be cities of gods more than of men because we shall be seeking like Gilgamesh to learn their mind on life and death and to discover what they have done or tried to do to make themselves immortal. We shall find no fully satisfactory solution to the problem of death, it is true, and thus we shall be no more successful in this respect than was Gilgamesh himself. What we shall learn, nevertheless, about the partial solutions which men have found and what we shall learn about the cause and significance of their failure to find a fully satisfactory solution may make our quest worthwhile and worth recounting.

I am grateful to the Rockefeller Foundation for a grant given in 1960 to do a year of research on the theology of the Hellenic city-state, the matter dealt with in chapters Three, Four, and especially Five of this book. I would like to thank Father Theodore M. Hesburgh, Father Thomas T. McAvoy, Father Chester A. Soleta, Professor Robert Rodes, Professor Frederick J. Crosson, Professor John T. Noonan, and other members of the Notre Dame faculty and the Princeton faculty who have encouraged me all through the research and writing. I am also thankful to the publishers and especially to the editor, Elizabeth Bartelme, for encouraging the work from its first conception and for being so patient with its slow completion.

NOTES TO THE PREFACE

1. Cf. C. G. Jung, *Modern Man in Search of a Soul* (London, 1949), 196 f.

2. Cf. Martin Heidegger, *Being and Time* tr. by John Macquarrie and Edward Robinson (New York, 1962), 303 (*existential* definition of death) and 311 (*existentiell* definition of "authentic being towards death").

The *existential* is meant to be the level of a philosophy of philosophies of life, so to speak, while the *existentiell* is meant to be the level of a simple philosophy of life. By relating the *existential* to the particular version of the problem of death now prevailing I am denying its universality and reducing it to the level of a philosophy of modern philosophies of life.

3. Od. I, 3.

Contents

CHAPTER ONE

The Kings of Erech

FOR God's sake," says Richard II, "let us sit upon the ground and tell sad stories of the death of kings!"[1] It is the death of kings that has been at all times the mystery of sacred kingship. From the first appearance of the king at the dawn of history to his final disappearance in modern times what has invariably decided the meaning of his life has been the answer to the question as to whether or not his existence is bounded by death. If the king must die, as was held in the early days of kingship, then the meaning of his existence is strictly limited. If the king never dies, as was maintained in kingship's latter days, then the meaning of his existence is boundless.

Myth is an interpretation of mystery. The tenets that the king must die and that the king never dies are, both of them, myths. It must not be supposed, though, that the institution of kingship has ever existed independently of the interpretations placed upon it. Rather the institution is the embodiment of the interpretation, the kingship is the enactment of the myth. The king actually does live toward death or toward life according as he understands death or deathlessness to be his destiny.

Kingship as it existed in the ancient Sumerian city-state of Erech makes a particularly advantageous starting point for the study of such myth. A considerable amount of the traditional lore of the Sumerians—practically all the extant epic poetry—has to do with the deeds and sufferings of the kings of this city.[2] There is reason to believe, in fact, that the kingship at Erech became the model of sacred kingship to all Sumer and lay thus at the foundation of the earliest of human civilizations. Above

I

all, the evidence now available on this primordial institution brings to light a rather unexpected interpretation of the death of kings.

[1] *The King Must Live*

The *Epic of Gilgamesh* is the tale of one of the most renowned of the kings of Erech and of his search for a means of indefinitely prolonging his life. Gilgamesh's life, as it is described both in the Akkadian epic and in the earlier Sumerian poems,[3] is an existence orientated toward life rather than death. At first this is owing simply to his unconsciousness of his mortality. Gilgamesh at this stage suffers from the common illusion of being immortal, regarding death as something which happens to people in general not to himself in particular. When this illusion is dissipated at the sight of dead bodies floating on the Euphrates, a second phase of Gilgamesh's life begins in which he sets out to acquire a name and a fame that will live on after his death. This kind of immortality pales, though, when he witnesses the death of Enkidu, his best friend, and a third phase begins in which his whole existence becomes a desperate quest for life everlasting. The eternal life which he seeks in this last stage, moreover, is not life after death but actual deathlessness, an unending existence in this world.

There is a question as to whether such a search for life is a rational possibility for us or whether we are left with the two alternatives, either to face death or to ignore it. If Gilgamesh's quest is not a possibility for us, then something important has happened to man between the past when such an undertaking was thinkable and the present when it is no longer so. The alchemists, who searched not only for a way of transforming base metals into gold and of curing all diseases but also for a means of indefinitely prolonging life, are a proof that such a quest was carried on even in early modern times. There is a good likelihood too that the alchemical ideal of endless life has passed like the other ideals of alchemy into an ideal of modern science. If this is the case, then a quest like that of Gilgamesh is not only a possibility for modern man but is actually, though implicitly and to some extent unconsciously, being carried out by him.

Before we conclude that Gilgamesh's search for life was a perfectly reasonable undertaking, though, we should observe that the quest, according to the ancient traditions, was a failure. Like the voyages undertaken to search for gold and the fountain of youth in the New World, Gilgamesh's quest took the form of a journey to a faraway land. To learn the secret of deathlessness he had to find Utnapishtim,[4] the Akkadian equivalent of Ziusudra, the Sumerian Noah, who had survived the great flood and had been given the gift of eternal life. The gods had put Ziusudra in the land of Dilmun, "the place where the sun rises." It is as though God had placed Noah, after the flood, in the garden of Eden, located like Dilmun in the east at the mouth of the rivers, where he could live perpetually on the fruit of the tree of life. What Gilgamesh learned, however, when he finally met Utnapishtim after a long and adventurous journey toward the sunrise, was that eternal life was a gift of the gods and not something that a man could take for himself. "Who will call the gods to assembly for your sake," Utnapishtim asked him, "that you may find the life which you seek?" Utnapishtim did tell him where to find a plant which would renew his youth, but Gilgamesh had no more than found it when it was stolen from him by a serpent.

The alchemical quest for the means of indefinitely prolonging life was a failure too, we should add, like the quest of Gilgamesh, and it might well be asked whether the scientific search for the same thing will not fail in its turn. We must admit, nevertheless, that if the same ideal of prolonging life has inspired the scientific research of recent times, it has done so in an entirely different manner. There is no longer any search for a philosopher's stone which will enable man to transmute base metals into gold, nor for a panacea which will cure all diseases, nor for an elixir which will give unlimited extension to life. Control over matter and control over life, to be sure, are still very much sought after, but the endeavor is to attain limited objectives within the scope of the universal ideals rather than to attain the universal ideals themselves by limited means. The prolongation of life is sought but not the indefinite prolongation of life by a finitary method. Immortality has become a limit which man hopes to approach ever more closely, it seems, but which he does not seriously hope to attain by human means alone.

Eternal life, we might say, is a mystery, and what we have in the tales told of Gilgamesh is a set of myths the purpose of which is to offer an interpretation of the mystery. The term "mystery" here is not the equivalent of the term "unsolved problem." In this realm what would constitute a problem in the usual sense of the word would be the attainment of a given limited objective within the scope of the universal ideal. The attainment of the universal ideal itself, though, would not be a problem if by "problem" we mean something that in principle should admit of a finite solution. Eternal life, rather than being a soluble but unsolved problem, would be an inexhaustible source of soluble problems. It seems reasonable, therefore, to call eternal life a "mystery" and to call any description of the method by which the gods might go about conferring eternal life upon man a "myth." The myth would not consist in stating that eternal life is something that a man cannot take for himself, something that would have to be given to him if he is to attain it at all. That would be merely the assertion that there is a mystery. Rather it would consist in explaining how eternal life is conferred.

One explanation offered in the *Epic of Gilgamesh* is the well-known myth of the eternal return. The way in which life was thought to be prolonged, according to this standpoint, was by a process of rejuvenation. The plant which Utnapishtim revealed to Gilgamesh was supposed to bring him "new life," to restore his youth, and it did indeed restore the youth of the serpent that stole it from Gilgamesh, for it was supposed to have become the cause why the serpent shed its slough. The bestowal of eternal life upon Utnapishtim himself was associated with a rejuvenation of the whole earth. The flood was conceived to be more a renewal than a catastrophe, a return to the watery chaos from which the world had begun. Utnapishtim, the last man of the old world, became the first man, the Adam, of the new world. Thus he found himself like Adam in a garden of paradise where he could live perpetually on the fruit of a tree of life. Since a process of rejuvenation, if it were indefinitely repeated, seemed able to prolong life indefinitely, the eternal return appeared to explain how man and his world might last forever. A man must eventually die, it seemed, unless his youth be periodically restored. The world too would eventually die of old age, it was thought, if it did not periodically renew itself by returning to its primordial state.

A second explanation of eternal life, somewhat inconsistent with the myth of the eternal return, is what might be termed the myth of perpetual growth. This is apparently the conception that underlies the story of Gilgamesh's expedition into the cedar forest called the Land of the Living[5] at the stage in his life when he was searching merely for a lasting name and not yet for lasting life itself. The forest was called the Land of the Living most likely on account of the evergreen nature of the cedar. Being exempt from the annual cycle of death and rebirth of vegetation, the evergreen tree seemed to possess unending life. The exploits of Gilgamesh in this land, the felling of trees and the killing of a monster named Huwawa who dominated the forest, probably amounted to the destruction of a monopoly on life: the monster and his great evergreen trees were in all likelihood thought to be hoarding up life to themselves. The seemingly unending life of the trees, of course, was not explicable on the myth of the eternal return since the trees were evergreen and apparently not subject to the cycles of nature. Their supposed immortality was rather the embodiment of the idea that death is the result of decline and that decline is not possible as long as there is growth.

The fact that the monster could be killed and the evergreen trees cut down by Gilgamesh, however, would suggest that the myth of perpetual growth is subordinate to a third explanation of eternal life, the myth of destiny, in which not only death from natural causes is excluded but also death by violence or accident. On his deathbed Gilgamesh had a dream in which it was revealed to him that the gods had not destined him to eternal life.[6] To be destined to eternal life would apparently mean to have one's life so arranged by the gods that nothing would ever happen to one that could cause one's death. If it were to be supposed that all death is accidental, that the so-called "natural causes" of death are really accidental causes or perhaps an accumulation of accidental causes, then this explanation would be complete in itself. Among primitive peoples the belief is often encountered that no one dies unless by some means or other he is killed. Actually, the nearest thing to a concept of natural death that is to be found in the tales told of Gilgamesh is the idea that death is the common lot of mankind, that most men are destined to death rather than to eternal life. Death, in other words, was not conceived to be the result of natural causes so much as the outcome of one's destiny.

Closely associated with the myth of destiny there is a fourth explanation of eternal life which might be called the myth of dualism. What Gilgamesh was told on his deathbed was that he had been destined to kingship not to eternal life. The suggestion here is that kingship and eternal life are mutually incompatible alternatives. There is an Akkadian legend about a king of Eridu named Adapa who was given knowledge of the plan of heaven and earth by the god of cunning and who was offered the bread and water of eternal life by the sky god but refused it on the advice of the god of cunning. This story together with an earlier Sumerian tale about the manner in which the god of cunning brought about the end of the golden age in which mankind was under the personal rule of the sky god bear a strong resemblance to the story of Adam's fall.[7] There is an incipient dualism between the sky god and the god of cunning as between Yahweh and the serpent, though it is not carried to the point of an ultimate struggle between good and evil such as we find in the later Iranian myth of Ormazd and Ahriman. There is at the same time a decision to be made by man between the gifts of the two opposing deities, life and knowledge. The end of the personal rule of the sky god in the Sumerian story is equivalent to the beginning of human kingship upon earth. Thus the decision between eternal life and the knowledge of good and evil seems to amount to a decision between eternal life and kingship.

Eternal life appears to be what defined the gods. If one were to ask "Who are the gods?," the answer would have to be "the immortals." Gilgamesh, as a matter of fact, is represented as conceiving his own quest for life to be an attempt to "join the assembly of the gods."[8] If we say that eternal life is a mystery and that explanations of eternal life like the four we have considered are myths, then what are we to say about the idea of a god? Is the idea of a god a mythological conception? If we hold to the distinction between myth and mystery, maintaining that the relation of myth to mystery is analogous to the relation of solution to problem, then we would have to make a distinction between the idea of a god that involves a finitary interpretation of eternal life and one that does not. The former alone would be a mythical god. The gods who are identified by their role in the myth of the eternal return, the myth of perpetual growth, the myth of destiny, and the myth of dualism, therefore, and only such gods as these would be, properly speaking, mythical. The God of whom men were forbidden to make images (Exodus 20:4) would hardly be one of these, even though the same myths were taken over to serve as parables describing his ways with men.

The tales told of Gilgamesh might seem to contain an explicit acknowledgment of mystery in that eternal life is represented in them as something which a man cannot take for himself but which must be given to him if he is to attain it at all. It turns out, though, that the reasons why man cannot achieve eternal life by his own efforts are causes that are mythical in type. Gilgamesh cannot have eternal life because there is no rejuvenation of the earth to occasion the assembly of the gods required for the bestowal of immortality. Or again, he cannot have it because life is hoarded up in the Land of the Living. Or more simply, he cannot have it because he is not destined to it. Or finally, he cannot have it because it is incompatible with kingship. The last reason is the ultimate reason. It is because he was destined to kingship that he was not destined to eternal life. It is because the personal rule of the sky god was brought to an end and replaced by human kingship that there was "evil in the Land." It is because kingship was said to be "taken away" in a flood and afterward again "lowered from heaven" that a king could not participate in a rejuvenation of the earth.[9] The question to be asked and answered, therefore, is why kingship was thought to be incompatible with eternal life.

[2] *The King Must Die*

It is well known that the classical myth of Adonis, the beautiful youth loved by Aphrodite, slain by a wild boar, and on account of the goddess' grief required by the gods to spend only part of the year in Hades, is derived from the Semitic myth of Tammuz, the beloved of the goddess Ishtar, slain before his time, and mourned every year by women even at the temple of Jerusalem in Ezechiel's day. It is further known that the figure of Tammuz is derived from a figure in Sumerian myth, that of Dumuzi, one of the kings of Erech. It has been discovered, however, that Dumuzi, and Tammuz too, originally, was not thought to rise like Adonis from the dead but to have been taken away to the nether world in order to replace his divine mistress so that she could return again to the realm of the living. One could go on to suggest that what was true of Dumuzi was true of all the kings of Erech, that the "descent into the nether world" and "ascent from the nether world" of Innin, the city goddess, were institutions (*me*'s) at Erech,[10] and that each king in turn was thought to be taken when he died to make possible the return of the goddess to the city.

Gilgamesh tried to avoid the fate of the kings of Erech by rejecting Innin's advances and finding some means of indefinitely prolonging his life. When Innin became enamored of him and made an attempt to seduce him, he spurned her. In fact, in the later Akkadian epic he is made not only to spurn the goddess, now replaced by her Semitic counterpart Ishtar, but to launch into a tirade about the fate of her previous lovers.[11] The occasion for this was that by the time the epic was being composed the kingship at Erech had become the model of sacred kingship in Mesopotamia and the death of the king of whatever city enjoyed hegemony in the whole land had come to be interpreted in the same manner as the death of the king of Erech had been. So Gilgamesh was represented as describing in metaphor five of the more famous of Ishtar's "shepherds," kings who had been her consorts, and the sorry ends to which they came. He concluded with the observation that should he become her lover he would fare no better than they.

It appears to have been the desire to taste death as a kind of ultimate experience that was supposed to have led the goddess to descend into the nether world. She is said, in the opening lines of the poem describing her descent, to have "set her mind towards the great below," towards the land of the dead, exactly as Gilgamesh was said to have "set his mind towards the Land of the Living."[12] She is like Eve in her desire for the knowledge of good and evil, the fruit of the tree which brings death. Eve had to be reassured by the serpent that she would not die but would become like a god knowing good and evil before she would taste the fruit. The goddess, in like manner, made certain of her own resurrection by message to the god of cunning, the counterpart of the serpent, before she entered the land of the dead. Once in the underworld she was seized, stripped, brought in before Ereshkigal, queen of the dead, and put to death. For three days and three nights her naked corpse hung upon a stake projecting from a wall, until she was revived again through the machinations of the god of cunning. She was released from the nether world, however, only on condition that she provide someone to take her place. Like Eve having her husband taste the fruit of the deadly tree, the goddess chose her mate, the king, to share her experience of death, and had him carried away to the land of the dead.

The question has been asked whether or not it makes sense to speak, as we often do, of "tasting death," as though death were something that could be experienced. "Death," it has been said, "is not an event of life. Death is not lived through." One could never taste death, it would seem, for to experience anything one would have to exist. "Our life," it has been said, "is endless in the way that our visual field is without limit."[13] We cannot see at infinite distances, yet we do not perceive any horizon in the sky overhead such as we see on the curved surface of the earth. Our life, according to this standpoint, though finite would be unbounded, for there could be no boundary that would be accessible to experience. The desire to taste death which we find expressed in the story of the goddess' descent to the nether world would be, from this point of view, altogether vain. If death were the same as nonexistence, we must indeed agree, then one could no more experience it than one could experience not being. If death is not assumed to be absolute nonexistence, however, then there might well be some sense in the idiomatic phrase "to taste death."

The descent of the goddess to the nether world seems to be inconsistent with the common conception of the gods according to which they are the immortals. It seems to suggest instead an idea of the gods along the lines of the story of Adam and Eve where they are said to be those who know good and evil. Actually, the two notions do not coexist in the ancient traditions through an oversight. One can fully understand eternal life only if one fully understands death. The "hows" of eternal life correspond to the "whys" of death much as the "hows" of a cure correspond to the "whys" of a disease. To possess eternal life in one's own right and not merely as a gift from another it is necessary to have that comprehensive understanding of life the other side of which is an equally comprehensive understanding of death. There is reason to believe that the object of eating the fruit of the tree of knowledge was to learn which tree was the tree of life. After Adam's sin God said, "Behold Adam has become as one of us knowing good and evil; now he has only to put forth his hand and take the fruit of the tree of life and he will live forever" (Genesis 3:22). The conception underlying the story of the descent and ascent of the goddess seems to be the more elementary conviction that one acquires the understanding of life and death through the actual experience of death.

Besides the question as to whether an experience of death is possible at all, another question pertinent for us has been raised as to whether a vicarious experience of death is possible. For the king to die meant for the king to share the experience of the goddess, to become like the goddess knowing good and evil. The manner in which the king's death appears to have been taken by the city would suggest that the king's experience of death was the occasion for a vicarious experience of death on the part of the populace. In the lamentation over the death of a king the city is described as a "sheepfold given to the wind," the same phrase which is used in the lamentation over the destruction of a city.[14] The fervor of later lamentations over Tammuz and Adonis may be an indication of the original intensity of this public experience. The king himself by tasting death became like a god knowing good and evil, and in this capacity was often conceived to become king of the nether world. Dominion over the nether world was conferred, it would seem, when Ereshkigal, queen of the dead, placed in the hands of the dead ruler the "tablet of wisdom."[15] By vicarious experience of the king's death the populace was probably thought to attain some participation in this wisdom.

It has been said that death is a strictly private affair and that a genuine anticipation of death could not arise in an interpersonal experience like assisting at the death of another but only in some exclusively personal experience like being condemned to death.[16] Assistance at another's death could at best be only an occasion for the solitary experience that is required, according to this point of view, to free one from the illusion of being immortal oneself while others die. The king's death, however, was certainly not conceived in the early civilizations to be a private act. Yet there seems to be no reason to say that it was any less a personal experience on the part of each person involved for being at the same time interpersonal. According to the view that death is strictly a private matter, when one man dies for another, he dies for the other only in some particular role such that the other is still left with his own death to die. This can readily be conceded. But it follows that assisting at the death of another who is dying for oneself would be all the more an interpersonal experience in which one's own death is anticipated. To assist at such a death is to assist at the putting off of one's own death and thus to perceive one's own death as something which the future holds in store.

The great myths were the formulation of the knowledge of life

and death which was thought to be gained in this sort of experience. The knowledge which was supposed to be acquired by the
king himself in the experience of death was essentially a knowledge of the decrees of fate. The "tablet of wisdom" which was
given to him when he became king of the nether world, or which
in any case belonged to the ruler of the dead, was thought to
have inscribed upon it the hour of everyman's death.[17] What we
have set forth for us in the myth of destiny is the participation
in this wisdom which was believed to be obtained by everyone
in the sharing of the king's death through sympathetic experience. Each man had his hour of death fixed for him by the decrees of destiny, an hour unknown to him until such time as it
was revealed to him in dream or in the actual experience of his
own death. The wisdom that he could acquire in the vicarious
experience of death was not an exact knowledge of his own fate
but simply a knowledge that he too must die. The dream, however, being an anticipatory experience of death, could be a complete revelation of his fate.[18] It was in a dream that Gilgamesh
learned that he was destined to kingship and not to eternal life.
Kingship, from this standpoint, was called a *bala,* a limited tenure
the term of which was fixed according to the decrees of destiny.

The literal meaning of the word *bala,*[19] namely "reversion" or
"return to origin," suggests the myth of the eternal return. At the
end of the king's life the authority which he had enjoyed reverted
once more to the civic assembly which had originally bestowed
it upon him and thus in some sense it reverted to the assembly
of the gods which was thought to make itself felt through the
assembly of men. A more radical reversion to the assembly of the
gods was conceived to occur when the kingship of a given city
which enjoyed hegemony in Sumer was transferred through the
fortunes of war to another city. The ultimate reversion was supposed to take place when human kingship was swept from the
face of the earth in the deluge that brought the earth back to
its original state so that afterward kingship had to be "lowered
from heaven" once again as it had been in the beginning of the
world. Meanwhile, as kingship itself reverted to the gods who had
conferred it upon man in the first place, the human beings who

had been in possession of kingship were said to have "returned to clay." The eternal return, in this fashion, was at once the "how" of eternal life and the "why" of death. If man should ask why it is that he must die, he is answered "Dust thou art and unto dust thou shalt return."

While kingship was a fate, a destiny to death, there was a kind of immortality which the king could attain, an immortality associated in the Sumerian version of the myth of perpetual growth with the evergreen forest known as the Land of the Living. Gilgamesh, having come to the realization of his own mortality at the sight of dead bodies floating on the Euphrates, decides that before he meets his destined end he will set up his "name" in the Land of the Living in the places "where the names have been raised" and in the places "where the names have not been raised" he will set up the "names" of the gods. It could be that he meant by this that he intended to raise physical monuments to himself and to the gods. The Land of the Living would have been the place to do this because its evergreens seemed to be independent of the cycles of the eternal return. In the Akkadian epic, however, we are given to understand that Gilgamesh will have made himself a "name" even if he should die in his attempt to overcome the monster who rules the forest, for men would tell ever after of the heroism of his death.[20] Every king, it seems, was assured of some degree of immortality in this last sense on the ground that his death would be experienced vicariously by his people. He would live on for this reason in the memory of mankind and, like the evergreen, escape the cycle of decay.

Such immortality as this, though, would hardly be enough to make kingship an alternative preferable to eternal life as would seem to be supposed in the myth of dualism according to which man chooses the gift of the god of cunning in preference to that of the sky god. What makes the choice of kingship intelligible is the knowledge of life and death which the experience of the king's death purports to confer. Whether we take the myth of dualism to mean that man himself knowingly preferred kingship to eternal life or whether we take it to mean that the god of cunning deceived man into making such a choice, the value of the alternative which was actually chosen seems to lie in this: that through the experience of death man can obtain the knowledge of life and death that will enable him to possess eternal life in his own right like the gods. The sky god himself, according to the Sumerian mythological tradition, descended at one time to the nether world,[21] and the goddess of the city, as we have seen, was thought to descend periodically to the land of the dead and to return as often to the land of the living. In choosing between the tree of life and the tree of knowledge, therefore, man was choosing between eternal life as a purely gratuitous gift of the sky god and eternal life to be possessed in his own right as the sky god possessed it himself. What man chose was to be like the gods knowing good and evil.

NOTES TO CHAPTER ONE

1. Shakespeare, *Richard II*, III, ii, 155 f.

2. The chief human figures in extant Sumerian epic are Enmerkar, Lugalbanda, Dumuzi, and Gilgamesh, all kings of Erech.

3. English renditions of most of the relevant texts are available in J. B. Pritchard, *Ancient Near Eastern Texts* (Princeton, 1955) where the Akkadian epic is translated by E. A. Speiser and the Sumerian poems by S. N. Kramer.

4. Ziusudra is the name of the flood hero in the Sumerian tale (Pritchard, *op. cit.,* 42ff.) but in the Akkadian epic which alone contains the story of Gilgamesh's encounter with him he is called Utnapishtim (*ibid.,* 88ff.). That he lives in Dilmun "where the sun rises" is stated only in the Sumerian poem, but Gilgamesh's journey "along the road of the sun" in the Akkadian poem could be an eastward journey, retracing the steps of the sun, especially since he encounters the sun-god after walking in dense darkness, rather than a westward one as Speiser argues (*ibid.,* 89, n. 152).

5. This is its name in the Sumerian tale (Pritchard, *op. cit.,* 47ff.). In the Akkadian epic it is called the Cedar Forest (*ibid.,* 78-83).

6. The Sumerian tale in which this event is narrated (Pritchard, *op. cit.,* 50 ff.) is not reproduced in the Akkadian epic.

7. The Akkadian tale of Adapa is translated in Pritchard, *op. cit.,* 101 ff. The tablet containing the Sumerian tale of the golden age is reproduced on the frontispiece of Kramer's *Sumerian Mythology* (Philadelphia, 1944).

8. Pritchard, *op. cit.,* 88 and 93.

9. Kingship "taken away" in the flood, Pritchard, *op. cit.,* 44; "lowered from heaven" after the flood, *ibid.,* 265. Utnapishtim obtained eternal life but he first renounced his kingship before the assembly and the elders of his city, *ibid.,* 93.

10. Kramer, *op. cit.,* 66.

11. Pritchard, *op. cit.,* 83 f.

12. Compare the beginning of the poem describing Innin's journey to the land of the dead, Pritchard, *op. cit.*, 53, with the beginning of the poem describing Gilgamesh's journey to the Land of the Living, *ibid.*, 48.

13. Both of the statements cited above are from Ludwig Wittgenstein's *Tractatus Logico-Philosophicus* (London, 1922), 6.4311.

14. Compare the lamentation over Dumuzi in A. L. Oppenheim, *The Interpretation of Dreams in the Ancient Near East* (Philadelphia, 1956), 246, with the lamentation over the destruction of Ur in Pritchard, *op. cit.*, 455 f.

15. Gilgamesh was thought to have become king of the nether world according to Stephen Langdon, *Semitic Mythology* (Boston, 1931), 235, and so apparently was Tammuz, to judge from the last lines of the Akkadian poem describing the descent of Ishtar to the nether world, Pritchard, *op. cit.*, 109. The tablet of wisdom was the means by which dominion over the nether world was conferred in the Akkadian tale of Nergal and Ereshkigal, *ibid.*, 104.

16. Cf. Heidegger, *op. cit.*, 281 ff. Note that Heidegger considers his existential analysis of death particularly relevant for the analysis of myth, magic, and ritual, *ibid.*, 291 f. and 361.

17. Langdon, *op. cit.*, 161.

18. Cf. Oppenheim, *op. cit.*, 212 ff., on the death dreams of Dumuzi and Enkidu.

19. For relevant instances of the use of this word see Thorkild Jacobsen in *Journal of Near Eastern Studies* II (1943), 170, n. 66.

20. Cf. Pritchard, *op. cit.*, 48 (the Sumerian account of the "name") and 79 (the Akkadian account).

21. Kramer, *op. cit.*, 43 ff.

CHAPTER TWO

The Kingdom of the Two Lands

THE nature of a society, it could be argued, is decided by the relationship which obtains in that society between the living and the dead. In a modern progressive society or in a modern revolutionary society the relationship will be fairly negative, will consist, in fact, in the independence of the living from the dead,[1] but it will be none the less decisive, for it will be this relationship of independence which the living have towards the dead that will make the society progressive or revolutionary. In a classical society like the one supposed in the *Antigone* of Sophocles the relationship of the living to the dead will be a more positive one and will be the source of independence in another direction, independence from the rulers of the living,[2] the sort of independence Antigone asserted when she performed the funeral rites over the body of her brother Polynices against the command of her uncle Creon, king of Thebes. In an ancient society like that of Mesopotamia and especially that of Egypt the relationship will be still more positive and will no longer be the source of independence either of the living from the dead or of the living from the living but will be the source of the greatest conceivable interdependence among the living and the dead. It is the society of this last type, and particularly that of ancient Egypt where the very division of the kingdom into the two lands, Upper and Lower Egypt, was probably meant to symbolize its division into the land of the living and the land of the dead,[3] that we must examine to discover the full possibilities latent in the relationship between the living and the dead.

[1] *The Land of the Dead*

The pyramids, particularly the great ones at Giza, are the standing witness to the Egyptian concern over life after death. In order to defend the Egyptians against the criticism of being morbidly occupied with the thought of death it has been argued that the evidence we have of their culture is one-sided, that the materials concerned with death and the next world were preserved in the desert sands while materials dealing with life in this world have decayed in the fertile and alluvial soil of the Nile valley. Before rushing to the defence or the attack, though, we should perhaps examine our own assumptions on morbidity. It might be that the man who faces death squarely is saner than the one who attempts to ignore death. It might also be that the man who faces it with hope is able to face it with more sanity than the one who faces it without hope. It could well be that the stability of Egyptian culture, its persistence for better than two millennia, its ability to recover twice from the kind of downfall that destroyed other civilizations, is not unrelated to the fact that the Egyptian could face death squarely and face it with good hope and had no need to repress the thought of death in order to be happy.

To be sure, the Egyptian was capable of losing his hope for life after death and of attempting as a consequence to forget death by immersing himself in the pleasures of life. "The Song of the Harper,"[4] a poem dating from after the first downfall of Egyptian civilization, is an invitation to do just this. The reasons advanced are that it is not given to a man to take his property with him into the afterlife and that there is not one who departs this life who comes back again. If one cannot take one's worldly goods with one, then one must make the most of them now while one still has them. If no one who departs ever comes back again, then nothing really is known about the life after death. No one knows the state or the needs of those who are in the land of the dead, and no one will know until he has gone there himself. Each Pharaoh in the early period had taken up residence near the site chosen for his tomb, where, during the better part of his lifetime, the work on the pyramid and its temple continued. The harper's advice, though, was to forget about one's tomb and the care of one's body after death and enjoy life while one was still in possession of it.

This was the counsel offered to the man who debated with his own soul the question of suicide. The famous "Dispute over Suicide,"[5] as a matter of fact, probably comes out of the same epoch of disillusionment as the "Song of the Harper." The prospective suicide, however, rejects the life of pleasure on the grounds that to embrace it would bring his name into evil odor. The appeal of death to him is that the men of his day are such that there is no one to whom he can speak, that death can only be a liberation, and above all that the dead are actually supposed to be as gods. The customary way of describing the death of an important person was to say that he had "become a god." The suicide tells his soul that one who is in the realm of the dead will be a living god, punishing the sin of the sinner, standing in the bark of the sun as it nightly crosses the nether world sky, and engaging in wise converse with the sun-god himself. If the dead are indeed as gods, then death is something that can positively be desired. The soul of the suicide therefore relinquishes the prospect of a carefree life and accepts the idea of death, even the death by fire which he has been contemplating.

To what extent one's personal identity was supposed to be conserved in this kind of immortality is not immediately evident. For to "become a god" at death meant specifically to become the god Osiris.[6] This god was originally the one with whom the deceased king was identified and in this capacity was ruler of the dead. But gradually all the dead, kings and commoners alike, came to be confounded with Osiris so that it was not easy to maintain the god's position of authority over the dead except in his role as the judge who admitted the newly dead to the nether world—since any of the dead could be conceived to be a king in this manner, receiving the just and excluding the sinner. Besides his nether world kingship, though, Osiris had another role, that of being the vegetation and the growing grain. His own death in view of this was said to have been a death by drowning, as the vegetation seems to emerge every year from a watery grave after the annual inundation of the Nile. To become Osiris the vegetation and the growing grain, however, would seem to involve an even greater loss of personal identity than to become Osiris the ruler of the nether world.

There is a striking analogy between this ancient belief in a dead god of nature and the modern belief in a dead God of history. The statement "God himself is dead," the paradoxical formulation of modern atheism as belief in a dead God, meant in its original context of dialectical idealism that both the personal God and his individual incarnation are abolished in a Calvary from which there emerges the autonomous human spirit, the "absolute spirit."[7] This Calvary, it is true, is a moment in the history of the human spirit, the moment when man abandons his faith in the personal God and in the incarnation of this God, abandons his hope of being delivered from death by a power outside of himself, and experiences the autonomy of his own spirit in the face of death. If one were to exchange the idea of a history of the human spirit for the idea of a natural cycle of the human spirit, though, then one would pass directly from this modern vision of the death of God to the archaic vision of the death of the god. Instead of the God of history being abolished once and for all in his unique historical incarnation, the god of nature would be periodically abolished in his successive incarnations. Instead of the universal spirit making its unique appearance in the course of history, it would be making its seasonal appearance in the course of nature.

Once upon a time, according to the myth of Osiris, the dead god had been a living god embodied in a living king. This king, however, was not the present king but the past king. If one asks about the past king, then neither was he Osiris while he was alive but rather Osiris was his predecessor. The time at which Osiris was alive continually recedes as one inquires further into the past. In every present time the god is dead. The tale that Osiris was once alive, thus, is evidently not supposed to have the same kind of validity and relevance as the tale that Osiris is dead. The one tale purports to possess a kind of prehistoric truth, the other an eternal truth. As for the reigning Pharaoh, when he died he would be said to become Osiris, and Osiris would be said to have been murdered by Set, his adversary. So it was that both the god and his human embodiment were always destroyed with the same blow. What then emerged was the universal spirit of life manifest in the vegetation and the growing corn.

When a man dies he becomes, according to this conception, an *akh*, a "transfigured spirit." The word *akh* as an adjective refers to utility and glory, as a noun it is often translated "effective personality."[8] Although the suggestion of personal immortality contained in the latter rendering is probably misleading, if one were to distinguish here between the person and the individual, one would be close to the truth. For while individuality seems to be lost in death as the Egyptians conceived it, the person might be said to survive if one understands the person to be a spirit that can exist in a less particularized manner than it does when it is incarnated in a human individuality. It is true that the dead were spoken of in the plural *akhu*, "transfigured spirits," especially when they were referred to as the "followers of Horus," the supporters, that is, of the living king who was identified with the god Horus.[9] This plurality, nevertheless, was an anonymous collectivity consisting of all the dead who had become Osiris. It was a universal spiritual force operative in the living king and in the world he ruled with its recurrent seasons of drought, inundation, and growth.

Life after death, from this point of view, did not mean surviving in one's own right so much as surviving vicariously in the living. One of the names of Osiris was Wennofer, "he who lives anew," the significance of which seems to have been that Osiris while dead in himself yet lived anew in his son, Horus, who took his place in the land of the living.[10] When the burial practices were extended to others besides the kings, the idea of living in one's successor was extended as well. A man had no hope of an afterlife, it seems, unless he had a survivor to stand at the grave on the day of burial and to maintain the care of his tomb. The survivor assured continued contacts of the dead with the living, contacts by which the dead enjoyed and appropriated the life of the living. No such contacts existed for the man who did not have a survivor or who was not properly cared for after his death.[11] What these contacts did was to link what remained of the man's individuality, his mummy, to the life of the living. Their purpose, clearly enough, was to prevent the passing of his individual identity into total oblivion.

This idea of vicarious life which we find among the ancient Egyptians is not unlike what has been called "objective immortality" and defined as "the appropriation of the dead by the living."[12] Objective immortality is a notion that is meant to mediate between the idea of personal immortality and that of impersonal immortality, though to one accustomed to the Christian hope of a personal life after death it will appear altogether impersonal, "objective" as indeed it is termed rather than "subjective." The simplest analogy would be the common notion of the dead surviving in the memory of the living. If one were to substitute a divine memory for the ordinary human memory envisioned in the common notion, and if one were to attribute this divine memory not to a God that transcends the world but to one that is wholly immanent in the world, then one would obtain a notion similar to that of objective immortality. Death, from such a standpoint, would be the end of one's subjective existence. What would remain after one's death would be the trace of one's life in the living spirit immanent in all other subjective existences. Though divested of one's own living immediacy, one would become a real component in other living immediacies.

The "appropriation of the dead by the living" is in many respects a fair description of the relationship that obtained between the living and the dead in ancient Egypt. "The Song of the Harper" and the "Dispute over Suicide" represent attitudes that diverge from the normal Egyptian outlook by making the existence of the dead independent of the existence of the living, the harper seeking in this an escape from concern about death and the suicide an escape from the burden of life. In the usual point of view the existence of the dead would have been inconceivable apart from the existence of the living. The myth that the dead are gods was only the other side of the myth that the god is dead. Like its modern counterpart, though against an entirely different background, the ancient myth of the dead god has the effect of denying that there is any life other than the life that is lived in this world. If the dead live, it is only because they participate in their way in the life of the living. In one sense the dead are only mummies deprived of the spirit of life, but in another sense they are the departed spirit of life now immanent in the living and in the live world.

[2] *The Land of the Living*

Where the dead king was said to be Osiris, the king of the dead, the living king was said to be Horus, the king of the living.[13] There may be some connection, as a matter of fact, between the Egyptian idea of the Living Horus and the Biblical idea of the Living God. The final and most remarkable statement of the latter, the one which occurs in the argument of Jesus with the Sadducees over the Resurrection,[14] is the very one which appears to parallel the structure of the Egyptian notion most closely. There Jesus argues against the Sadducees, a conservative sect which received only the more strictly Mosaic portions of the Bible and which was therefore unwilling to accept the doctrine of the Resurrection, that God was said to be the God of Abraham, Isaac, and Jacob, patriarchs who were presumably dead, and yet was said to be the God of the living not the God of the dead. If Yahweh is the God of the living and not of the dead, then Abraham, Isaac, and Jacob would apparently be among the living and not among the dead. Thus, since the Bible records their respective deaths, they must be risen from the dead or at least marked out for resurrection.

The argument, amazingly enough, seems to have silenced the Sadducees and brought Jesus the congratulations of some of the scribes. Its force lay in its appeal to an idea characteristic of the tradition in the Hebrew religious heritage which the Sadducees themselves accepted. This is the tradition which also bears most unmistakably the imprint of ancient Egypt. It contains, of course, the story of the sojourn in Egypt and the exodus of the Hebrew people under the leadership of Moses. More than this, though, there are among its leitmotifs ideas that show considerable affinity to notions that were natively Egyptian. The idea that Yahweh is the Living God and the God of the living not only corresponds to the idea of the Living Horus who is king of the living, but fits into a total perspective similar to that of Egypt in which the existence of the dead is a participation in the existence of the living. Human life, as the Sadducees rightly contended, was confined in this tradition to the earth with no thought of an immortality of the soul or a resurrection of the body. As the hope of the Pharaohs was to participate in the existence of their successors, the hope of the patriarchs was to participate in the existence of their posterity.

There is a point, nevertheless, to the argument of Jesus, for the Living God of the Hebrews was not immanent in a king and in the world in the same manner as was the Living Horus of the Egyptians. The belief in a living god who is radically immanent is a complete solution to the problem of life after death. When one relegates this quality of being a living god to an entity that transcends the world and man, though, one simultaneously renders the immanentist solution to the problem of the afterlife untenable. What Jesus did was point out the resulting vacuum in the Mosaic tradition which had to be filled with the later idea of the Resurrection. The concluding statement in Luke's version of the argument, "all are alive to him," actually completes the solution to the problem of death on the supposition of a transcendent God in a way that parallels the original Egyptian solution for an immanent god. The dead Pharoah is alive to the Living Horus in that there is in the living king the power to live (the *ka*) which originally quickened the dead king. The dead patriarch is alive to the Living God in that there is in Yahweh the will and the power to raise the patriarch from the dead.

The parallel between the Living God and the Living Horus, to be sure, is not as equivocal as a simple contrast of immanence and transcendence might make it appear. The Living Horus was not so thoroughly incarnate in the Pharaoh that he could not also be regarded as the falcon god of the sky. Neither was the Living God of the Bible so thoroughly the God of the heavens that he could not be thought to have come down to earth and become incarnate in Jesus. The same is true for the parallel between the dead God and the dead Osiris. The Living Horus necessarily gave rise to the dead Osiris since the spirit of life had to be conceived as continually losing its identity through the destruction of its ephemeral human embodiments. In like manner, once the Living God of the Old Testament was believed to have become incarnate in the Christ of the New Testament a destruction of his identity became conceivable too. Because his original identity, though, was independent of his incarnation, the destruction of identity could not be conceived to occur through the physical death of Jesus but only through the spiritual death of denial in the collective mind. The gulf between the Living Horus and the Living God of Christianity, therefore, is as wide and no wider than the gulf between the dead Osiris and the dead God of modern atheism.

The idea that all things are alive to God, specifically the Johannine idea that all things are life in the Logos,[15] seems to be foreshadowed to some degree in the Egyptian conception of the creator-god Ptah and in the corresponding identification of the Pharaoh with Ptah as the Lord of the Two Lands. Ptah was termed "the heart and tongue of the gods," that is, the mind and speech of the gods, the rational principle in the universe like the logos of the Hellenistic philosophy and theology. The idea that the world was created through the thought and word of Ptah replaced an earlier and more primitive notion that the world was created through the physical action of Atum, either an act of self-pollution or else of self-dismemberment. In the latter version, however, there is already an approach to the heart and tongue doctrine in that Atum dismembers by naming the parts of his body.[16] The heart and tongue of the gods was lodged in the Pharaoh according to the doctrine of the Pharaoh's *sia,* "perception" or "understanding," and *hu,* "authoritative utterance" or "creative command."[17] Here the concrete terms are replaced by the corresponding abstract terms. What was communicated through the heart and tongue of the gods and thus through the speech of the Pharaoh, was *maat*, "truth." This is what the gods were said to live on and is what a man would claim to live on when he was protesting his innocence. Truth was reality in the Egyptian worldview, and reality was life.

How one evaluates a logos doctrine will depend largely on the nihilistic or positivistic character of one's presuppositions, "positivism" meaning here the acknowledgement of irrational fact and "nihilism" meaning not "the denial of what exists" (a definition that can only mean "the erroneous denial of what I rightly consider to exist") but rather the denial of irrational fact and the contention that the rational alone is real. From a positivistic standpoint a logos doctrine, since it is the affirmation of a rational principle in the universe, will appear to be a piece of mythology, a rationalization of the irrational. From a nihilistic standpoint, on the contrary, a logos doctrine will appear to be a necessity of reason—thus, for example, Hegel's conviction that the subject matter of logic should be the logos. A third standpoint seems to be suggested in the Christian doctrine of a logos that is transcendent and that becomes immanent in the world through incarnation, for over and above the dichotomy of the rational and the irrational this doctrine introduces the third category of the suprarational, the category which we have been calling "mystery."

How one evaluates the specific version of the logos which originated in ancient Egypt and which holds the historical primacy among logos doctrines besides depending on one's general assumptions about the rational and the irrational will depend on how literally one takes the "heart and tongue" terminology. If we disregard the possibility of a crude literalism in the Egyptian viewpoint, a possibility which is not very probable in view of the more abstract *sia* and *hu* terminology, we still find a marked contrast between the immanence of the original Egyptian logos and the transcendence of the Logos in Christianity. The lodging of the heart and tongue of the gods in the Pharaoh is not the incarnation of a transcendent logos so much as the emergence of a logos that is already immanent. The Egyptian idiom for this was "to appear as a god," the phrase used to describe the accession

of a new king.[18] The purport of such language seems to have
been that the god became manifest in a person in whom he had
previously been latent. The transition was less from transcendence
to immanence than from a concealed to a manifest immanence.

The symbolism of emergence is carried through in a vivid manner in the identification of the Pharaoh with the creator-god
Atum-Re. When the floodwaters of the Nile begin to subside,
little hillocks of mud appear as the first promise of yearly life.
Thus, too, when the primeval waters of Nun subsided, the
primordial hillock of earth, from which all things have come
forth, was supposed to have appeared. This hillock, Atum, is represented by a hieroglyph which shows a rounded mound with
the rays of the sun streaming upward from behind it—hence the
conjunction of Atum with the sun-god Re.[19] A new Pharaoh appears as a god like the rising sun or like the emerging hillock.
What emerges in the Pharaoh, who obviously existed as a human
being before he became Pharaoh, is something immanent, the
rational principle in the universe, the heart and tongue of the
gods. This luminous principle is again enveloped in darkness,
again immersed in the water of chaos, when the Pharaoh dies
and becomes the drowned Osiris, only to reappear once more
when the dead king's successor becomes the Living Horus. The
rational principle in the universe was thus alternately manifest
and hidden. In its hidden state it could be identified with the
god Amon, the "hidden one," who came into prominence in the
later history of Egypt. In its manifest state, on the other hand,
it could be identified with Aton, the sun-disk, who became the
subject of a remarkable religious revolution in the New Kingdom.

The Pharaoh Amenhotep IV changed his name to Akhenaton,
moved his capital from Thebes to Tell el Amarna, and attempted
to make Aton the supreme and only god of Egypt. The Amarna
Revolution, however, seems to have been not a rebellion against
polytheism but a reaction against what Akhenaton took to be
obscurantism. The main target was Amon, the Hidden One, and
the contending god was Aton, the least hidden of all possible
divinities, the blazing disk of the sun.[20] The object of the revolution was apparently to make the rational principle in the uni-

verse out to be something as plain as the light of day. Hence the crudely realistic conception of truth and the naturalistic style of art which prevailed under Akhenaton. Far from being an advance in the direction of monotheism and transcendence Akhenaton's religion appears to have been a recession from the sense of mystery toward a very naïve mythological consciousness. Atonism was shortlived, however, for Akhenaton's successor restored Amon, and Egypt never again departed from its fundamental religious standpoint as long as the New Kingdom lasted.

The concealed immanence of Amon is the closest thing we find to a conception of mystery and transcendence in the perspectives of ancient Egypt. This hiddenness of his,[21] though, is the dark phase in the myth of the eternal return when chaos prevails to be followed by the bright phase in which the rational principle in the universe is made manifest. It is the indeterminate phase in the myth of destiny when the lifetimes of men can be lengthened or shortened to be followed by the determinate phase in which the fates are declared. It is the negative phase in the myth of dualism when the king is dead and Osiris is overcome by Set to be followed by the positive phase in which the new king lives and Set is overcome by Horus. It is the impersonal phase in the myth of perpetual vitality when the immanent spirit of life has lost its old identity in the old king to be followed by the personal phase in which it gains a new identity in the new king. In the figure of Amon-Re where the dark phase represented by the hidden god Amon is combined with the bright phase represented by the sun-god Re it becomes evident that one same spirit is supposed to be the subject of both phases. As a consequence there is a final unanimity in the dialectic of mythological thinking between the god who is alive and the god who is dead.

NOTES TO CHAPTER TWO

1. Cf. Chapter Nine, Section 3.
2. Cf. Chapter Seven, Section 2.
3. Egypt was called the Kingdom of the Two Lands, the united realm, that is, of Upper and Lower Egypt. It is improbable, though, that Lower Egypt ever existed as a political unit prior to its incorporation into the

dominion of Upper Egypt. It has been surmised instead that the significance of the designation is to be sought in some sort of dualistic symbolism. Since Lower Egypt in the traditional Egyptian foundation myth is treated as the land of Osiris, the king of the dead, it might plausibly be taken to stand for the land of the dead, while Upper Egypt could accordingly be taken to stand for the land of the living.

On the nonpragmatic origin of the two-land symbolism cf. H. Frankfort, *The Birth of Civilization in the Ancient Near East* (London, 1951), 78 ff. The foundation myth is the so-called Theology of Memphis for which cf. Pritchard, *op. cit.*, 4 ff. Note that in spite of the titles in the present chapter nothing depends essentially on my highly conjectural interpretation of the two-land symbolism.

4. Pritchard, *op. cit.*, 467.

5. Ibid., 405 ff.

6. On Osiris cf. Frankfort, *Kingship and the Gods* (Chicago, 1948), 181 ff.

7. Cf. Hegel, *The Phenomenology of Mind* tr. by J. B. Baillie (London, 1961), 753 and 782. Cf. my discussion of this in Chapter Nine, Section 1.

8. J. A. Wilson, *The Burden of Egypt* (Chicago, 1951), 67 f.

9. Frankfort, *Kingship and the Gods*, 90 f.

10. This interpretation is substantiated by the fact that Osiris is said to be the *ka,* the vital potency, of Horus. Cf. Frankfort, *Kingship and the Gods*, 114, 133, 135, 199.

11. Cf. the discussion of this point in the "Dispute over Suicide," Pritchard, *op. cit.*, 406. Also, cf. Frankfort, *Kingship and the Gods*, 110, 132-139, 362 (nn. 8 and 10), 377 (n. 14).

12. A. N. Whitehead, *Process and Reality* (New York, 1929), ix.

13. On the king as Horus cf. Frankfort, *Kingship and the Gods*, 36ff.

14. Mt. 22:32 f.; Mk. 12:26 f.; Lk. 20:37 ff. On the evolution of Hebrew thought on life after death cf. R. Martin-Achard, *De la mort à la Résurrection d'après l'ancien Testament* (Neuchâtel, 1956).

15. Jn. 1:3-4. The same idea is at least suggested in the common alternative reading of the passage. Cf. also I Jn. 1:1 on the "logos of life."

16. For a discussion of these various creation accounts cf. Wilson, *op. cit.*, 58 ff., and his translation in Pritchard, *op. cit.*, 3-5.

17. On *hu, sia,* and *maat* cf. Wilson in Frankfort, *The Intellectual Adventure of Ancient Man* (Chicago, 1946), 83 f., and Frankfort, *Kingship and the Gods*, 51.

18. E.g. cf. Pritchard, *op. cit.*, 418 (the instruction of King Amenemhet to his successor).

19. Wilson in Frankfort, *The Intellectual Adventure of Ancient Man*, 51.

20. Cf. Wilson's Translation of the "Hymn to the Aton" in Pritchard, *op. cit.*, 369 ff. and his discussion of the Amarna Revolution in *The Burden of Egypt*, 206 ff.

21. Cf. Wilson's Translation of "Hymns to Amon" in Pritchard, *op. cit.*, 365 ff. and his discussion of the worship of Amon in *The Burden of Egypt*, 130 f. and 206 ff. In particular as regards the myth of destiny compare Amon's power to change fate (Pritchard, *op. cit.*, 369) with Akhenaton's claim, as son of the Aton, to be Shay, the god of fate (cf. Wilson, *op. cit.*, 223, 225, 298 f.).

CHAPTER THREE

King, Council, Assembly

W HEN cities were a new thing and when the destruction of cities, the culminating act of warfare in ancient times as in modern times, was therefore a new thing, perhaps men had a more conscious notion than they do now as to why it is that cities are destroyed. Although it would appear to be an act of singular barbarism, almost as if it were the destruction of civilization itself, in that the city is the very embodiment of civilization, the Sumerians, the creators of the first civilization, listed "the destruction of cities" as one of the divine institutions (me's) upon which civilization is founded.[1] Significantly, the institution which follows this one on the list is "lamentation." To judge from the "Lamentation over the Destruction of Ur,"[2] a poem occasioned by the fall of Ur to the Elamites and Subarians, the chief effect of destroying a city besides the obvious physical consequences was to force the abandonment of the city by its gods. The statement is made repeatedly in this poem that the ruined city's institutions and rites have become inimical, meaning probably that they have devolved upon the enemy. To destroy the city, apparently, meant not to destroy but to appropriate the civilization of the city, and the appropriation of civilization was itself, naturally enough, one of the fundamental institutions of civilization.

It may be worthwhile to investigate the causes of war in the earliest city-building cultures, the two cultures which we have already been considering and which seem to have been the first ones of all, and the others which arose as city-building spread eastward to Harappa and Mohenjo-Daro and westward to Knossos and Mycenae, particularly these western cultures since

over and above archaeological finds we have the Homeric epics
on which to draw for information. An inquiry of this sort may
bring to light features of warfare and of the basic structure of
civilized society which have become concealed and repressed in
the long evolution of civilization and war and which play a role
in collective psychology like that of unconscious forces in the
psychology of the individual.

[1] *The King's Will*

What motivated the sacking of the city was the very desire
which seemingly inspired the original building of the city, the
wish to consort with the gods. The first cities, those built in
the Tigris-Euphrates valley, were essentially temple communities
and were conceived to be the home of the gods, and each of the
more important cities of the Nile valley was thought to be the
site where creation had taken place and where the gods had
come into being.[3] There was probably in the building of the
cities in Mesopotamia with their ziggurats, temple towers consisting of an imposing pyramidal structure raised in successive
stages with outside staircases and a sanctuary at the top, some
feeling of throwing up a tower that should reach to the sky like
the biblical Tower of Babel. The principal temple at Erech, for
instance, was called Eanna, the House of Heaven, the dwelling-
place of An the god of the sky and Innin, his daughter, the goddess of the city, and its walls were spoken of with pride as
touching the clouds. To live in Erech was to consort with An
and Innin, to become as one of the gods. To destroy such a city
was to make it untenable to the gods, to break up the companion-
ship of its inhabitants with the gods, and to take possession of
all this eminence for oneself.

In some of the earliest cities there was no permanent king but
only a temporary leader chosen in time of emergency, but in
cities like Erech where he was the mortal consort of the city-
goddess the king was permanent.[4] Quarrels between such cities
over hegemony in the land could accordingly be understood as
disputes between their kings for the hand of the goddess. Some-

times the dispute took the form of claims and counterclaims of rival cities to be the dwelling place of the goddess and sometimes, with the implicit acknowledgement that the rival city was the actual habitation of the goddess, it took the form of a demand that the goddess be brought from one city to another.[5] The Trojan War, the first of wars in the tradition of the West, is readily seen to be a conflict of the latter type if one takes into account the fact that Helen, the purported cause of the war, is known to have been at one time a Mycenaean goddess. Even in the *Iliad* itself, where she is no longer a goddess but only a woman, the Trojan elders are forced to declare when they see her that it is no wonder that there is a war being fought over her since she is like an immortal goddess to look upon.[6]

As an anthropological curiosity the union of man and goddess in sacred marriage is an institution that is familiar to us. It is something which we look down upon as a superstitious device for promoting fertility and which we think we can explain as arising out of primitive ignorance of the laws of nature. The connection between sacred marriage and warfare, though, is enough to give us pause, especially in view of the fact that we do not fully understand our own motives for engaging in war and for destroying cities.

In reality the sacred marriage was much more than a means of magically promoting the fertility of crops and herds and people. It was an end in itself insofar as it was the climax of civic commerce with the gods. Because the gods were considered to be the powers of nature, human association with them did mean communion with the forces responsible for fertility and could be thought to redound to the fruitfulness of nature. But what seems to have been sought primarily was the fellowship of the gods. It was for the king to attune himself directly and immediately to the cosmic powers and the cosmic rhythms so that by attunement to him and in sympathy with him all the people of his city might find themselves in living resonance with the gods. Human intercourse with the gods in the city was thus brought to consummation vicariously in what was conceived to be the cohabitation of the king with a goddess.

If we ask what became of this notion in later ages, we find that the idea of consorting with the gods paled before the thought of consorting with the transcendent God and during the first part of the Christian era degenerated into the notion of trucking with demons. We can see the old wish for intercourse with the gods emerging again, however, in early modern times in the figure of Faust and we can observe it gradually separating from the discouraging fear that the gods are demons. Faust wishes to be as a god and is still medieval enough to go about this by making a compact with a demon, but he points forward to later supermen who will lay aside all fear of demons and boldly set out to make themselves a place among the gods. Marlowe's Faustus rejects a succubus, a demon assuming female form, but with demonic help evokes the shade of the divine Helen, kisses her and cohabits with her, hoping thereby to obtain immortality and yet fearing at the same time to bring upon himself eternal damnation. Goethe's Faust, less fearful of damnation, seeks union with a goddess at first through demonic connivance, seducing Margaret and then abandoning her for the legendary Helen, but in death parts company with demons to reach out toward the Eternal-Womanly.

What a man could hope to gain by consorting with a goddess is evident from the lot promised, according to the tradition related in the Odyssey, to Menelaus, the husband of Helen. Although Helen has ceased in Homer to be the goddess she once was, she is still the daughter of Zeus and to be her husband is still to be the son-in-law of Zeus. So Menelaus is told by the Old Man of the Sea that on account of his marriage to Helen he is considered by the gods to be a member of Zeus' own family and therefore, instead of being destined to die in his homeland, is to be conveyed to the Elysian plain at the furthermost reaches of the earth where Rhadamanthys dwells and where men live a life like that of the gods themselves on Olympus.[7] It could be that this was the hope that originally launched the thousand ships and burnt the topless towers if the Trojan War was once, as we have reason to believe, conceived to have been a war over a goddess. The contenders for the goddess' hand by wooing and winning an immortal bride, by winning her back or keeping her from a rival, would have hoped to win personal immortality, and their supporters by sharing in the fortune of the principals would have hoped to win a vicarious participation in the immortality.

Eternal life on the Elysian plain, to be sure, is quite a different thing from eternal life in one's homeland. It is rather like eternal life in the land of the dead. Helen the goddess, as a matter of fact, was probably thought to descend periodically into the nether world like the great goddess in the Near East. She was worshiped at a temple in Rhodes under the title Helen of the Tree, the story going that she was hanged from a tree at the orders of the queen of the island. She was like Artemis, another figure related to the great goddess, who appears to have been annually hanged in effigy in her sacred grove at Condylea and to have been worshiped there under the title Artemis Hanged.[8] The circumstances of Helen being put to death by the queen of Rhodes is reminiscent of the great goddess being put to death by the queen of the nether world, and it may be that Helen's consorts like those of her Near Eastern prototype were called upon to share her experience.

Helen's metamorphosis in the *Iliad,* the fact that she has come down to earth, losing her old position as goddess in order to become the most beautiful of earthly women, implies that there has occurred in Homer, or else in the tradition of which he makes use, a revolution in the conception of war. The object of warfare has become something completely human where before it had been something divine. Men have not ceased to believe in the existence of goddesses, and they still consider it possible for goddesses to mate with human beings. Yet there has been a transvaluation of all values in warfare and in life, a substitution of human ideals for the divine ideals that had previously been conventional. The goal for which cities had originally been built as well as destroyed has been repudiated and a novel principle accepted for engaging in the pursuits of civilization without for all that abandoning any of those pursuits.

What has happened, it seems, is that the hope of consorting

with the gods has been given up and been replaced with the simple hope of consorting with human beings. The despair of all fellowship with the gods appears in the consistent contrast recognized by Homer and by all his characters between the comic existence of the gods and the tragic existence of men. Nothing is serious for the gods in the war even though they take part in it and fight one another in support of the contending armies. The reason is that there is for them no possibility of death as there is for men. If there is anything serious for a god it is something that can have no meaning for a man, the threat of eternal punishment if he disobeys the commands of Zeus. This can have no meaning for a man because a man does not live long enough to be punished forever. He can only be punished with death. It is difficult, therefore, for any real sympathy or community of interests to exist between beings so alien to one another. The gods, of course, can commiserate with men, can take pity on men and do them acts of kindness, but there can be no real sharing of lives when men are mortal and the gods are immortal.

This divorce between mortals and immortals seems to be connected with a change in the relationship of the living to the dead. The old Mycenaean practice of elaborate and magnificent burial has been replaced by the common Indo-European practice of cremation.[9] Where it had been the belief that the continued existence of the dead depended to some degree on the care exercised by the living for the tomb and probably that the dead participated to some extent in the existence of the living as in Egyptian thinking, the only thing that the living can do for the dead in the Homeric epics is to burn the dead body and make it possible for the ghost to leave this world and enter the nether world. The role of the living is not to maintain a link with the dead but to break the last link so the dead can lead an independent existence. To one who loves life in this world an afterlife of this sort can hold little attraction since it must be completely alien to earthly existence, a mere shadow of life on earth. It is no longer possible to think of death as anything more than the end of life in this world. As for the gods, it is not because they have passed through and beyond death that they are immortal.

They simply live on indefinitely in the world while men must depart from it. The idea that the gods are dead and that the dead are gods has become altogether meaningless.

With the hope of consorting with gods dashed, the paramount hope and desire of all the chief characters in the Iliad was naturally to consort with human beings, the prime concern of each one being his family or his friends. The main concern of Priam, king of the Trojans, was the welfare of his sons; that of Agamemnon, king of the Achaians, was the welfare of his brother Menelaus; that of Hector, the champion of the Trojans, was the welfare of his wife Andromache and his son Astyanax; that of Achilles, the champion of the Achaians, was the welfare of his comrade Patroclus. It is no wonder that in such a context the overall issue should be a question of human marriage. The wish to consort with human beings, to be sure, was not a universal desire for human company so much as a craving for the fellowship of very definite individuals. In this form, though, it seems to have been strong enough to have been a credible motive for warfare and the destruction of cities and at the same time a convincing cause for building cities and living in them, credible, that is, and convincing to Homer's audience.

Actually, while it may be perfectly comprehensible that men should have lost the ideals that originally motivated the building and destroying of cities, that more human goals should have been substituted for the over-ambitious objective of consorting with the gods, it is not so obvious how the new humanistic motivation could have been sufficient to inspire the very same acts to which men had been impelled by the old wish to be as the gods, and particularly how it could have been enough to justify warfare. The difficulty involved in the transformation of Helen into a human being, which we find in Homer, is how to make sense any longer of a war which was supposed to have lasted for ten years, to have entailed fairly heavy loss of life for those days, and to have ended in the complete destruction of a city, if the object of the war was simply to win back a woman for her husband. It is not that the original motive for war, the goddess, is not deserving of criticism. She is, but on grounds that she is a

myth, a criticism which Homer could hardly make, not on
grounds that she cannot sufficiently motivate men who believe
in her. It is all very well to say that the only motive for killing
that is rational is the desire to resist encroachments upon the
finite and human sort of happiness that is concretely possible for
us in this world. The question is whether such motives are usually
sufficient for taking the lives of others and risking one's own
life.

Homer himself does not appear to be at all convinced of the
sufficiency of such reasons. The *Iliad,* he tells us in the prologue,
is about the wrath of Achilles, how one man's anger sent many
a strong soul down to Hades and left their bodies a prey to dogs
and carrion birds. This deadly wrath was provoked all because
Agamemnon, the leader of the host besieging Troy, took away
Briseis, a captive woman belonging to Achilles. The quarrel over
the slave girl is quite probably intended by Homer to be a parody
of the quarrel over Helen. He does not attempt in the *Iliad* to
recount the whole story of the Trojan War; he limits himself to
this miniature war which constitutes only an episode of a few
days in the larger war and which seems to be an unflattering
mirror in which the larger war is reflected. Like the overall
conflict, the dispute between Agamemnon and Achilles leads,
through Achilles' refusal to help Agamemnon against the Trojans,
to heavy losses on both sides, the slaughter of Agamemnon's
followers and the death of Achilles' comrade and best friend;
and it culminates in the overthrow of a mock city, the wall built
by Agamemnon's party around the beached ships, just as the general struggle ends in the sacking of Troy. It may well be that
this disastrous strife over Briseis is meant to exhibit, by the out-
rageous disproportion between its petty cause and its catastrophic
results, the ultimate absurdity of the great war over Helen.

That the parallel between the quarrel over Helen and the
quarrel over Briseis was conscious on Homer's part is proved by
the words which he puts into Achilles' mouth to the effect that
there is a parallel.[10] When Agamemnon sends a delegation of the
chiefs of the Achaian host to make peace with Achilles, he is
rebuffed with the reply that Achilles' feud with him is as justified

as the feud of the Achaians with the Trojans. The cause of the war against the Trojans, Achilles points out, is the lovely Helen. But it is obvious, he argues, that every man loves his own, not just Agamemnon and Menelaus. Therefore, he concludes, it is as right for him to be angry at being deprived of his Briseis as it is for Menelaus to be angry at being deprived of his Helen. Agamemnon by taking away Briseis from Achilles put himself into the wrong, it seemed to Achilles, in exactly the same manner as Paris did by taking away Helen from Menelaus. The Achaians had refused only the day before to accept an offer of the Trojans to return the treasure that had been stolen with Helen and to add more to it, refused further to consider any offer to return Helen herself since, as Diomedes put it, even a plain fool could see that the bonds of destruction lay about the people of Troy.[11] So the following day when it seemed as if the bonds of destruction lay rather about the Achaians than the Trojans, Agamemnon's offer to return Briseis and add more gifts was rejected by Achilles. Full vengeance could be as rightfully exacted for Briseis, Achilles thought, as for Helen.

That the comparison of Helen and Briseis was intentionally derogatory seems to follow from statements which Homer reports about the one woman and the other being unworthy of the great bloodshed which she has caused. Although Achilles had at first contemplated drawing his sword and dispatching Agamemnon for the insult which he had offered him, he thought better of it and declared before Agamemnon and the whole host that he would never use his hands to fight for a girl.[12] He carries on his feud with Agamemnon from then on by refusing to aid him against the Trojans rather than by lifting his own hand against him. Later when the death of his comrade Patroclus at the hands of the Trojans makes him regret ever having had his quarrel with Agamemnon he expresses the wish that Briseis had died in her homeland instead of occasioning the death of so many heroes.[13] Helen makes a similar statement about herself on at least three different occasions. She says that she wishes she had died before she had been carried away to Troy and given rise to the great war that was fought for her sake.[14] And when the

Trojan elders say that it is no wonder that a war is being fought over her they immediately add that they wish nonetheless that she would sail away and not be the ruin of themselves and their children.[15]

Though the wall that Agamemnon's party built around the beached Achaian ships was an imitation city with towers, moat, and gateways large enough for horses to pass, there was nothing sacred about it as there was about Troy except perhaps the fact that the walls were joined to the common barrow which had been raised for the Achaian dead after they had been burnt on the funeral pyre. Not only was there no intention of consorting with the gods or of setting up some kind of shrine, the Achaians even forgot to sacrifice to the gods when they went to work building. This, according to Homer, caused considerable consternation among the gods and led to a resolution proposed by Poseidon, the god of the sea, to destroy the wall with water as soon as the war was over.[16] That resolution was carried out in due time, and in the meanwhile the Trojans were able to break down the gate, pour into the encampment and set fire to one of the ships before the tide of battle turned against them.

This godless city of the Achaians was as far removed from the holy city which it was the original objective of war to destroy as was the slave girl from the goddess who was the original cause of war. Its destruction is probably intended by Homer to be a mockery of the destruction of Troy but the irony is greater than he would have intended since the actual Troy will have been built not simply to be a home for human beings blessed and protected by the gods, as he supposed, but to be a common dwelling for gods and men. Sacred Ilios, as Troy was called in the *Iliad*, may have been a circular citadel no more than two hundred yards in diameter (this is how Achilles could chase Hector around it three times), but its walls and towers were lofty and it was a holy city and to dwell in it was to live in the company of the gods.

In the beginning the reason why the city had to be destroyed was a mythological one, to force the abandonment of the city by its goddess, to force her removal to the city of the destroyers. In

Homer the reason is only half-remembered; it is still Helen but she has become a woman where she had been a goddess. The war has now become a worthy object of parody since its cost in human lives is out of all proportion to its motivating cause. So Homer proceeds to parody it with an even more preposterous instance of vain bloodshed, the foolish contention over the slave girl Briseis. From goddess to woman and from woman to slave girl. The story has become much livelier than the formalized Sumerian epics describing stately disputations over the whereabouts of a goddess. In a sense, though, the subject of the narrative has not actually become any more concrete, for the sacred marriage of the king with the goddess had been consummated every year in his union with a very real human priestess.[17] The change which has occurred is rather the loss of all the higher significance once attached to the royal matrimony. There remains only the after-glow of divinity in the relationship which Helen has kept to Zeus of being his daughter.

Zeus, the divine king, absurdly decides the conflict between the two human kings over Briseis as if it were a contention for the hand of his own daughter Helen. Achilles appealed to Zeus to settle their dispute because he had been given to understand that though his life would be short he was to have honor from Zeus, and now instead of honor he had received dishonor from Agamemnon, Zeus' human representative.[18] After it had become plain that the prayer of Achilles had been heard and answered, Agamemnon repented of what he had done. The man whom Zeus honored, he felt constrained to admit, was worth more than many thousands, and Zeus had obviously honored Achilles and humiliated the Achaian nation.[19] Agamemnon realized that he had placed himself in a false position by failing to honor the man whom Zeus honored, for he thereby ceased to act for Zeus and to wield the authority which he had received from him. In order to retrieve his own lost status Agamemnon offered besides Briseis to give Achilles his own daughter in marriage. In refus-ing to accept Agamemnon's daughter, Achilles was refusing to let Agamemnon regain the role of Zeus. When Achilles finally was reconciled with him, however, Agamemnon found Zeus' will once more in conformity with his own and he began again to taste success.

Zeus is described in the *Iliad* and represented, it seems, in a picture preserved from the Mycenaean period as having in his possession the golden scales of destiny somewhat as the supreme god in Mesopotamia is depicted as possessing the tablets of fate.[20] The balance, especially if one is thinking of the emblem of blindfold Justice, might seem to suggest that the decrees of fate are not personal choices made by Zeus but impersonal determinations recorded and carried out by him. The same implication might be drawn from the Mesopotamian tablets of fate since these tablets were of such a form that they could be used like dice for casting lots. More likely, though, the nonrational methods of arriving at decisions are invoked simply with the intent of contrasting divine choices with human choices. The idea is probably that all contingent matters are matters of choice, some of them, like war and peace, matters of human choice, others, like defeat and victory, matters of divine choice. What lies outside the range of man's effective freedom, like victory and defeat, will appear to be decided by methods of choice which are independent of man's will such as the use of a balance or the casting of lots. The significance of the tablets of fate and the golden scales of destiny, thus, is probably that their possessor has it in his power to decide all contingencies which are not matters of human choice and not that there is some overriding impersonal force to which even the gods are subject.

A more fundamental cause of the widespread impression that there is a fate in Homer that works independently of the will of Zeus may be the evolution in the conception of warfare which we have been considering. As war became more pointless, its object declining from goddess to woman to slave girl, the decrees of fate determining the outcome of war also became more pointless. The workings of fate began to seem less and less the result of an intelligent choice and more and more the effect of something like blind chance. Actually they have become in Homer only more arbitrary. There are two occasions in the *Iliad* on which Zeus makes use of the scales of destiny: the first time the

lot of the Achaians sinks and that of the Trojans rises; the
second time the lot of Hector sinks and that of Achilles rises.[21]
On both occasions Zeus' object is simply to cover Achilles with
glory, a paltry and arbitrary aim perhaps but an aim nonetheless
freely and consciously adopted. There is no doubt in Homer's
viewpoint, it seems, that events are the work of a free and personal will. There is a great deal of doubt, though, as to whether
there is wisdom in the choices made by that will. And since the
pointlessness of war's outcome has resulted from the pointlessness
of war itself, there is a more basic doubt in this standpoint about
there being wisdom in the choices made by man.

[2] *The Council's Advice*

To the extent that the king was thought merely to propose
of war and peace and not to dispose of defeat and victory it was
deemed necessary that he take counsel with wise men who were
able to reckon the probable consequences of his actions. Among
Indo-European peoples like the two peoples represented in the
Iliad and also among the Near Eastern peoples who created the
first civilizations there existed an institution comparable to the
Anglo-Saxon witenagemot, a council (gemot) of sages (witan), to
advise the king.[22] Even in ancient Egypt besides the ordinary
advisers of the Pharaoh there was the vestige of an institutional
council of elders in the ceremonial council of the Great Ones
of Upper and Lower Egypt.[23] Where the king was practically
identified with the sky-god as in Egypt, it is true, the council
could be little more than a foil for the bravery of the king who
was customarily depicted as rushing forth into heroic deeds
against the cautious advice of his counselors. Where there were
many distinct city-states as in early Mesopotamia and the king
was more loosely linked to the supreme god, the king, to judge
from a story about Gilgamesh and the civic council of Erech,[24]
could still go into war against the advice of his council but he
did so more at his own risk.

In estimating the consequences of various courses of action
proposed to them by the king, the councilors were in effect at-

tempting to calculate and predict the arrangements of fate. Oftentimes destiny was thought to take a conditional form such that the city or the king would have alternative fates depending on the course of action that was taken. A city or a king might, for instance, have a choice like that of Achilles in the *Iliad* between an existence that was long but inglorious and an existence that was glorious but short. However commonplace this kind of choice might seem, it would not be true from a purely logical point of view that there is a fixed outcome for each possible human decision. Rather the result of a given decision would depend as in games of strategy on the decisions made by others and on chance events. If it is supposed that there is a fixed outcome, this is in virtue of some such doctrine as that of fate. There is room, all the same, in a conception of fate like this for human calculation and human freedom since no matter how fixed the outcome of each possible course of action different courses of action are possible. A city might be destined to be sacked, for instance, if it chose to resist the demands of another city, but it could always choose to acquiesce in them and remain standing. Some viewpoint such as this was seemingly necessary in a society which combined a firm belief in fate with an equally firm belief in the necessity of taking counsel before acting.

A councilor's wisdom in matters of fate placed him on a level with the gods and put him into touch with the powers to which it belonged to determine destiny. There was always in the mythology of societies organized in this manner a council of gods to which it pertained to work out the lots of mankind.[25] In Mesopotamian mythology the divine council was composed of seven gods, probably in accordance with the quorum of seven members of the human council who could act at times in the name of the whole body of elders in the city. In Egyptian mythology it was composed of the nine principal gods, the Ennead, including the king of the gods, and may well have corresponded to a human council of similar structure existing in prehistoric times. Likewise in the various Indo-European mythologies there seem to have been councils usually consisting of twelve gods in conformity with the councils of men which existed among the several peoples. It was not simply a question of men being unable to imagine the gods organized in any fashion other than that familiar in their own human society. It was more a matter of wishing to share in the divine deliberations by which the course of human life was decided.

This desire, perhaps it was, that led beyond methods like the ordeal and the duel, in which the gods were called upon to judge human affairs, to the organization of courts of judgment in which human beings sat like gods deciding the fate of other human beings. The witenagemot, besides being a council to advise the king, was the highest court of judicature in the land, and it seems that it was generally true in early civilization that the council of elders functioned as a court of law. This was probably the main function of the council in those of the early Mesopotamian cities which had no king other than a temporary leader elected in times of crisis and it was the only one which lasted into the later days of absolute autocracy. In the *Iliad* in the description of the design on Achilles' shield there is an account of a civic council sitting in judgment on two men in a case of murder in which the question was whether the aggrieved kinsman of the dead man should accept a blood-price or whether the offender should be outlawed so that anyone could kill him without price. When the council convened for judgment, according to Homer's account, the elders sat in the Sacred Circle on polished stones, each one took the herald's staff in turn as he rose to give judgment, and the one whose judgment was deemed fairest was awarded two nuggets of gold.[26]

Holding the power of life and death, the judges who sat in council were thought to consort with the nether gods who judged the dead as well as the heavenly gods who decreed the fates.[27] In Mesopotamian mythology the function of the nether world court was to pass the sentence of death on the living and it was Namtar, the vizier of the nether world queen, who carried the verdict into execution. In Egyptian mythology the issue which lay before the forty-two judges of the dead was not whether or not a man should die at a given time but whether or not his death should be tantamount to utter annihilation. Those who were condemned were destroyed on the spot and those who were acquitted went on to enjoy a life after death. While it is true that human judges could kill only the body and not the soul so that from this standpoint the fellowship between the council of the living and the council of the dead was closer in the Meso-potamian conception than in the Egyptian, still the grounds for condemnation to death were the same as the grounds for con-demnation to annihilation so that it was possible in the Egyptian viewpoint too to identify the verdict of the netherly court with that of the earthly court. There is some evidence, also, that in the Egyptian court the names of the guilty could be obliterated along with their lives to accord with the sentence of annihilation that was expectedly being passed upon them by the infernal judges.[28]

To say that the council of the living sat in joint session, as it were, with the council of the dead is ultimately nothing more than another way to say that the council of men sat in joint session with the council of the gods. When special deities of des-tiny were introduced into later Egyptian mythology, it seemed logical to place them in the nether world court that judged the dead. In Mesopotamian mythology there seems really to have been no clear distinction between the seven gods who judged the dead, the ⁻Anunnaki, and the seven gods who determined destinies. Like Saul who had recourse to the witch of Endor to learn what was in store for him in his conflict with the Philistines when all appeals to God by dreams and by priests and by prophets had failed to bring an answer, the king might resort to necromancy to discover the outcome of a projected war if he had been failed by divination. In searching the nether world for Samuel, the dead judge and counselor, Saul's witch saw forms like gods (*elohim*) ascending out of the earth.[29] If indeed the dead are gods and the gods are dead, then divination, the art of learning the future from the gods, and necromancy, the art of learning the future from the dead, must finally come down to the same thing.

In spite of the frequent use of divination in the *Iliad* and the success with which it was borne out in the story, Homer seems to have been somewhat skeptical about any kind of information which men thought they had obtained from the gods. It was not that he doubted the existence of the gods so much as that he was unconvinced of their truthfulness and their benevolence toward men. He tells of important instances in which men were deceived by the gods and he represents his heroes to be well aware that the gods are both capable of deluding men and prone to do so. Plato was so scandalized by what he read in Homer to this effect that he laid down as the two rules of censorship to be observed in his ideal republic that the young should read no book in which the gods were not made out to be truthful and no book in which they were not made out to be good.[30] It is true that there is a kind of theodicy at the beginning of the *Odyssey* in which the gods lay the blame for excessive human misery upon the blindness of men themselves.[31] The cogency of the vindication is weakened, however, by the fact that in Homer's point of view "blindness" is supposed to be at least partially the work of the gods.

Homer had fairly good grounds for his mistrustfulness toward the gods. If the losing side in a war or a battle had every reason to believe that the gods should have been favorably disposed toward it, then it had no reason to believe that they were either benevolent or truthful toward it. Why the gods should find it expedient to deceive mankind was only too apparent. It was that men might the more easily fall victim to the fate which the gods had planned for them. It might even be impossible for the doom decreed by the gods to be accomplished unless the victims were deluded. If it was the will of the gods that a city like Troy be destroyed, then it was necessary that the city be prevented from acceding to the demands of its enemies and concluding a peace. If it were known to the citizens of the doomed city that to resist would mean inevitable disaster, then they might not resist and the disaster would never take place. Thus the gods intervened at the duel between Menelaus and Paris, recounted in the *Iliad,* in order to prevent the outcome of the duel from being accepted by the Trojans as a settlement of the war.[32]

Why men should continue under these circumstances to take

counsel with the gods before acting, why, for instance, they should credit dreams when they know, as Homer has it in the *Odyssey,* that some dreams are true coming as they do from the Gate of Horn and some, coming from the Gate of Ivory, are false,[33] is because there exists no rational method of fully determining the consequences of human actions. Since they depend on other human actions and on chance events, the consequences of a given human action are to some extent unpredictable. It is of supreme importance, at the same time, to be able to predict them. The best one can do is calculate the comparative risks that are involved in all the various courses of actions which are possible in the situation and attempt to discover some appropriate principle of selection by which to chose among the risks. Oftentimes, when all the calculations are done, one is reduced to a random device such as flipping a coin, throwing dice, or making use of a table of random digits.[34] The only advantages which such devices have over a completely arbitrary selection is that the actual odds involved in the calculated risks can be exploited in using them. The line which separates the kind of modern man who makes use of such devices and the ancient man who made use of divination is a narrow one, especially since one standard method of consulting an oracle in ancient times was to draw lots. The ancient man too would make use of his oracles, omens, and dreams, for the most part, only when he had no more rational criteria for arriving at decisions.

With the gods, as Homer supposes, making use of human passions to achieve purposes entirely opposed to the human intent at work in the passions it was important to go as far as one could on purely rational considerations before resorting to divination. One could always determine in a purely rational manner what was possible and what was probable even if one could not determine which possibility or probability would be actually realized. After this point one had to take one's chances with the gods, but there was no sense in relying on the unreliable any more than one absolutely had to. The gods, indeed, might be able to manage things so far that a man would be blinded to what he otherwise would have seen for himself. In this case he could afterward blame the gods, as Homer's heroes do, for blinding him and leading him thus into disaster, but the gods could in turn blame the man himself, as they do in the beginning of the *Odyssey*, since he was blind to things which lay within the province of human reason.

The whole purpose of the council from Homer's point of view was to prevent blindness of this sort. Blindness (*ate*) effectively leads to disaster, according to his theory, because of failure to listen to advice. Ate is followed by Litai, prayers or appeals, which can undo its harm, but if they are rejected then the Litai go to Zeus and beg him that Ate may lead its own way toward ruin.[35] If a king is led into disaster by blindness, therefore, it will generally be his own fault for not listening to the advice of his council.

There is some similarity between Homer's idea of the will of the gods being accomplished through the blindness of men and Hegel's idea of "the cunning of reason in history." In both conceptions the moving force in human affairs is blind passion and the outcome of human actions is largely unintentional as far as the human beings themselves are concerned while it is intentional from the standpoint of a higher divine purpose which triumphs through the interplay of human cross-purposes. The chief difference between the two views lies in the nature of this divine purpose. From Hegel's standpoint human beings are at cross-purposes because their aims are particular and the higher purpose triumphs through them and over them because it is universal. From Homer's standpoint, on the contrary, the divine purpose is just as particular as the human purposes and it triumphs because it is the expected resultant of a composition of opposing forces. Hegel thought that the higher purpose in the Trojan War, for instance, was the unification of the whole of Greece in a national undertaking.[36] Homer thought, as he puts it in one place, that the purpose was the destruction of Troy in the tenth year of the struggle after the best of the Trojans and many of the Achaians had been killed.[37]

If the divine purpose in history, as Homer presumes, is as particular as the human cross-purposes through which it moves to fulfillment, then there can be nothing approaching a science of history like that postulated by Hegel but the only human wisdom that could conceivably cope with the cunning of divine providence would be the prudential grasp of particulars that is the competence of the counselor. When Homer wishes to praise a man for this kind of knowledge he calls him a man "who sees both before and behind."[38] Seeing before is neither prophecy nor an exact calculating of the future but simply foresight. Seeing behind, in like manner, is simply hindsight, and it is probably because he assumes foresight to arise ordinarily from hindsight that Homer is so ready to grant that men of age and experience like Nestor possess it. At the same time he is willing to grant its existence in some young men like Diomedes who are naturally provident. When the prudence of continuing the siege of Troy comes up in the *Iliad* the area of hindsight is marked out in Agamemnon's repeated statement that Zeus has sacked many a city and the area of foresight in the statement that he will yet sack many another.[39] Hindsight consisted here in knowing the circumstances under which cities had been sacked in the past, in knowing for instance at what cost and with what profit they had been sacked, and foresight consisted in applying these lessons to the proposed sack of Troy.

Every time the statement is made in the *Iliad* about the past and future sack of cities the suspicion is expressed that the Achaians have been deceived by the gods into believing that they will sack Troy whereas in reality the gods have no such intention. At first Agamemnon says this without being convinced of it himself, merely seeking to test the mettle of his men and their willingness to go on with the war. Ironically Homer would have it that Agamemnon really deceived as he said without knowing it although the deception did not extend to the ultimate outcome of the war but only to the outcome of the battle in which he was about to engage. Later on after he has suffered heavy losses Agamemnon repeats his doubts about the will of the gods, this time with sincere conviction. Homer clearly did not think that the Achaians were deceived in their belief that they would sack Troy, for they did eventually succeed, according to him, in taking it. He does seem to have considered them deluded, nevertheless, about the price they would have to pay in human lives in order to overthrow the city. Agamemnon was fooled by a false dream sent from Zeus into thinking that he could take Troy immediately if he offered battle.[40] The losses he incurred by following this dream were so great that he began to believe that it was Zeus' intention that the Achaian nation should perish far from home, as he put it, without a name.[41]

The actual intention of the gods, from Homer's point of view, was identical neither with the intention of the Trojans, that the entire besieging army perish, nor with that of the Achaians, that the city be taken with a minimum of losses, but with the resultant of the two opposing forces, that the city be taken at a maximum cost to the besieging army. Both sides were thus deceived and blinded by the gods in such a way that each by striving to fulfill its own purpose did its part to fulfill the purpose of the gods. Whether the blindness was due to a failure of the kings to listen to their councils or whether the councilors themselves were blinded, the blindness was of such a sort that it could have been avoided by the exercise of human prudence. It should have been clear from past instances of warfare that the result of war is never simply what the victorious side has desired.

It is doubtful that there can be a war, if one adopts the Homeric standpoint, without there being deception on both sides. From almost any point of view there would have to be deception on at least one side since it would be impossible for both sides to be victorious. From the Homeric point of view, according to which the outcome of the struggle will always be the resultant of the two opposing forces, there would inevitably be blindness on both sides since the intention of neither side could be perfectly achieved unless there were no opposition from the other. One might think that it would be possible for this to be known and taken into account, that there might be at least some men, say some wise counselors, who would know that the king's intention in making war could not possibly be fulfilled unless it were left unopposed by his rival. This could very conceivably happen, but there would be no war if this were known to everyone involved, for instance to the king himself, without changing the objective of the war. It is only if we imagine war being deliberately fought for some purpose other than victory that it could be carried on without some foolish hope of an impossible kind of success.

Interpreting the subject of the *Iliad*, the wrath of Achilles against Agamemnon over the slave girl Briseis, as we have been doing, to be a parody of the wrath of the Achaians against the Trojans over Helen, we find in the blindness Homer attributes to the two antagonists an exemplification of the mutual blindness which in his thinking seems to be the necessary condition of war. Agamemnon, as he himself later admits, is blinded by his "wretched passion" into thinking that he can deprive Achilles of the slave girl with impunity. Achilles, on the other hand, is blinded by his own indignation into thinking that he can with impunity allow Agamemnon's army to be bested by the Trojans. In both instances the impunity proves to be illusory, Agamemnon losing his battle against the Trojans and losing the lives of many of his best men, and Achilles losing the life of his best friend Patroclus. In both instances too the blindness resulted from a failure to listen to counsel and was remedied by a new willingness to take advice brought on by the shock of disaster. Agamemnon would not heed Nestor's admonishment to leave Achilles in possession of the slave girl but after the tide of battle had turned against him he became willing to listen to his council's advice to make amends to Achilles. For his part, Achilles refused to heed the delegation of councilors who came to arrange a reconciliation with Agamemnon but after the death of his comrade Patroclus he became willing to accept all proposals which he had previously rejected.

The point of parody, if we are correct in saying that parody was intended, was the unworthy cause for which blood was shed in the quarrel between Achilles and Agamemnon and in the war between the Achaians and the Trojans. The blindness ascribed to each of the contending parties lay in the naïve hope that the objective of the struggle could be attained with impunity. By failing to realize what price in blood would have to be paid to attain its end each party to the dispute failed to foresee the enormous disproportion between the cause of the strife and its disastrous effects. Agamemnon and Achilles did not perceive the absurdity of their contention over the slave girl until the harm was already done because neither foresaw the losses he would have to sustain in order to maintain his position against the other. Likewise the Trojans and the Achaians could not grasp the absurdity of their war over Helen until it was too late because neither foresaw the almost total ruin that they would undergo, the Trojans the destruction of their city and the Achaians their losses in battle and the disasters of their return home. It was only in the light of the resulting catastrophe that Briseis appeared unworthy of a quarrel and Helen unworthy of a war.

Since the gods always knew beforehand what the outcome of these human struggles would be, one might think that the divine council would always prevent there being any blindness in the behavior of the divine king comparable to that of human kings. One of the most notable passages in the *Iliad,* however, is the *Dios apate,*[42] the tale of Zeus being blinded by the wiles of Hera, who lured him to sleep with her while Poseidon managed to turn the tide of battle against Zeus' will. The plot came to nothing when Zeus awoke, but the episode reveals a belief on Homer's part that there can be a divine as well as a human blindness. This is in line with his general idea that the divine purpose in human affairs is just as particular as the human cross-purposes.

There may be in all this a feeling that the objectives pursued by the gods in their intervention in human affairs do not make a great deal of sense, a feeling approximating the idea that the only purposes in history are human purposes and that the outcome of human struggles to the extent that it is not humanly intended is the work of blind chance. The blindness of blind chance is actually correlative to the blindness and lack of foresight in human agents. It is simply what human beings fail to plan. But given the existence of the gods it is natural when one adverts to its senselessness to think of it as a subjective blindness and lack of foresight in the gods. When one does not advert to its senselessness, however, it is natural to think of it as a piece of cunning and trickery played by the gods on mankind.

Homer's theory of blindness is bound up, it seems, with his viewpoint on the cause of war. The split between the divine purpose and the human purposes in war is dependent on the assumption that the cause of war is something strictly human, Helen the woman rather than Helen the goddess. If it is assumed, as it was when civilization was new, that the cause of war is something divine, the goddess of the city, then it will probably be supposed that the will of the gods is identical with one or the other of the competing human wills, that the divine purpose is the same as one of the human cross-purposes instead of being the intended resultant of a divinely arranged composition of opposing human forces. The divine purpose in the Trojan War, for instance, would have been the removal of the goddess Helen from Troy to Achaia. The deception and blindness, on this supposition, would be all on the losing side. From the standpoint of one who does not believe in the gods, of course, the deception would be total on both sides in this situation whereas it would be only partial on both sides in the situation contemplated by Homer. It is nevertheless more intelligible that men should consent to war if they believe that there is a chance of the king proposing the war not being deceived than if they believe that partial deception is inevitable.

[3] *The Assembly's Consent*

It is not because they see only good in war that the men who are to engage in it and suffer its consequences are willing to consent to war but because they see comparable evils in peace. When Gilgamesh was confronted with a demand from Agga, the king of Kish, for the payment of corvée in recognition of the hegemony of Kish over Erech, the story goes that the council of elders at Erech advised Gilgamesh to submit rather than endanger the existence of the city by going to war, but the assembly of arms-bearing men, we are told, readily agreed to war in spite of the council's advice to the contrary since to submit would have meant for them military duty in the service of Kish.[43] The young men in the assembly, according to what they said, had no taste for either the toil or the danger involved in the life of a soldier, and to them the whole matter appeared to be a choice between more or less continuous duty in the army of Kish and one dangerous stretch of duty in the army of Erech. Since they had to fight and risk their lives in any case, they preferred that it be for as short a time as possible and in defense of their own city.

This was a special situation, admittedly, for the choice between war and peace is not always a choice between two forms of military service. Yet the idea that there are evils in peace comparable to those of war seems to have been at all times an essential condition for willingness to take the risks of war. it has been said in defense of thermonuclear war itself that "peace also has its tragedies," meaning that life is risky in peacetime as well as in wartime and that death is anyway inevitable. From the standpoint of a quantitative estimate of the relative risks involved in thermonuclear war and in modern peacetime existence it has been concluded that "war is horrible. There is no question about it. But so is peace. And it is proper, with the kind of calculations we are making today, to compare the horror of war and the horror of peace and see how much worse it is."[44] The idea was not that peace as such is horrible but that the risks involved in peacetime existence are horrible and are comparable with, though less than, the risks involved in war so that it is conceivable that there be reasons compelling enough to justify accepting the risks of war.

In spite of the "horrors of peace," though, the assembly at Erech would probably not have given its consent to war so readily if it had not been confident that Erech would be victorious over Kish and that Gilgamesh the king was the "beloved of An," the supreme god. The deliberations of an assemblyman on the question of making the king's purpose his own purpose made sense only on the supposition that it was conceivable that the king's purpose be identical with that of the gods. If it were to be supposed instead, as Homer seems to have thought, that human cross-purposes are never simply identical with the overriding divine purpose, that human intentions are never simply realized unless they go unopposed, and that human wishes are never fulfilled in war since they are at odds in that situation with other human wishes, then it would no longer be reasonable to make one of the cross-purposes in a situation of conflict one's own. It is only when one assumes the purpose of war to be divine, for instance the retention of the goddess in the city or her transference to the city, whatever be the concrete matter such as the payment of corvée in which the issue comes to a head, that one can believe in the possibility of absolute victory, for only then could one believe in the possible identity of one's cause with the will of the gods.

The same is true, for that matter, of deliberations about the reasonableness of modern war. Some positive assumption about victory is necessary, whether it be the maximum hope that history is on one's side, that one's purpose is identical with the higher purpose in history, or the minimum hope that it be possible for one side to win and not necessary that both sides be destroyed.

Given such an assumption, though, and given that it is firmly held on both sides, it is possible for a war to be won or lost without any blood being shed. If each of the opposing forces is convinced that the gods will not divide their sympathies but will be in favor of one side and against the other, then it is only necessary that one side be persuaded that the cause of the other side is the cause of the gods and it will capitulate. This is what is supposed to have happened in the siege of Erech by the army of Kish. Both armies were under the persuasion that the gods would be with one or the other of them, each hoped itself to be the favored side, and each feared that the gods would be with the other. The army of Erech almost gave way at the sight of the enormous host from Kish and its commanding king, but when Gilgamesh made a personal appearance on the wall of Erech the army of Kish was so terrified that it prostrated itself in the dust and Agga, the king of Kish, was forced to "restrain his soldierly heart." The war was over as soon as the forces of Kish became convinced that the cause of Erech was the cause of the gods.

Naturally wars carried on under this assumption were not always so bloodless, for it was not always so easy to recognize the divine favorites without the test of arms. The possibility of a bloodless solution without any compromise on the one side and with complete capitulation on the other nevertheless existed where this mentality existed, and, at least according to the legends, the conflicts among the Sumerian cities were more than once settled in this manner.[45]

Not sharing this simple conviction that in warfare one side loses and other side wins, or that when human beings are at odds one of the opposing human wills must be identical with the divine will, Homer has it that the gods were divided in the Trojan War, some of them like Poseidon, Athena, Hera, Hermes, and Hephaestus, supporting the Achaians, and others like Apollo, Ares, Artemis, Leto, and Aphrodite, supporting the Trojans. It was possible, indeed, for the Homeric heroes to be fooled into believing that the gods were united in their favor as when Agamemnon had the false dream sent by Zeus in which he was told that the gods were no longer divided and that he could take Troy immediately if he attacked.[46] The heroes, nevertheless, seem to have been well aware that the gods are not necessarily on one side or the other in war so that when there was evidence of divine support on the enemy side, when the aegis-cape of Zeus was un-furled and shaken against them, they retreated but they did not capitulate. They knew that while on one day the gods might be against them, on another they might be with them, and on still another day there might be gods on both sides.

With this kind of thinking determining its course, a war would tend to be fought out to the bitter end like the siege of Troy rather than settled bloodlessly like the siege of Erech. An attempt was made to resolve the issue between the Achaians and the Trojans by single combat, a device which appears to have been an established institution in Sumerian warfare[47] and which would make perfect sense on the presupposition that the gods were with one side or the other since the outcome of a duel would then be a revelation of the divine will like the outcome of an ordeal. The duel proposed in the Trojan War was appropriately to be fought by Menelaus and Paris, the contenders for Helen. Yet the gods intervened both to prevent the issue of the combat from being too clearly a victory for Menelaus and also to prevent the Trojans from keeping their oath to abide by its result. It did not make too much sense to settle a war in this manner anyway if one did not believe that the gods were necessarily united in favor of one of the rivals. To demand that the gods show their preference for one side or the other by giving its representative victory in single combat was to present them with too simplified an either-or proposition. Neither gods nor men, given the Homeric stand-point, could ever have held themselves to such an alternative.

It has been observed that it is a strange phenomenon of early modern history that some king or emperor will levy an army, fight a battle with the army of his foe, gain a victory, kill three, five, or ten thousand men, and consequently subdue a state and a whole people consisting of several millions. It seems surprising that the defeat of any army, one hundredth of the whole strength of a people, should force the people to submit. In reality one might say that a people is not forced to submit in these circum-stances unless it is acting under some kind of conviction similar to that which in early times allowed wars to be settled by single combat. It has been correctly pointed out that when defeat in battle has failed to convince a people that it has been defeated, as happened with the Russian people in the Napoleonic invasion of Russia, then the defeat becomes something approaching a formality, an empty gesture, having little significance for the actual outcome of the war.[48] What follows from this, however, is not that historians give us a false view of history or that true history consists of inevitable mass movements but rather that everything in war short of physical destruction depends for its significance on the accepted political mythology. If a people considers itself to lose a war when its representative in single combat or in formal battle loses, then it does lose the war; if it does not consider itself to lose in this eventuality, then it has not lost.

To remain unconvinced by formal defeats of this kind is not necessarily a sign of some sort of hard-headed realism. It can just as well be the result of another form of political mythology.

The Homeric view of warfare according to which the gods may be divided in their sympathies for the human causes is not equivalent to the view that the gods are not concerned about human affairs or to the view that there are no gods. The hope which the Homeric armies entertain that they will succeed in spite of initial defeats derives from the belief that there are gods who at any moment can turn the tide in their favor. If a people were to think that the gods were unconcerned or that they did not exist, then, unless it were to place its trust in some impersonal substitute for the gods such as luck or historical inevitability, it would have no grounds for hope apart from its own calculated power and the enemy's estimated weakness. Hope based on these latter considerations would not be as far-reaching as hope in the gods since the factors of chance and freedom in human affairs leave a vacuum of unpredictability which cannot be filled by rational planning.

It is undeniable, though, that the Homeric view is closer in practice to the view that there are no gods than it is to the view that the gods are undivided. Compromise, for instance, as a way of settling disputes is surprisingly feasible in the view that the gods are undivided while it is very difficult to reach when it is thought that the gods can be divided or that there are no gods. When the former position is adopted it is possible for a compromise to be imposed through arbitration, as it sometimes was among the Sumerians, on two parties, neither of which is considered to have divine support, by a third party thought to have the backing of the gods.[49] The possibility of the compromise is given, of course, by the fact that the conflict is not over hegemony in the land but is only a rivalry among subordinate powers.

When it is thought that the rival interests, however opposed to one another, can both obtain divine support or when it is believed that there is no divine authority by which they can be reconciled, then it becomes very hard in practice to obtain the necessary mutual agreement. This is what caused the compromise proposed by the Trojans in the *Iliad* to fail. According to the terms of the proposal Paris would have returned the treasure he had stolen together with more of his own but would have kept

Helen herself.[50] The offer was rejected by the Achaians in the hope of winning everything, Helen and all, a kind of hope that is irrepressible as long as there is no undivided divine power to render disagreement hopeless.

In atheistic views of war it may be generally true that instead of the good cause hallowing even war, the good war, as Nietzsche has it, hallows any cause.[51] In the Homeric view where the cause of war has lost a great deal of its original holiness, there may be something approaching this state of affairs. Of herself Helen, declining from goddess to woman though remaining still the daughter of Zeus, was no longer enough as a pure woman to hallow an undertaking like the expedition against Troy nor to justify the jeopardy in which Troy placed itself in order to keep her. Something more than the cause of the war was needed to motivate the men who were to fight in it to give their consent to the war. Where there is no divinely supported cause, as in the atheistic views, there evidently must be some intrinsic value seen in war itself if there is to be any sufficient reason for accepting the risks of war. Where the gods can be divided, some for and some against the cause, the partial hallowing which the cause thereby receives would seem to leave the risks of the war insufficiently justified. This appears to have been the feeling of the Achaian assembly when at the king's proposal that the siege of Troy be abandoned, a motion which he made merely to test their mettle, they rushed headlong to their ships to set sail for home.[52]

The manner in which they were persuaded to return to the battle and take up again the siege clarifies the complex motivation which inspired their original consent. It was necessary to appeal to that hope of theirs, always available for the very same reason that their desire to fight tended to flag, in order to compensate for the slackening of their desire to see the war through. Because neither their cause nor that of their opponents was holy enough to entail the exclusive backing of the gods, their desire to fight over the issue tended to become remiss when the war was prolonged and when the toils and dangers of battle increased. Because of this same uncertain patronage of the gods, though, it was always possible to hope for a sudden change of fortune. Desires for spoil, for captive women, for personal glory, while not in themselves sufficient to make war attractive made an otherwise doubtful cause seem worthwhile when they were combined with an enthusiastic hope for victory. The chiefs who harangued the crowd, Odysseus and Nestor, both appealed to readily forgotten omens of eventual victory in order to rally the assembly's spirit. It was not that anyone was so very credulous in regard to omens as that the uncertainty of the issue always made it possible to have recourse to them in order to restore confidence.

Popular consent to war may seem to justify the contention that there are many things which men desire more than life itself, that the will to power is greater than the will to existence. It has been argued that there is no such thing as a will to existence, for what does not exist cannot will to exist and what does exist cannot very well want what it already has.[53] This kind of argument, though, seems to pass rather lightly over the fact of death. If there is such a thing as death, then one can conceive a desire to hold on to one's life and can possess a will to live although one already possesses life. This is a will to power but the power willed is the power to live. The fact that men consent, often rather reluctantly, to risk their lives in war does not prove that they value some things more than their lives but it may mean that they have hopes like the Achaians of enriching their lives with power in the form of spoil or women or glory or the like. The choice for the Homeric assemblies is not between power and life but between a life of less power and a life of more power. It is possible to prefer death to a life without liberty or without happiness. A man who does this, however, even if he commits suicide, has not lost the will to live, for he still has the will to live happily or to live in freedom. He does not prefer liberty or happiness to life itself; he prefers a life with them so much to a life without them that he will accept nothing else.

The Homeric assemblies did not, as a matter of fact, prefer a life of successful war so much to a life of peace as to be willing to accept nothing less. The Trojans and Achaians consented to war, knowing that there was in it for each man a risk of death, because they thought death was merely a risk and not because they preferred death to a life without glory. When they would die in battle, they would go down to Hades, Homer tells us, lamenting their fate. Achilles, it is true, was supposed to have accepted his fate in advance; he killed Hector knowing that his turn would probably come soon afterward and saying that he would accept his fate when it came. The acceptance of fate, nonetheless, was never the kind of thing which later on became the mark of the Stoic wise man.[54] Ideally the Stoic embraced his fate before it came, loving it, as it were, with his whole mind, his whole heart, and his whole soul, so that nothing could ever happen to him that was in any true sense against his own will. When a Homeric hero died, on the contrary, this was definitely against the hero's will and generally whenever things went contrary to his will he would not hesitate to remonstrate with the gods.

What happened to the two sides in the Trojan War was not at all in accord with their wills in spite of the fact that both had given assent to the war in their assemblies and had known beforehand at least of the possibility that things would turn out as badly as they did. Blindness played its role, to be sure, since if they had known for certain what was in store for them they probably would never have consented to the war. Hope at the same time did its part, leading them to act in the dark of their blindness and compensating for the failure of the cause itself to justify the deadly risks they had undertaken. Each element of the tragedy found its counterpart in the parody which Homer drew upon it in the conflict between Agamemnon and Achilles, the unworthy cause, the mutual blindness, and the common discomfiture. The followers of Achilles and those of Agamemnon consented, however reluctantly, to their leaders' wills in the quarrel, while not fully sharing their infatuation, but neither the "people," Agamemnon's army, nor the Myrmidons, Achilles' party, would have willingly given their consent to the mutual disaster that ensued.

Both parties displayed considerable dissatisfaction with their leaders, each urging its chief to abandon his stubborn opposition to the other. While the body of the army reproached Agamemnon for alienating Achilles, the Myrmidons reproached Achilles for keeping them out of the fight with the Trojans or, if his wrath was incurable, for keeping them there before Troy against their will instead of allowing them to set sail for home.[55] The unwillingness of the Myrmidons was not absolute, otherwise they would have either joined the battle or set sail in spite of Achilles. It was rather that their preference was to do battle, or if not that then to sail home, and only if he would have nothing else were they willing to go along with his policy of idleness. That they were in sympathy to some extent with Achilles' wrath against Agamemnon appears from the exhortation to bravery given them by Patroclus when he had succeeded in persuading Achilles to let him lead them into battle. Patroclus told them to fight bravely in order to bring honor on Achilles and shame on Agamemnon.[56] When they actually did fight, therefore, they were fighting to vindicate the wrath of Achilles. So the disaster they incurred, the loss of Patroclus, was the result of consenting to their chief's will and was altogether contrary to their own desires as well as his.

This, it seems, is the final incongruity of warfare in Homer's eyes. Those who lead men to war, he seems to think, are generally blind to the disproportion that exists between the cause of the war and its disastrous results. The men who follow their leaders into war are generally not so blind and do so against their better judgment only to share all the more absurdly in the ruin incurred by their leaders. The Trojans certainly preferred to turn Helen over to the Achaians rather than risk destruction for their city, death for themselves, and enslavement for their wives, as their open hatred and contempt for Paris and Helen show, but they reluctantly agreed to take the risk and as a consequence suffered the loss of everything they had. Agamemnon's men, in like manner, certainly preferred to turn Briseis over to Achilles rather than risk the damage they might suffer from the enemy if they had to fight without the aid of Achilles and his men, but they reluctantly agreed to go along with Agamemnon and as a consequence many a strong soul, as Homer puts it, was sent down to Hades while their bodies were left a prey to dogs and carrion birds.

The incongruity which Homer sees in warfare he extends to the world in which it occurs where divided gods can be brought only into a reluctant unity. In the four days of fighting described in the *Iliad* Zeus convokes the divine assembly twice, the first time on the second day of fighting in order sternly to forbid the gods to take part on either side in the battle between the Trojans and the Achaians, the second time on the fourth day of fighting in order to give them permission to join the battle, each god on whatever side he favored.[57] The gods who sympathized with the Achaians were thus compelled by Zeus at the first assembly to consent, against their preferences, to the temporary defeat of their favorites by the Trojans. Zeus himself, however, who would have preferred to save Troy, consented reluctantly to the ultimate defeat of the Trojans and the destruction of their city.[58] The upshot is that nothing which happened had whole-hearted divine approval. The war had only the reluctant consent of the men who engaged in it and the fortunes of the war, which were positively against the will of the men involved, had only the reluctant consent of the gods who presided over them.

How valid the Homeric theory of warfare turns out to be will depend to some extent on how fundamental and universal the form of society it presupposes proves to be. This society with its king-council-assembly structure is known to have obtained among most of the Indo-European peoples and also among the peoples who founded the first cities in Mesopotamia. As far as possible the idea that the king could not carry on a war without the support of an assembly of arms-bearing men was eliminated in the developed notion of the Pharaonic kingship, but evidence from the Proto-dynastic period, by contrast with later periods where the gigantic figure of the Pharaoh normally appears in solitary triumph, shows the king winning battles with the altogether obvious aid of his army.[59] This together with vestiges of the council of elders like the ceremonial council of the Great Ones of Upper and Lower Egypt point to the possible existence of a king-council-assembly type of society in early Egypt like that in early Mesopotamia. In succeeding ages, although this social structure gave way to forms of a more autocratic sort in some parts of the world and to forms of a more democratic sort in other parts of the world, the exigencies of warfare have always seemed to revive it, a war requiring leaders, counselors to advise them, and men willing to follow them. So from the standpoint of political form there is a case for attributing some kind of general relevance to Homer's point of view.

From the standpoint of content, if the interpretation given here has been generally correct, an important change occurred in the whole conception of war's purpose while the king-council-assembly form still prevailed. Where the cause of war had originally been considered something divine, Helen the goddess, it later came to be considered something human, Helen the woman. The change made a difference primarily in the king's object in leading his people to war, but it also made a difference in the significance of the council's advice on war and peace as well as in that of the assembly's consent to make war or peace. The warfare which Homer knows and which he finds so incongruous is this later type, fought for objectives that were quite earthly, rather than the earlier type, fought for more heavenly ideals. In an effort to rescue us from the madness of total warfare generated by modern political ideologies embodying a renewed attempt at consorting with the gods and thus a revival of the original conditions of warfare, many thinkers have proposed a return to more earthly and human objectives in warfare.[60] What awaits us if we do this, if we repeat once more the original evolution of war, Homer seems to warn, is only another kind of madness.

NOTES TO CHAPTER THREE

1. Kramer, *History Begins at Sumer* (New York, 1959), 100.

2. Pritchard, *op. cit.*, 455 ff.

3. On the Mesopotamian cities cf. Frankfort, *The Birth of Civilization in the Ancient Near East,* 49 ff. On the Egyptian cities *see* the texts in Pritchard, *op. cit.*, 3-8 on the claims of Heliopolis, Hermopolis, Memphis, and Thebes to be the site of creation.

4. Cf. Frankfort *op. cit.*, 69 f.

5. The disputes between Erech and Aratta took both forms. For the first

form *see* the epic described and partially translated in Kramer, *op. cit.*, 18 ff. For the second form *see* the one treated *ibid.*, 204 ff. The dispute between En-kimdu and Dumuzi (Pritchard, *op. cit.*, 41 f.), often cited as a parallel to the Cain and Abel story, is probably a contention between two cities for the god-dess since both of the rivals for the hand of Innin are said to be kings and Dumuzi is known to have been king of Erech. The conflict between Gilgamesh and Agga which we shall discuss in the concluding section of this chapter was probably understood to be a rivalry over the goddess since Gilgamesh is described in the relevant epic as one "who performs heroic deeds for Innin" and since the cities of the rival kings, Erech and Kish, were both under the special patronage of Innin. It is true that many of the Sumerian cities were under the patronage of other gods and goddesses but the patronage of Innin, at least in the earliest period, seems to have been tantamount to hegemony in the land.

6. *Il.* III, 156 ff. On Helen as a Mycenaean goddess cf. M.P. Nilsson, *The Minoan-Mycenaean Religion* (Lund, 1950), 528 ff.

7. *Od.* IV, 561 ff.

8. Nilsson, *op. cit.*, 530 f.

9. Cf. Nilsson, *op. cit.*, 616 ff.

10. *Il.* IX, 337 ff.

11. *Il.* VII, 400 ff.

12. *Il.* I, 297 ff.

13. *Il.* XIX, 59 ff.

14. *Il.* III, 173 ff.; VI, 344 ff.; XXIV, 764.

15. *Il.* III, 159 f. It is noteworthy that both women lament the principal hero whose death they have caused, Briseis mourns Patroclus (*Il.* XIX, 282 ff.) and Helen mourns Hector (*Il.* XXIV, 761 ff.), and they do so in much the same terms, weeping for the special kindness shown them by the hero in contrast with the unkindness shown them by everyone else.

16. *Il.* VII, 446 ff.

17. A love song chanted by a priestess impersonating the goddess Innin to the king Shu-Sin is translated in Kramer, *op. cit.*, 213 f.

18. *Il.* I, 352 ff.

19. *Il.* IX, 116 ff.

20. On the golden scales of destiny cf. Nilsson *op. cit.*, 34 ff. On the tablets of fate cf. Geo Widengren, *The Ascension of the Apostle and the Heavenly Book* (Uppsala, 1950) , 9 ff.

21. *Il.* VIII, 69 and XXII, 209.

22. On the Indo-European peoples cf. W. J. Shepard in *The Encyclopedia of the Social Sciences* IX, 355 ff. and VII, 11. On the Sumerians and Akkadians cf. Thorkild Jacobsen in *Journal of Near Eastern Studies* II (1943), 159 ff.

23. On the council of the Great Ones cf. Frankfort, *Kingship and the Gods*, 81 ff. and 130 ff.

24. Cf. Pritchard, *op. cit.*, 45.

25. On the Mesopotamian council and assembly of the gods cf. Jacobsen, *op. cit.*, 167 ff. On the Ennead *see* texts in Pritchard, *op. cit.*, 3-6 and partic-ularly 14-17 where the Ennead acts as a tribunal to settle the divine dispute over kingship in Egypt. On the Indo-European councils of gods cf. H. Munro Chadwick, *The Heroic Age*, (Cambridge, 1912) , 370 and 384.

26. Il. XVIII, 497 ff.

27. On the Mesopotamian judges of the dead *see* the translation of the Sumerian poem on the descent of the great goddess into the nether world in Kramer, *op. cit.,* 163 ff. The record of a Sumerian murder trial is translated *ibid.,* 57 f. On the forty-two judges of the dead in Egyptian mythology *see* the text of the Negative Confession in Pritchard *op. cit.,* 34 ff.

28. The names of the guilty in a conspiracy trial that has been recorded were changed into new and opprobrious titles. Cf. Pritchard, *op. cit.,* 214 ff.

29. I Sam. 28:13.

30. Rep. II, 379 ff.

31. Od. I, 32 ff.

32. Il. IV, 14 ff.

33. Od. XIX, 562.

34. Cf. Von Neumann and Morgenstern, *Theory of Games and Economic Behaviour* (Princeton, 1953) 144 ff.

35. Il. IX, 501 ff.

36. Hegel, *The Philosophy of History* tr. by J. Sibree (New York, 1956), 230 f.

37. Il. XII, 13 ff.

38. Il. I, 343; III, 109; XVIII, 250.

39. Il. II, 116 ff.; IX, 23 ff.

40. Il. II, 35 ff.

41. Il. XIV, 69 f.

42. Il. XIV, 153 ff.

43. Cf. Jacobsen's commentary attached to Kramer's edition of the poem "Gilgamesh and Agga" in *American Journal of Archaeology,* LIII (1949), 17 f.

44. Herman Kahn, *On Thermonuclear War* (Princeton, 1961), 47 n. 1.

45. Besides the story of Gilgamesh and Agga *see* the two epics describing disputes between Enmerkar, an earlier king of Erech, and Ensukushsiranna, king of Aratta, in Kramer, *History Begins at Sumer,* 18 ff. and 204 ff. Also the story of the dispute between Dumuzi and Enkimdu is relevant here if we are correct in taking it to be a conflict between two cities (cf. supra note 5).

46. Agamemnon is told expressly in his dream that the immortals are no longer divided (*Il.* II, 30 f.).

47. Single combat by selected champions was proposed as a solution of the conflict between Erech and Aratta (Kramer, *op. cit.,* 19 ff.).

48. Tolstoy, *War and Peace,* part XIV, sect. 1 (Modern Library ed., 960 ff.).

49. This seems to have been the manner in which a boundary dispute between the cities Lagash and Umma was settled (Kramer, *op. cit.,* 40 ff.).

50. Il. VII, 361 ff. and 389 ff.

51. Nietzsche, *Thus Spake Zarathustra,* I, 10, "On War and Warriors."

52. Il. II, 142 ff.

53. Nietzsche, *op. cit.,* II, 12.

54. Homer has both Patroclus (*Il.* XVI, 855 ff.) and Hector (*Il.* XXII, 361 ff.) bewail their lot as they go down to Hades. Achilles accepts his fate in the *Iliad* (XVIII, 115 ff.; XIX, 420 ff.; XXII, 365 f.) but bewails it in the *Odyssey* (XI, 488 ff.). For a classic statement of the Stoic thesis that nothing ever happens to the wise man against his will *see* the beginning of Epictetus' *Enchiridion.*

55. Il. XVI, 200 ff.

56. *Il.* XVI, 269 ff.

57. *Il.* VIII, 1 ff. (the first convocation) and *Il.* XX, 1 ff. (the second convocation).

58. *Il.* IV, 31 ff.

59. Frankfort, *The Birth of Civilization in the Ancient Near East,* 79 f.

60. *See,* for instance, Albert Camus' essay "Helen's Exile" in his *Myth of Sisyphus* tr. by Justin O'Brien (New York, 1955), 185 ff. where the (Homeric) motivation of the Trojan War is contrasted with the motivation of modern political movements in order to criticize the overweening ideals of contemporary man. Cf. also the discussion of limited and total warfare in my article "Realpolitik in the Decline of the West" in the *Review of Politics,* XXI (1959), 131 ff.

CHAPTER FOUR

Homeland and Wonderland

WHEN civilization began man had evidently not been convinced of any far-reaching limitations on his potentialities or else he probably never would have undertaken what to him was the enterprise of becoming like the gods. There is evidence, however, that the original ideals on which civilization had been built were lost at a rather early date. The *Epic of Gilgamesh,* the story of a man who sought and failed to attain the means of indefinitely prolonging life, must have appealed to a wish in those for whom it was composed, a wish whose failure to come true was still freshly felt. One would be inclined to think that the wish itself is always there in man, ready to respond sympathetically to a quest like that of Gilgamesh, since it has reappeared again and again in the course of history and has been very much in evidence in more recent times with the emerging ideal of the superman. In the *Odyssey,* though, we have another epic poem which certainly found a sympathetic response in the contemporaries for whom it was sung and which has had some impact down the ages. Yet it is the story of a man who did almost the very opposite of what Gilgamesh did. Odysseus turned down the chance of immortality when it was offered to him by the goddess Calypso, and he wandered as far to reach home as Gilgamesh did to reach the garden of paradise.

What apparently killed the idea of consorting with the gods was the belief which gradually took hold in the early city-state cultures that there is a nature in man which sets limits to his possibilities. "Strive not for immortality," Pindar said, "but exhaust the limits of the possible."[1] Before man could be brought to settle for this, he had to experience like Gilgamesh the frustration of his striving for immortality. Once failure had been thoroughly ascertained, though, he was in a position to give himself over wholeheartedly like Odysseus to exhausting the limits of the possible.

Now that the idea of human nature has come to be a commonplace it has become necessary to take the stand that there is no such thing as human nature, or what amounts to the same thing, that man's nature is to have no fixed nature but to be infinitely malleable and perfectible, both of which positions have been adopted in modern times, if there is to be any hope for consorting with the gods. All the same, the barriers which have invariably been encountered each time man has begun to strive for an ideal of this kind, above all the ineluctable barrier of death, seem always to evoke once more, as they have done again in our own time, the idea of human nature.[2]

To pass judgment on the validity of the idea, one must examine carefully the double experience out of which it seems to arise, the frustration exemplified by Gilgamesh and the retrenchment exemplified by Odysseus. If these two experiences stand up under scrutiny, then the idea of human nature would seem to be authenticated. If they do not, then the denial of human nature and the affirmation of man's perfectibility have yet to be adequately challenged.

Although there are a number of Near Eastern legends that parallel the tale of Odysseus refusing the gift of immortality offered him by the goddess Calypso, the reason for the refusal given in these stories is different from the one found in the Odyssey. The motive which Odysseus alleges when he turns down Calypso's proposal is homesickness.[3] The word for homesickness, *nostalgia,* is, of course, a modern creation. What Odysseus said was that he longed for the day of his homecoming. The word for homecoming, *nostos,* and its cognates occur very frequently in the *Odyssey*[4] and designate what was undoubtedly supposed to be uppermost in the mind of Odysseus and his companions. Calypso was amazed that he should prefer his wife, a mortal woman, to her, an immortal goddess, and that he should be willing to undergo all the troubles that lay in store for him if he attempted the voyage to his homeland. Odysseus' reasoning was apparently that immortality would do him no good if he were unhappy because then it would only amount to eternal misery. It was far better, he thought, to be happy for a short period and then die than to be unhappy forever. Living with Calypso on the wild island of Ogygia meant misery to him, all the worse for being prolonged indefinitely, whereas living with Penelope in Ithaca his homeland meant happiness, no less desirable for being foreshortened by death.

When the great goddess of the Near East was spurned, it was not with any idea that the immortality she offered was tantamount to eternal misery, it seems, but rather with the conviction that when she promised eternal life she could not possibly be telling the truth. There is a Ugaritic tale of a youth named Aqhat who refused the goddess Anath when she offered him immortality in exchange for his bow.[5] He rejected her proposal, remonstrated with her for lying to him, and went on to say that he knew he would grow old and die like everyone else. The supposedly unanswerable question which he asked her: "How can a mortal attain life everlasting?" practically articulated the idea of human nature as an unsurpassable barrier. It would be an exaggeration to say that it was thought to be a contradiction in terms and an absolute impossibility for a mortal to become immortal, for there are instances of mortals being made immortal in Near Eastern mythology. The barrier probably amounted to this, that one could not become immortal without ceasing to be human, that to live forever one had to become one of the gods and cease to be one of mankind. If one pushes the matter far enough, one comes to the underlying feeling that the gods are dead and that one must die to become one of them.

Greek mythology seems to have been in agreement with Near Eastern mythology on the impossibility of becoming immortal without ceasing to be human. What was added in the Greek standpoint was the further consideration that in relinquishing humanity one relinquished also the possibility of human happiness. There was an eternal happiness that was available to the immortal but there was also an eternal misery to which he was liable. It has been said with some degree of truth that the Greeks never asserted that the limits imposed by human nature could not be transgressed, but only that if one did transgress them one would have to pay a heavy penalty. Although there was no idea in Greek mythology of anything like the Christian hell to which any human being could go after death, there were stories about human beings who became immortal and were eternally miserable. One could, for instance, be given immortality without being given perpetual youth and thus one would spend one's eternity like Tithonos[6] getting older and older while one's life became less and less enjoyable. Immortality by itself was not necessarily equivalent to eternal happiness even for gods, and its inhuman character could make it seem almost equivalent to eternal misery for persons who had once been human.

It might be suspected that immortality had actually become "sour grapes" to the Greeks, that it was something they disparaged because they knew they could not possess it. After all there was no question of someone like Odysseus really being given a chance of immortality and turning it down. All the tales of eternal misery which we find in Greek mythology were told by men who never had any opportunity to become immortal and who were only expressing their attitude toward something which was beyond their reach. Perhaps, one might think, there was less self-deception in the frank disappointment expressed in the Near Eastern mythologies. The Homeric attitude is one that would appear only a considerable time after the initial shock of disappointment. At first there would have been an open acknowledgement of a desire for unending life. After the impossibility of ever realizing such a wish became an established fact, there would have been an attempt on man's part to reconcile himself with his inescapable mortality by telling himself that he never really wanted to be immortal anyway. This attempt had not yet been made in the mythmaking of the Near East though there was a clear realization already in the *Epic of Gilgamesh* that man's happiness was to be found in earthly joys rather than heavenly ones.[7]

In the legends about Heracles there is evidence of an earlier Greek attitude that would have corresponded directly to the Near Eastern mentality. Heracles' quest for the golden apples of the Hesperides was an open endeavor to attain the means of indefinitely prolonging life, and, according to Achilles' statement in the *Iliad* that even Heracles failed to escape death,[8] his quest must have turned out in much the same manner as that of Gilgamesh. The denouement which we find in the *Odyssey*, therefore, probably represents a later point of view taken when men had passed the stage of simply being frustrated in their striving for immortality and were trying to devote themselves fully to exhausting the limits of the possible.

What killed Heracles, according to the *Iliad*, was fate and the implacable anger of Hera. It could probably be said, in like manner, that what killed Gilgamesh was fate and the implacable anger of Innin. The name "Heracles," "Hera's glory," suggests that the relationship of Heracles to Hera may originally have been similar to that of Gilgamesh to Innin. When Gilgamesh spurned Innin and thereby merited her unrelenting hatred, he did so not because he had no desire for immortality but because he did not want an immortality which could be attained only through the experience of death.[9] What he wanted was an indefinite prolongation of his earthly existence. This seems also to have been the goal of Heracles' labors. If we put this into the perspective of the *Odyssey* it would amount to desiring everlasting life in one's own homeland as opposed to everlasting life in the Elysian fields or on Calypso's island or the like. Both Gilgamesh and Heracles attempted to bring back to their homeland the means of indefinitely prolonging life: Gilgamesh tried to bring back the plant that renewed one's youth to Erech and Heracles tried to bring back the golden apples of the Hesperides to Tiryns.

This quest of Heracles and Gilgamesh represents dissatisfaction with the ideal of immortality on which civilization was originally built, the ideal of consorting with gods who were dead. Gilgamesh wanted nothing to do with a goddess with whom he would be called upon to share the experience of death. Failure to Gilgamesh

and Heracles did not mean failure of the original hope of life
after death, for there is hardly any way for a living man to learn
whether or not the hope for an afterlife is vain unless he assumes
that the afterlife is bound up with the preservation of the body
in the tomb. In the latter eventuality there can be an apparent
failure of this hope as there was in ancient Egypt during the
interregnum when the tombs were despoiled. Maybe a failure of
this type was experienced also in the Mycenaean civilization and
was the source of the dissatisfaction expressed in the tales of
Heracles. The failure of the quest of Heracles and Gilgamesh, in
any case, meant the frustration of the more ambitious idea of an
immortality in this world. After this there was nothing left to
do but embrace wholeheartedly like Odysseus the finite life-span
on earth which was obviously within man's reach.

In spite of these changes of attitude, from striving for an everlasting life beyond the grave to striving for everlasting life in
this world and from that to making the most of a finite life in
this world, there had not been a great deal of change in the real
object of man's desires. If we were correct in taking the afterlife
which was desired in the first civilizations to be a participation
by the dead in the existence of the living,[10] then at all stages
what man really desired was to live in this world. At first it
seemed that it was possible for the dead to live on in this world
after death by sharing in the existence of the living. Then, either
because this participation in the life of the living did not seem
enough like real life or because the despoliation of tombs made
it seem unlikely, there was an abortive attempt or wish to find
some way of actually preventing death. Finally, when it became
evident that there was no feasible way of prolonging life on earth
indefinitely, there was a more or less desperate effort to extract
the most out of the little time man was granted to live. This last
stage could be reached, of course, without passing through the
intermediate stage, as it was in the "time of troubles" in ancient
Egypt, when the possibility of staving off death indefinitely was
not seriously considered.

Although Odysseus turned down the chance of immortality
offered him by Calypso, he did not do this because he wanted to

die nor did he do it because he did not mind dying as long as he reached home. When Circe told him that he must visit the nether world in order to learn from the dead prophet Tiresias what he was to do in order to reach home he made it very plain that he had nothing but horror at the thought of death. He accepts his fate, to be sure, when he is told of it by Tiresias, but he does so only because it is useless to reject it. The sentiment expressed by the ghost of Achilles, that he would rather be a live slave than a dead king,[11] was undoubtedly shared by Odysseus himself.

The reason for hating death was the same as the reason for rejecting immortality, paradoxically, the desire to lead an ordinary earthly existence. Death deprived a man of home and wife and friends and everything with which he was familiar. If the desire for these things was good reason for turning down a chance for immortality in a strange land in the company of an inhuman being, it was also good reason for hating death and making every effort to save one's life. Odysseus was told that he would live to ripe old age and that death would come to him gently from the sea.[12] But this death from the sea, however gentle and tardy, could never be actually welcome. The best that could be said for it was that it was more palatable than a premature death.

There is a contemporary way of thinking, the existentialist, according to which the very thought of death banishes us once and for all from everything in which we are at home. From this standpoint one can enjoy the kind of life Odysseus wanted to lead, an existence at home and among familiar persons and things, only by concealing from oneself the truth that one must die. Authentic human existence, from this point of view, is the "happening of strangeness,"[13] the homelessness that arises from consciously facing death. To live in truth, according to this, would be to live as Odysseus did amid strange lands with his fate always before his eyes, taking his future into his own hands and making choices of life and death. To live as he wanted to live, at home, without cares, among familiar persons and things, would be to live in self-deception. Odysseus, according to this position, was possessed of authentic existence in spite of himself. If he could have had his own way he would have been a perfect non-entity, and, when he did finally have his own way after his return and after the massacre of the suitors who had been plaguing his wife and his home, he actually did lapse into what is considered bourgeois mediocrity.

Everyday existence from the standpoint of the *Odyssey*, nevertheless, is not, as it is in existentialism, the least a man can do. It is rather something that may have to be won with the kind of cunning and patience that was exhibited by Odysseus in reaching and winning his home. The sort of existence that would be regarded as "authentic" in existentialism is from the standpoint of the *Odyssey* a life that a man may well be constrained to lead against his own will and by mere force of circumstances like the extraordinary life which Odysseus had to lead while he was seeking to regain the possibility of an ordinary life. It is true that as soon as Odysseus had fully retrieved his familiar surroundings the story told by Homer ceases as though the life of Odysseus from that point on contained nothing interesting or remarkable. This would amount to a critical commentary on Odysseus' goal in life only if it is assumed that there is something preferable to being happy such as making of one's life a good story.

If there is a criticism of Odysseus' life made by Homer himself in the *Odyssey*, it is that the happiness which Odysseus sought was out of proportion to the price he had to pay for it in misery. Calypso tells him that if he knew what troubles he would have before he got to Ithaca he would stay with her. He answers that he has already suffered so much that this will only be one trouble more.[14] What Odysseus had desired all along was simply home but the Cyclops whose eye he had destroyed had called down a curse upon his homecoming, that he reach home late and in misery, in another man's ship, that he lose all his companions and find tribulation when he finally arrived.[15] His homecoming was indeed spoiled in this manner though this did not prevent him from being happy at last when all the trouble was over. It is admittedly impossible to argue with happiness, but one can take Odysseus' life as a whole with its mixture of happiness and misery and say something about the relative proportions of misery and happiness, namely that the happiness is disproportionately small in comparison with the misery. In Odysseus' situation there was nothing to do but make every effort to achieve this happiness however small, but if it had been his to decide he certainly would not have chosen a life with so large a portion of unhappiness. Plato's story of Odysseus choosing to be reincarnated as a common man who had no cares seems very much in keeping with the character he is given by Homer.[16]

There is a reader's illusion into which it is easy to fall and which greatly hinders an understanding of the *Odyssey*. We read the story of Odysseus' adventures with such pleasure that we are unconsciously led to suppose that Odysseus himself had a desire for adventure and that in spite of his complaints his adventures were somehow a delight to him. Each time Odysseus told his story in the *Odyssey* itself he told it as a tale of hardship but his listeners, first the Phaeacians and then his wife Penelope, took delight in hearing it.[17] The story is undoubtedly intended to produce just this effect in its hearers but it remains for all that a tale of misery and woe. In order to understand the view of life which it contains, it is essential to recognize and avoid the fallacy of confounding the effect which the adventures of Odysseus have on us with the effect they were supposed to have had on him. There is indeed in this view of life the idea that an adventure story is a delight to hear, a delight, however, when one listens to it as the Phaeacians did in the coziness of one's hall or as Penelope did in reunion with one's own at home.

If instead of being considered a series of delightful adventures Odysseus' wanderings are regarded in the manner they were apparently intended to be as a series of woeful hardships, there comes to light an underlying absurdity in the world in which they were supposed to have occurred. Without the goal of immortality the travels of Odysseus became somewhat pointless by comparison with those of Heracles and Gilgamesh who deliberately set out in quest of strange lands to find the means of prolonging life and when they found it tried to bring it home with them. Only the goal of home remains in the *Odyssey*. As a result the sojourn in strange lands which made sense in a search for eternal life became a meaningless exile.

Wonderland in the legends of Gilgamesh and Heracles is a kind of obstacle course leading to immortality. Each obstacle overcome is death overcome in a new way. Gilgamesh's first task is to kill the monster that hoards life in the evergreen forest. Then he must resist the attempts made by Ishtar to seduce him, the object of the seduction being not simply the sexual intercourse that one would have with a woman but the experience of death that one would share with a goddess. As a result of spurning the goddess Gilgamesh must destroy another monster, the bull of heaven, this time a monster that deals out death rather than one that hoards up life, the sort of monster that Heracles had to contend with as a result of his enmity with Hera. Then comes the task of harrowing hell, raiding the land of the dead, a task which Gilgamesh leaves to his friend Enkidu to the latter's ruin[18] but which Heracles performs himself by kidnaping the hound of hell. Next comes the task of overcoming death in the form of darkness and reaching the garden where the sun rises or sets, for Gilgamesh the garden of jewels, for Heracles the garden of the Hesperides. There follows for Gilgamesh the task of overcoming death in the form of the dead sea, the antithesis of "living water," by crossing safely over "the waters of death." Then there is the task, at which Gilgamesh fails, of overcoming death in the form of sleep by staying awake six days and seven nights. Finally there is the task of securing the actual means of prolonging life, for Gilgamesh the plant of renewed youth, for Heracles the golden apples of life, and bringing it back to the city, a task at which both heroes ultimately fail since neither succeeds in keeping the elixir in his possession.

Wonderland takes on a different aspect in the *Odyssey*.[19] It is still an obstacle course but an obstacle course on the road to home. Each obstacle is a trap to prevent the hero's homecoming. In the first adventure, the raid on the Ciconians, the temptation is to tarry over the enjoyment of plunder instead of immediately resuming the homeward voyage. The trap in the land of the lotus-eaters, the next stop, is the lotus which makes one forget home altogether. The danger in the next place, the land of the Cyclops, is to fall into the hands of the Cyclops or, if one escapes, to have one's homecoming cursed by him. The snare in the next port of call, the island of the winds, is the gift the king offers, the bag of winds, since these winds released can blow the ship into unknown waters when it is already in sight of home. Where Odysseus loses his fleet, all except his own ship, is at the next stop, apparently the land of the midnight sun, a place inhabited by cannibals. The lure in the island to which he comes after this is the charm and the witchcraft of the goddess Circe who detains Odysseus for a year and almost makes him forget home. The visit to the land of the dead is retained in the *Odyssey* and follows the stay with Circe but instead of being a harrowing of hell it is only a daring piece of necromancy, a consultation with the dead prophet Tiresias on the problem of reaching home and at the same time a reunion with dead friends and relatives. The Sirens whose island comes next on the itinerary bewitch men who stay to hear their song so that they never see home again. The danger at the moving rocks and between Scylla and Charybdis which come next on the homeward journey is, of course, shipwreck and death. The temptation that waits on the island of the sun for those who make their way through the strait is to forfeit their homecoming by eating the cattle of the sun. On the island of Ogygia, after this, there lies the greatest temptation of all, the goddess Calypso and her offer of immortality. Once this temptation is overcome and the land of the Phaeacians is reached there are no more obstacles and a quick passage is provided by this seafaring people from wonderland to homeland.

While there is a consistency in the adventures of Odysseus in wonderland that compares with that in the adventures of Gilgamesh and Heracles, each incident being the surmounting of an obstacle on the way to a single goal, there is nevertheless an overall loss of sense in that Odysseus is led far out of his way to reach home whereas one would expect Heracles and Gilgamesh to be led out of common paths if they are to reach something as extraordinary as the garden of paradise. Obstacles that would make sense on the way to paradise seem gratuitous on the way to home. It is somewhat similar to the senselessness that over-shrouded the Trojan War when Helen ceased to be considered a goddess.

It is not surprising in view of this that the idea of blindness (*ate*) figures as prominently in the *Odyssey* as it does in the *Iliad*. There is the blindness of Odysseus himself in provoking the Cyclops who is son of the sea-god; then there is the blindness of his companions in eating the cattle of the sun; and then there is the blindness of the suitors to Penelope in acting as though Odysseus would never return.[20] The first is the reason why Odysseus' homecoming is so tardy and miserable; the second is why he returns without his companions; and the third is why he finds trouble waiting for him at home.

This is like the mutual blindness of the two sides in the Trojan War and it is capped with a similarly arbitrary behavior on the part of the gods. The difference is that the pointlessness brought out in the *Iliad* arose from the loss of the original ideal of life after death on which civilization had been built and which in the early city-cultures meant sharing the life and death of the city-goddess while the pointlessness brought out in the Odyssey arose from the loss of the subsequent ideal of perpetual life on earth to which men had evidently turned in their dissatisfaction with the first.

Whether in the form of fellowship between the living and the dead or in the form of indefinite prolongation of life, the ideal of consorting with the gods was lost. It is true that the failure of a given attempt to find the elixir does not prove that there is no way of indefinitely prolonging life anymore than the failure of a given method of embalming and entombment proves that there is no afterlife. In these experiences of failure, nevertheless, there is the occasion for an insight into the finitary character of all human achievement. This insight is tantamount to the discovery of human nature if we reduce the meaning of the term "human nature" to that of a limiting factor in man's makeup. The insight seems to be a valid one too as long as its purported significance is not extended one whit beyond the statement that what man can achieve by his own efforts is necessarily finite. If one goes on instead to assume that what man can be is no more and no less than what he can achieve, some fairly questionable conclusions follow. It follows, of course, that he should not desire immortality, for if what he can be is only what he can achieve then he can never become immortal and to desire it would be to indulge in a delusion that is by no means harmless. It also follows that man should devote himself, as Pindar advises, to exhausting the possibilities of the finite, an endeavor from which ineffectual wishing for immortality can only distract him.

The pointlessness, however, revealed by the *Iliad* and the *Odyssey* in a life devoted to exhausting the possibilities of the finite raises some doubts about the wisdom of this advice. It seems in fact to call for a revaluation of the ideal of immortality. One could argue, to be sure, that the futility of the fighting described in the *Iliad* and of the wandering described in the *Odyssey* implies simply that actions which make sense only in a quest for immortality have no place in a meaningful human life and not that life itself is largely meaningless without the hope for immortality. In the Homeric view of things, though, a man may be compelled by force of circumstances to fight or to wander in this absurd manner in order to wrest from life what little happiness he can. There can be no question in such a view of eliminating everything which has no place in a meaningful life. The feeling of futility which we find in the two epics, on the other hand, would not exist if there were not at work in them a demand for meaning in life. Unless the bold determination to be a man and the proud refusal to consort with the gods is to be written off as a somewhat pretentious instance of "sour grapes," there must be some possibility of this demand being satisfied.

NOTES TO CHAPTER FOUR

1. *Pyth.*, III, 61 f.

2. Albert Camus's works, especially *The Myth of Sisyphus* tr. by Justin O'Brien (New York, 1955) and *The Rebel* tr. by Anthony Bower (New York, 1956), contain an appeal for a return to the Greek idea of nature. Note the imagery from the *Odyssey* in the conclusion of the latter work.

3. *Od.* V, 215 ff.

4. Cf. the words νοστέω, νόστιμος, and νόστος in Ebeling's *Lexicon Homericum* (Leipzig, 1895) I, 1163.

5. Pritchard, *op. cit.*, 151 f.

6. Cf. the Homeric "Hymn to Aphrodite," 218 ff.

7. The ale-wife advises Gilgamesh to give up the quest for immortality and seek the joys of home (Pritchard, *op. cit.*, 90) .

8. *Il.* XVIII, 117 ff. In the *Odyssey* (XI, 601 ff.) the ghost of Heracles is encountered in the land of the dead. The lines (602-4) containing the statement that this was merely his phantom and that he himself lived with the immortal gods were rejected by some ancient critics as having been inserted into the text by Onomacritus. The idea that Heracles actually succeeded in attaining immortality seems to be a post-Homeric belief but it appears already in Hesiod (*Theog.*, 950 ff.).

9. The discussion of Gilgamesh's repulse of Innin in Chapter One is based on the Akkadian epic. The Sumerian prototype, which is said to differ in detail but not in substance, has not yet been published (cf. Kramer, *History Begins at Sumer*, 190).

10. This interpretation was developed in Chapter Two in connection with Egyptian civilization but it is probably applicable to Mesopotamian civilization too for the period preceding the dissatisfaction with the afterlife expressed in the tales of Gilgamesh and to the Minoan and Mycenaean civilization for the period preceding the similar reaction expressed in the tales of Heracles.

11. Od. XI, 489 ff.

12. Od. XI, 134 ff.

13. Heidegger, *An Introduction to Metaphysics* tr. by Ralph Manheim (New Haven, 1959), 150 ff. and especially 158.

14. Od. V, 221 ff.

15. Od. IX, 532 ff.

16. Republic X, 620 D.

17. Cf. *Od.* XI, 333 ff. (the reaction of the Phaeacians) and XXIII, 308 f. (the reaction of Penelope).

18. Here I am replacing the story of Enkidu's death from illness given on Tablet VII of the epic (Pritchard, *Op. cit.*, 85 ff.) with the alternative and, to judge from the Sumerian material, earlier story of his death in the attempt to retrieve Gilgamesh's *mikku* and *pukku* from the nether world given on Tablet XII (*ibid.*, 97 ff.).

19. There is enough similarity between the *Odyssey* and the *Epic of Gilgamesh*, however, to make the contrast relevant. Cf. A. Ungnad's short essay *Gilgamesch-Epos und Odyssee* (Breslau, 1923).

20. Odysseus refuses twice to listen to the advice of his companions against provoking the Cyclops (*Od.* IX, 228 ff. and 500 ff.); the companions later will not heed Odysseus' warning against landing on the island of the sun and eating the cattle there (*Od.* XII, 277 ff. and 339 ff.); and the suitors will not listen to the reproaches they receive in the council meeting (*Od.* II, 84 ff.).

CHAPTER FIVE

Eternal Cities

THERE is a way open toward immortality even for the man who thinks that life ends with death and that there is no afterlife or at best only a shadowy existence in a nether world. This way is suggested by the commonplace notion of everlasting fame, but it amounts in actuality to something more than an immortality dependent upon human memory. It takes its strongest form in a view of life according to which the past on account of its immutability is immortal. In the Homeric epics the idea of everlasting fame plays an important role, but the constant contrasting of the mortality of mankind with the immortality of the gods, of the tragic existence of mankind with the comic existence of the gods, made it difficult to pass from this to the idea of an undying past. It was not easy to think in terms of an immortal past when the idea of immortality which occupied attention was that of an endless future such as the gods were supposed to enjoy. The despair of consorting with the gods, though, and the consequent decline of kingship did eventually lead men in their search for life to the concept of a past that never dies. The final result was an eternal city, not a society with an infinite future but a society with an immortal past.

This philosophy of life, though it arose long ago in the transition from early kingship to the urban republic, is still a serious possibility for modern man. It has been given new life in renaissance after renaissance down the ages, and it remains the direct alternative to the philosophy of life which forms the basis of modern revolutionary societies in which the past is thought to be in some significant sense abolished. The most articulate phase in its long career, however, was during the brief ascendancy of

Athens in the ancient world, and it is this privileged moment that we must consider if we are to form an adequate estimate of its worth.

[1] *City and Place*

Cities were sacked in republican times as they had been in earlier periods, but the destruction of the city seems to have lost the significance it had when wars were fought over the presence of the goddess in the locality. The evacuation of Athens during the Persian War was carried out on the assumption that the Athenians would still constitute a city even after their town had been sacked and burned by the enemy. Themistocles' famous answer to the taunt that the Athenians no longer had a city was that they had a city greater than any other in Greece as long as they had two hundred ships fully manned. He could threaten, moreover, in sober earnest that the Athenians would take their households and establish their city in Italy (at Siris) if the other Greeks would not agree to join them in a sea-fight against the Persians off Salamis for the purpose of regaining their land and their burnt-out town.[1] All this was possible in spite of the fact that it had always been the peculiar boast of the Athenians that they were autochthonous, that they had lived in the same place from the very beginning and had not taken their land from earlier inhabitants as the Dorians, for instance, had done.

A city that can exist in a fleet at sea or that can be transferred to another land is a far cry from the city in which gods and men had mingled at the center of the world. The departure from the earlier idea that the city is a sacred place, to be sure, is not so radical as to be already tantamount to the Copernican Revolution. Still the consciousness of the city's independence with respect to place is a clear anticipation of the modern consciousness of the insignificance of man's particular location in the universe. The old rites which were observed at the founding of a city and which embodied the notion that the city was a holy place were carried out in republican times whenever a colony was established,[2] but their meaningfulness was inevitably lessened with the decline and fall of the traditional kingship and the decreasing importance of the divine presence in the locality.

It has been said that since Copernicus man has been rolling away, faster and faster, from the center.³ If this were true, one might suspect that the roll from center was already beginning when the concrete location of the city was ceasing to be considered a matter of decisive significance. In reality it seems that neither the early change of perspective on man's place in the world nor the later Copernican Revolution amounted to a denial or diminution of man's importance in the world. The denial of significance of man's particular location in the universe can be taken instead as an affirmation of his transcendence with respect to place. This at least was the way it was taken in the time of the early republics. The affirmative side of this early change of worldview appears in the slogan current in those days to the effect that it is men rather than walls that make a city.

At Sparta the new principle was exemplified by the fact that the city was not a citadel at all but was left unfortified and entirely dependent on the bravery of its citizens. The prehistoric Sparta of Helen and Menelaus had been a walled citadel, of course, like other Mycenaean centers. Historic Sparta, though, was without walls until the days of the Macedonian domination of Greece. The legendary lawgiver of Sparta, Lycurgus, when asked about the question of fortifying the city, is supposed to have said that a city will be well fortified if it is surrounded by brave men instead of bricks. There were similar sayings to the effect that walls should be allowed to slumber in the earth and should not be awakened or that they ought to be of iron and steel rather than of earth.⁴ The town itself was little better than a group of villages situated by the river Eurotas, and the land did not all belong to citizens but was divided between citizens and subjects and thus did not constitute a proper territorial unity.⁵ It was not until Hellenistic times that the four villages were finally enclosed with a ring wall and the city once again became a citadel.

At Athens the new principle was exemplified by the survival of the city in its citizens despite the destruction of the citadel. Although the town was sacked and burned twice over in the course

of the Persian War, the Athenians considered themselves un-
defeated. As Aeschylus put it, the town was safe as long as the
men still existed.[6] An extended version of the slogan about men
rather than walls making a city appeared in Sophocles and
Thucydides to the effect that a city is made of men and not of
walls or empty ships.[7] The addition about ships was probably
inspired by the imagery of the Delphic Oracle's advice to Athens
during the war that the city be protected with a wooden wall,
that is, as Themistocles interpreted it, with a fleet.[8] Themistocles'
own saying that the Athenians had a city as long as they had two
hundred ships fully manned was valid, according to this version,
because the ships were fully manned. When the fleet itself was
lost later on in the Peloponnesian War, at the siege of Syracuse,
the Athenian army was told by Nicias its general that it still constituted a city even though it was far from home and had no more
means of reaching home.[9]

If nothing were left to Athens and Sparta but ruins, Thucydides
conjectured, posterity would be very reluctant to believe that
Sparta's power was equal to what it really was and would be very
prone to think that the strength of Athens was twice as great as
it actually was.[10] Sparta was not much to look upon while Athens
was quite splendid in its physical appearance. In spite of the
energy lavished upon it at Athens, however, the physical structure
of the city was considered accessory and incidental to the human
substance of the city. After the Persians departed only small portions of the encircling wall of Athens remained and most of the
houses were in ruins, the only exceptions being the ones which
the Persians had used as their quarters. The city was soon rebuilt
and so were the walls, Spartan protests to the contrary notwithstanding, and afterward when Athens grew rich an elaborate
building program under the leadership of Pericles was undertaken
in which most of the great works of architecture and sculpture
for which Athens was famous in later ages were completed. At the
beginning of the Peloponnesian War, however, Pericles made it
plain how far these things were from being indispensable by
pointing out that the gold on the statue of Athena by Phidias
could be removed and used to finance the war.[11]

Although there had probably never been such a thing as idol worship in the Greek cities, still in Mycenaean times when the city was in essence a place made sacred by the presence of the goddess much more importance had been attached to shrines and images. This is reflected to some extent in the tradition of the Trojan War according to which it was necessary to steal the Palladium, the image of the city-goddess, from Troy before the city could be taken.[12] There probably was such a goddess worshiped at Troy if Troy was like other early city-states in Asia. This Trojan goddess, of course, would not have been either the Helen or the Athena worshiped by the Mycenaeans. It was natural, though, for the Achaians who sacked Troy to identify the Asiatic goddess with one of their own. In the *Iliad* we have a later form of the tradition in which the Trojan goddess was confounded with the goddess of Sparta while in the story of the Palladium we have the fragment of a tradition in which the Asiatic goddess was confounded with the goddess of Athens.

These Mycenaean goddesses Helen and Athena were probably very much alike in the beginning. Helen was as much a goddess in Mycenaean times as Athena and Athena was probably no more a virgin in those days than Helen. It is likely that traditional kings of Athens like Erechtheus were at one time thought to have been Athena's human consorts. There is a trace of this, it seems, in the *Odyssey* where Athena, after going far afield to help Odysseus in his homeward wanderings, herself returns to the house of Erechtheus at Athens as though Athens were her home instead of Olympus.[13] That Helen for her part was probably the divine consort of the Mycenaean kings at Sparta seems to be indicated in the Homeric tradition that Menelaus, the king of Sparta, was her husband. Both goddesses lost their original role in the city when the transition was made from the early kingship to the republic. Helen lost her divinity and became a legendary woman of the past while the kingship at Sparta was eventually replaced by a dual kingship in which the two "kings" were actually republican magistrates. Athena did not lose her divinity but she did become a virgin and the king, her human consort, disappeared entirely except for certain of his functions which were assigned to one of the magistrates in the republic.

There was an idea of the city, however, which came between the early conception of it as a sacred place and the late conception of it as a human community. This was the idea of the city as home or homeland. In this intermediate point of view the city was still essentially a place and not yet a human collectivity but the process of humanization was already underway because it had become primarily a place where men and women lived rather than a place where mankind and the gods lived in common. Already at this stage the king had ceased to be the human consort of the goddess and the goddess herself had begun to change into a virgin or into a woman. The kingship nevertheless, to judge from the Homeric epics where this period is directly reflected, continued somehow for the time being. When the city became a strictly human dwelling-place, the king became the principal resident and householder of the locality and his palace which had formerly possessed the quality of a sanctuary became the principal home. It was not far to go from this to the idea that the king was merely *primus inter pares* and thence to the conviction that he could be rightly repudiated by his aristocratic peers.

This town composed of homes, one of the homes being a palace, was the immediate predecessor of the urban republic. This fact probably contributed to the impression in republican times that the origin of the state was the household. Conceiving the city as a human community, thinkers like Plato and Aristotle sought to explain its origin by pointing to a more elementary community, the family, whose needs called it into existence.[14] Plato in the *Laws* envisions the city being formed by a group of householders, heads of families agreeing to compromise on their respective family customs and to accept a common set of laws. Aristotle begins his treatise on politics with a discussion of the family and speculates that the earliest society was the single household, then an aggregation of households developed into villages, and finally combinations of villages formed cities. Fustel de Coulanges, the author of the modern classic on the ancient city, following the lead of Plato and Aristotle, proposes the general thesis that the civic institutions of ancient times took their origin from domestic institutions.[15]

In reality there seems always to have been some larger society in the context of which families have existed and in the evolution of which they have participated. The domestic institutions that obtained in the earliest urban culture when the king was human consort of the goddess were probably very different from those that prevailed afterward. Succession in the female line is usual in such societies, and if it existed in the Mycenaean cities there would have been a considerable revolution in customs in the transition to Homeric society where succession was in the male line.[16] A further change seems to have occurred in the transition from the royal city to the urban republic. As the city came to be considered a community rather than a place, the household came to be considered a family rather than a home. The difference becomes manifest in the practice of moving the household from one place to another, something that was probably inconceivable in the earlier period when the household was inseparable from the homestead. The idea of carrying one's household gods and one's home fire from one place to another was as novel as the idea of moving a city from one place to another. Households were evidently no longer places within a place but communities within a community.

[2] City and Utopia

It should be asked whether this newly developed independence with respect to place has any connection with the over-all modification of human living and thinking which came about during the republican period. The indifference with regard to place that has been characteristic of modern life subsequent to the Copernican Revolution has come under criticism for being in actuality nothing but uprootedness and alienation.[17] To live in a human manner, it has been argued, means to dwell, and when man lives as though his living were not dwelling then his existence has been denatured. A corresponding denaturation has supposedly occurred in thinking, inseparable as thinking is from living, in that thought has become an unmindfully abstract consideration of the universe in terms of space and extension instead of a concrete apprehension of the world in terms of place.

In the days of the urban republic there was radical criticism by philosophers, especially by Plato, of the mode of thinking and living which then prevailed, but the criticism was not directed against the newly won independence of place. On the contrary, Plato had gone from the notion of an actual city like Athens or Sparta being independent with respect to place to the notion of an ideal city that completely transcended place. The transformation of the city from a place into a community had created the proper atmosphere for utopian thinking. Plato's ideal republic was a utopia in the literal meaning of the term, a "nowhere." He did not criticize thinking for having become independent with respect to place but called for a kind of thinking that was still more radically transcendent in this regard and engaged in this sort of thinking himself. He did not criticize living for being less a matter of dwelling than it was formerly but maintained instead that the wise man ought to make his abode in the ideal city, that he ought to live as a citizen of that city more than as an inhabitant of his native city on earth, and Plato did indeed renounce Athenian politics and strive to live in this manner himself.[18]

One could imagine the society of Plato's time being criticized in a manner quite different from that in which Plato criticized it. The rise of the urban republic would be taken for the decline and fall of much that was valuable to man. The gods began to withdraw from man's life, so this critique would go, when the city ceased to be conceived as a sacred place where mankind lived with the gods and began to be regarded as the homeland of men and women and eventually as a collectivity of human beings. At the same time the earth will have lost some of its sacredness and some of its dearness to man and become with the idea of land reform a thing to be divided fairly or unfairly among citizens and exploited by them. Man himself in becoming a citizen will have been standardized both in cities like Sparta where citizenship was greatly limited and in cities like Athens where it was more extended, for at least in principle any citizen could be substituted for any other in public office and in the various peacetime and wartime activities of the city. With standardization there will have come the preeminence of the standard man, each individual citizen being measured against the standard citizen and if he was found to deviate too much, especially if he was found to excell the standard too greatly, being liable to ostracism.

This imaginary critique of the urban republic, suggested by the existentialist critique of Copernican society, is turned inside out in Platonism. Plato advocated a more radical standardization and on account of this a more radical land reform and a more radical reformation of religion than had already been carried out in the development of the urban republics. Standardization of itself was in his eyes neither a good nor an evil. Everything depended on whether the standard man was the good man or the evil man or the mediocre man. In a tyranny as it seemed to him, probably from his experience with the two tyrants of Syracuse one of whom he tried unsuccessfully to win over to a philosopher's life, the standard man was the evil man. In a democracy, on the other hand, and here he was probably influenced by his experience of living in the democracy at Athens under which Socrates was condemned and put to death, the standard man was the mediocre man. What he advocated was a society in which the standard man would be the good man. Provided that the good man was the standard, a more radical standardization of society than had already been carried out was a good thing.

It would be a mistake to read Plato's *Republic* as though it were a piece of modern utopian literature, in spite of the fact that the latter owes much of its material content to Plato. It is necessary rather to keep in mind his general theory of ideal entities and to recognize that his utopia is supposed to be an ideal entity and not simply a plan for a possible society like the usual modern utopia. The ideal city, according to his theory of ideal entities, can never exist anywhere on earth, for earthly things necessarily fall short of their ideal patterns. Earthly beauty, for instance, always falls short of ideal beauty and earthly unity always falls short of ideal unity. So too the earthly city necessarily falls short of the ideal city. The only relationship which the ideal city can have to earthly cities, it seems, is to serve as a criterion by which they can be judged and evaluated and improved. Plato's theory of the philosopher king and his personal effort to turn the tyrant of Syracuse into a philosopher were based on the conviction that this was the most effective way to improve a city and to decrease the distance between actual society and the ideal society, not on the persuasion that the ideal republic could actually be realized on earth. Modern utopias do not become Platonic in any important sense until their proponents cease to speak of them as actual projects and begin to speak of them as regulative ideals.

The *Republic* can be partitioned into two dialogues, one of which we might name *Adeimantus* since it would consist mainly of those parts of the original dialogue in which Socrates in conversation with Adeimantus is made to criticize the actually existent city of his time, and the other of which we might name *Glaucon* since it would consist of the parts in which Socrates in conversation with Glaucon is made to propose measures by which the actual city might be brought to approximate the ideal city.[19] The *Adeimantus* contains criticisms of the kind of motivation that was operative in society, the sort of education that was given, the kind of economic and social circumstances in which men lived, the quality of the philosophical thinking that was done, and the forms of government that were in existence. The *Glaucon* contains descriptions of the education that ought to be given, the economic and social circumstances that ought to obtain, the philosophical thinking that ought to be done, the form of government that ought to prevail, and the motivation that ought to be at work in a society if it is to approach the ideal society.

The sort of criticism of the urban republic which we find in the *Adeimantus* had been anticipated in Athenian comedy, especially the comedies of Aristophanes. When Plato was a boy of thirteen, in fact, Aristophanes had produced his comedy the *Birds*, usually regarded as his masterpiece, in which he had constructed an amusing utopia that may have suggested the idea of a serious utopia. Two Athenians sick of life in Athens, according to the comedy, persuaded the birds to unite and build a great walled city in the air. The two founders were enabled to grow wings and live in the new city themselves, but when other human beings of the various types that plague life on earth attempted to gain admittance to the utopia in the hope of finding new territory to exploit they were disappointed. The gods sent a delegation to make terms with the new city since it had become a bottleneck for sacrifices rising from the earth but were induced to surrender to it their sovereignty. The play ends with the principal human founder marrying Royalty, Zeus' daughter, and becoming thus the ideal king in the ideal city.

In the *Adeimantus* we find serious criticism of the same evils that had been mocked in the *Birds*. Plato seems to have considered Aristophanes a good critic of Athens, so much so that when the tyrant of Syracuse asked how he could learn what Athenians were like, Plato is supposed to have told him to read the comedies of Aristophanes.[20] Although neither the philosopher nor the comic poet appears to have thought that life would be substantially better in some other earthly city that then existed, both were sufficiently disgusted with life at Athens to turn their thoughts toward a heavenly city. Without a theory of ideal entities, of course, Aristophanes could hardly make anything more of his utopia than a fable about gods, men, and birds. Plato, on the contrary, though ready enough to engage in mythmaking in order to describe his utopia, was also able to point the way through and beyond myth to a transcendent entity about which stories could be told but which itself was more than a mere story. Aristophanes, nevertheless, while never departing from the realm of story was able to find a witty way to say that his city was no place on earth namely because it was built in the air just as Plato, entering the realm of metaphor, was able to say that the pattern of his city was laid up in heaven.[21]

The proposals for bringing actual society into closer conformity with the ideal society which are put forward in the *Glaucon* were already being discussed at Athens before the *Republic* was written, to judge from another comedy of Aristophanes, the *Assembly-women (Ecclesiazusae)*, produced in 392 B.C. In the comedy three facets of the communism which was to be proposed in the *Glaucon* had been satirized—the abolition of private property, the participation of women in public life, and the community of wives and children. Evidently someone had been advocating these measures, perhaps Plato himself or perhaps one or several of the sophists at Athens, and Aristophanes felt called upon to make fun of them. Plato has Socrates express to Glaucon his fears of being overwhelmed with ridicule when he proposes communism,[22] but Plato seems to have been quite serious about it, for he was supposed to have refused the invitation to draw up a constitution for the new city of Megalopolis when he learned that the prospective citizens were opposed to equality of possessions.[23] Aristophanes, being something of a utopian thinker himself, did not consider communism undesirable, his objection was that, given human nature, it was not feasible.

Communism is actually only the negative side of the proposals made in the *Glaucon*. What Plato was advocating there was that there be no standard in society except the transcendent Good and thus that there be no property distinctions, no distinctions of sex, no distinctions of blood, but only distinctions of quality and merit based on relative approximation to the absolute Good. Pericles had made the claim in his *Funeral Oration* that while Athens was called a democracy since all were equal before the law and the government was in the hands of the many, still, when it came to public honors there were distinctions among Athenians and these were in accordance with their personal merit rather than on a basis of property or class.[24] What is proposed in the *Glaucon* in like but more radical manner, is an aristocracy in the literal sense, "the rule of the best," an aristocracy of quality not of blood or of property. It should be observed in this connection that voting, the method by which military leaders like Pericles were chosen, was considered an "aristocratic" institution in ancient times by contrast with the lot, the method by which magistrates were chosen at Athens, which was a "democratic" institution, for one voted presumably for the man one judged to be the best whereas anyone could be chosen for office by lot.

There was no real conflict between Plato's view of the city and the common view of the urban republic in the matter of conceiving the city to be essentially a human community. Plato's thesis that the city is man written large[25] might well be regarded as a variation on the common theme that the city is made of men rather than of walls. At most Plato carried this view somewhat further, to the point of advocating the elimination of all the old distinctions carried over from the days when the city was thought to be essentially a place and to the point of measuring the city by the standard of an ideal city that could exist in no place on earth. Where the real conflict lay was in the fact that Plato's ideal city was a transhistorical city. By proposing to measure the historical city by the standard of a transhistorical city he was effectively denying the normative character of the city's history. This was not a necessary result of thinking in terms of an ideal city, for the ideal city could have been merely imaginary. The trouble is that Plato considered the ideal city to be the "really real" city and attributed to the earthly city only an evanescent reality. Thus the ideal city to him was eternal while the earthly city was merely temporal.

[3] *City and Time*

The classical formulation of the myth that the urban republic is an eternal city is to be found in the speeches put into the mouth of Pericles by the historian Thucydides. Pericles spoke at a time when Athens was at the height of her greatness but when she was faced nevertheless with the onslaught of all four horsemen of the Apocalypse, plague, war, famine, and death. He had to answer the inevitable questions whether the dead had died in vain and whether the city would perish from the earth. Although he seems to have been confident that the dead had not died in vain since what they had done could never be undone and would always be remembered, he expressed some doubt about the future of the city, at least about the future of the Athenian empire. His final word on the matter was that even should Athens at last give way a little, it being the nature of everything to decay as well as to grow, it would still remain true that Athens had been the greatest of all Greek cities and the memory of this greatness would be left to posterity forever.[26] Whatever should happen to the city in the future, the past, he was convinced, would never be abolished.

It has been said that it is a regular thing for empires to be deluded with a "mirage of immortality," to imagine themselves destined to endure forever on the earth.[27] If, however, the claim to eternity is simply a claim to an immortal past, as it was at Athens, then the decline and fall of the empire does not prove the immortality a mirage. Rome's claim to be the Eternal City, it is true, was taken by Vergil in the *Aeneid* to imply an infinite future. It seems quite probable, though, that in the days of the Roman republic the conquests which were creating the empire were thought of as *res gestae*, deeds done and never to be undone, and that the empire itself was conceived along the lines of the Athenian empire as a manifestation of the city's greatness never to go down in oblivion. In contradiction to the expectation of an infinite future, at any rate, there are the many statements we find in Roman authors to the effect that Rome is liable to fall and in particular the famous interpretation by Vettius of the twelve vultures which had appeared to Romulus at the founding of Rome according to which Rome's fate was to be accomplished twelve centuries after the date of its foundation.[28]

Modern man, in spite of the greater length of recorded history at his disposal, is not in a better position than the Roman or the Athenian or the Spartan to judge the truth or falsity of the eternity claimed for urban republics and their empires. If this eternity was supposed to have been an immortal past, then there are no "lessons of history" to contradict it. On the contrary, from the standpoint of pure historical experience it would be tenable even now, centuries after the downfall of the urban republics, to say that they were eternal cities. What is more, though there are philosophical and political standpoints that would contradict it, there is nothing in the past experience of mankind that would disprove a similar claim made for a modern civilization. The Athenian like Pericles faced with the prospect of the downfall of Athens could nevertheless affirm that Athens was eternal. The Roman faced with the decline and fall of the Roman Empire could say the same thing of Rome. The modern man faced with "the decline of the West" could say the same thing, though he does not, of his own civilization. The reason he does not do so is not so much his greater historical experience as his belief in a different political myth.

There is at once a parallel and a contrast between the ideas to be found in the speeches of Pericles and those to be found in Lincoln's famous speech at Gettysburg. Both speakers concern themselves with the problem whether the dead have died in vain and whether the republic shall perish from the earth. Lincoln, however, called upon his listeners to resolve that the dead shall not have died in vain, as though all depended on the future. Pericles, on the contrary, was confident that the dead had not died in vain no matter what the future should hold in store.

The reason why the dead had not died in vain in Pericles' eyes seems to have been the fact that they died for a worthy cause. Lincoln did not for a moment doubt that the dead about whom he spoke died for a worthy cause. If the cause for which they died should be ultimately a lost cause, though, their death in his eyes would seemingly have been vain. For Pericles, on the contrary, a lost cause did not render the death of the dead vain, but it was altogether sufficient that they died for a worthy cause, and he spends most of his *Funeral Oration* proving that their cause was worthy.

Why this should have been sufficient for Pericles and yet not sufficient for Lincoln is probably a matter of their divergent views of the past. If one's life survives only in its effects then everything depends on whether the cause for which one lives and dies prevails. If one's cause should be lost, then one's life has been ineffective and has left little or no mark on the future. If, on the other hand, one's life survives in itself as part of an immortal past, then it does not matter whether or not one's cause prevails but only whether or not one's cause was worthy.

While the slogans about freedom and tyranny which have been current in ancient and modern republics are deceptively banal and deceptively similar, the significance these terms have in a modern revolutionary society, where the past is thought to be in some important sense abolished, may prove to be quite different from the one they had in a society where the past was thought to be immortal. Consider, for instance, Sparta's claim to be the Liberator of Hellas.[29] Sparta maintained a tradition of putting down the adversaries of tradition, of being the opponent of all attempts at tyranny in Greece whether by a single man over a city or by a foreign power over Greek cities or by one Greek city over another. The title Liberator of Hellas was a claim to an immortal past of preserving the past of all Greece, for the essence of tyranny as it was then conceived was usurpation, breakage with the past and suspension of the influence of the past on the present, and the essence of autonomy, the antithesis of tyranny, was self-determination, the shaping of the city's life by its own native past rather than by alien customs or by the arbitrary will of an upstart.

The Spartan claim to be the Liberator of Hellas was matched by the Athenian claim to be the School of Hellas.[30] Both were claims to immortality. When Pericles said that Athens was the School of Hellas he meant that Athens was an abiding example to the rest of Greece and, for that matter, to all posterity. What Athens exemplified was autonomy, the self-sufficiency of city and citizens in peace and in war. The city, not imitating other cities but conforming to its own traditions, and each citizen separately, having been formed by these institutions, was adequate to the tasks both of war and of peace. The Athenians, to be sure, had a reputation for innovation.[31] This was the difference between being merely the Liberator of Hellas and being the School of Hellas. Where the Spartans were prone to cling to the old ways, the Athenians were ever ready to try something new. To innovate, though, was to create precedent, to create a past, to set an immortal example. This is how it was possible at Sparta itself to make the original innovation (recorded in the *Great Rhetra*) that created the republic. To be the School of Hellas was to create precedent for all Greece and to set an example for all times.

How much this classical conception of autonomy differs from that which prevails in modern revolutionary societies becomes clear from the impossibility of fitting it into Hegel's scheme of history as the story of liberty. Hegel had no small share in shaping the concept of freedom that is at work in modern revolutionary movements, and his view on the history of freedom is so governed by this concept that the story of liberty for him is really no more than the development of this sort of autonomy. There are three phases in the historical evolution of freedom, according to Hegel, first the stage of oriental despotism in which only one person, the despot himself, is free and everyone else is a slave, then the stage of classical society in which some are free and others are slaves, and finally the stage of modern society in which all are thought to be entitled to freedom and no one deserving of slavery.[32]

When Pericles said that freedom is happiness and that courage is freedom,[33] he enunciated an idea that appears at no stage, not even the second stage, of Hegel's scheme. To say "freedom is happiness" was to say that tyranny means misery, for as long as the tyrant reigns, no matter how much peace and prosperity he brings to the city, the citizens are alienated from the past. To say "courage is freedom" was to say that cowardice means tyranny, for only those who act to create and conserve the past have part in its immortality while those who do not act do not make the past their own. For Hegel freedom is appropriation of the self while for Pericles it is appropriation of the past. For Hegel slavery is alienation from the self while for Pericles it is alienation from the past. It is the difference between placing ultimate value on the self that passes through life and placing it on the life through which the self passes.

That ultimate value was actually placed on the life through which the self passes rather than on the self appears in the attitude taken in the urban republic towards law. The idea of law (nomos) was the idea of a normative past, a somewhat stronger notion than that of custom or tradition. There was no thought of being liberated from law such as we find in Christianity with its thesis that man is freed by Christ from the burden of the Old Law or in modern revolutionary movements where we find the view that the less law there is in a society the better and that in a perfect society there would be no law at all. On the contrary, in the urban republics freedom was equivalent to the rule of law and the alternative to freedom understood in this way was the rule of man.[34] Perhaps it has always been the function of law, whether in ancient or in modern times, to measure a man by his deeds rather than by his person, for instance to condemn him to death for his misdeeds in spite of any effort he makes to renounce his past by repentance. What has varied from age to age in human history is the evaluation of this situation. In the days of the urban republic it was considered not a necessary evil but a good, and there is no denying that if the past is considered immortal and unrenounceable this evaluation makes perfect sense. There is also no denying that the opposing notion that the past can be renounced is a dangerous one and has led in modern totalitarian societies to the horrible parody of conversion and repentance known as "brainwashing."

Alienation from the past, however unlikely it may seem to one who is not accustomed to thinking in terms of an immortal past, may really have been tantamount to misery in the world of the city-state. Tyranny was never an actual constitution like oligarchy or democracy,[35] and this together with the fact that in some instances the tyrant felt it necessary to maintain the forms of the constitution which he had nullified indicates that the tyrant's rule was felt to be an alienation of the city from its past. It is hard for the modern interpreter to believe that this situation was considered misery at the time when it actually prevailed, especially a tyranny like that of Peisistratus under whom Athens attained considerable prosperity. An economic interpretation of history would require that prosperity be equivalent to happiness for the prosperous and if there be simultaneously misery that it be the lot of those deprived of a share in the prosperity. If, notwithstanding, the basic solution to the problem of death in the society of the city-state was the immortality of the past, then it is instead quite believable that alienation from the past was universally considered misery, prosperity or no prosperity.

Appropriation of the past, conversely, with or without prosperity, meant freedom, immortality, happiness. Tyranny was introduced in times of weakness, mainly in the seventh century when the Greek city-states were still immature and in the fourth and following centuries when they were on the decline.[36] It took courage to conserve the past, not to be cowed by the upstart's power and not to be disheartened by the adversities of fortune which gave him his opportunity. It also took courage to create a past, to do immortal deeds that set a standard for the future rather than to content oneself like a domestic animal with the paternal and benevolent guidance of another man's will. The past, in this point of view, was immortal of its own accord, but one did not automatically have part in it. The city which allowed itself to be dominated by a tyrant had relapsed into passivity and was no longer creating a past and the past which had once been created for it was no longer its own. Likewise the individual citizen who was, for instance, a coward in battle was essentially a non-entity because he failed to do any deeds which would give him a part in the history that was being made. If appropriation of the past was the way to immortality, it was worth the sacrifice of prosperity and, since death had to come at some time anyway, worth the sacrifice of life itself.

[4] *City and Eternity*

Taken this way as an assertion of the immortality of its past rather than of the infinity of its future, an urban republic's claim to eternity could not be refuted by events. If its immortal past were understood to be merely the memory of its past surviving in human minds, it is true, then its past would be liable to lapse through forgetfulness, but if the past were understood to be immortal in itself, as it seems to have been, then there would be no way of countering the city's claim to eternity except by means of a theory of the lapse of time. This is actually what happened when Plato made the distinction between time and eternity. Plato's notion of time is to be understood in the context of his theory of ideal entities, and if it is so understood it appears to leave no room for the notion of an immortal past. Time, according to him, is "a changing image of eternity,"[37] and it falls short of eternity just as all earthly things fall short of their absolute archetypes. There is no such thing, from his standpoint, as an immortal past, for this would be a time that does not flow away but remains forever as eternity alone can do. Instead of being everlasting the past of an earthly city like Athens or Sparta is temporal and evanescent. Only the ideal city, in Plato's point of view, is an eternal city.

The high-handed manner in which Plato treats the past might suggest a comparison with the attitude toward the past adopted in modern totalitarianism, and indeed the Platonic doctrine of the "noble lie" has been compared with the totalitarian theory of propaganda and Plato has been denounced as being a totalitarian in his political thinking.[38] Actually he was no more a totalitarian than was Pericles. It is characteristic of modern totalitarianism to attribute absolute value to what Plato would consider an earthly society. It was precisely Plato's main contention that no earthly society could possess any such value and that no earthly society can do more than approximate the ideal society. The difference between Plato and Pericles was substantially that Pericles regarded Athens as an eternal city whereas Plato considered Athens and every other urban republic of his day to be an essentially temporal city and regarded the eternal city as an ideal entity. In his dialogue *Menexenus* the contrast with Pericles is plain in that Plato has Socrates make fun of funeral orations in which orators praise "the Athenians among the Athenians."[39] Such praise of an earthly city seemed particularly incongruous from Plato's viewpoint because of the inevitable chasm between the earthly city and the ideal city.

There is a broad hint, however, in Plato's dialogues that philosophy itself had originally been based on belief in the immortality of the past. This hint is contained in his doctrine that knowledge is reminiscence. The strange thing about the theory as we find it in Plato is that the reminiscence of which he speaks is a recollection not of the past but of the ideal entities.[40] One would not have expected him to use the term "reminiscence" (*anamnesis*) to describe the nature of knowledge and learning if he were not going to connect it with the past. Instead of relating knowledge to past time, though, he relates it to eternity. One can only suspect that this description of knowledge and learning was current among philosophers before the distinction between time and eternity had been drawn by Plato and that the role of eternity had originally been played by the "immortal past." This suspicion is strengthened when one learns that Pythagoras, who believed in reincarnation, claimed to be able to remember his previous existences, and that Empedocles, who entertained similar ideas on transmigration, considered himself a wanderer in time endowed like Pythagoras with the experience of many lifetimes.[41] Plato connected his own doctrine of reminiscence with metempsychosis too, but he treats metempsychosis as a "myth,"[42] to him a temporal image of the eternal, and so one can only suspect that the whole Pythagorean procedure of thinking back to the past is to Plato an image of thinking back to eternity.

In the beginning, it seems, the philosopher was a kind of prophet in reverse, a prophet who prophesied the past rather than the future. The oracles of Epimenides, Aristotle tells us, were not about the future but about things in the past which were obscure.[43] The philosopher did not attempt to probe the mysteries of the future so much as to uncover the secrets of the past and to learn the origin of things. The Ionians who were the first to cultivate philosophy in the western world were concerned primarily to trace things back to their origin (*arche*) in time. Thus Thales traced the present state of affairs in the world all the way back to a primeval watery chaos not too different from the watery chaos of mythology; Anaximander thought the primeval chaos was boundless and said that things emerged from it and returned to it "according to the arrangement of Time"; Anaximenes evidently thought as Anaxagoras did after him that the chaos was windy and gaseous rather than liquid since air is the most copious element in the world as it now exists; and Heraclitus thought that the primordial state was a fiery chaos. The fragments which remain of Heraclitus' work (and also that of Xenophanes) indicate, moreover, that the Ionian account of the origins included, as did the cosmogonic myths which went before it, the origins of the gods and of mankind and the origins of all divine and human institutions.

A way of thinking that seemed still more consonant with belief in the immortality of the past was discovered by Parmenides.[44] The "way of truth" as he called it led to the thesis that time does not lapse, that change and the passage of time are an illusion. It was a method of thought in which reliance was placed exclusively on reason with its demand for consistency and no confidence at all was given to experience and the phenomena of change which it involved. Plato, who maintained that time does lapse, attempted in his dialogue *Parmenides* to prove by this very method (and thus he has Parmenides himself do the talking) that the position of Parmenides leads to contradictions.

Another way of thinking, called by Parmenides the "way of opinion," was the opposite method of placing all confidence in experience and in the phenomena which it yielded to thought. This is the method which Plato seems to have considered characteristic of the philosophical schools of thought subsequent to Parmenides, especially the Atomists and the Sophists. In the dialogue *Theatetus* Plato raises the inevitable objection against this procedure that it does not satisfy reason's demand for consistency. He rejects also a modified form in which true and false appearances are discriminated and a further modification in which a process of analysis into elements is added, for the elements and the truth of the true appearances are left unexplained.

A third way of thinking, of which Parmenides spoke only to say that it should not be followed, was deliberately used by Plato in his dialogue *The Sophist* in order to arrive at the criteria of truth and falsehood to which the other two ways had failed to take him. Plato thought it necessary to postulate five interrelated archetypes, Being, Motion, Rest, the Same, and the Other, the last of which was the archetype of non-being. Thus it was possible to do what Parmenides had forbidden, to make affirmative statements about non-being. Specifically it was possible to make statements about the non-being involved in motion and the lapse of time, namely the past, without on that account assuming the actual being of the past.[45]

This way of thinking about the past contrasts sharply with the way of inquiry (*historia*) into the past followed by the Greek historians. There is a conscious movement away from the fabulous discernible in the contrast between Herodotus and Homer and further in the contrast between Thucydides and Herodotus. To Plato, on the contrary, the non-being of the past was apparently an invitation to mythmaking, and he did not hesitate to recreate it and transform it into a parable of eternity. Herodotus, describing the struggle of the Greeks with the Persians, allows himself much less poetic freedom than Homer assumed in describing the struggle of the Achaians with the Trojans. Thucydides, narrating the struggle of the Athenians with the Peloponnesians, allows himself still less freedom than Herodotus. Plato, however, seems to have intentionally created a past in his dialogues *Timaeus* and *Critias* in which Athens engaged in a heroic struggle with the legendary Atlantis. Whatever sources he may have used (Solon's writings, for instance) Plato's own creative activity is certainly manifest in the fact that the Athens of this story is supposed to have been an earthly incarnation of his ideal city. His purpose in recreating the past thus was evidently to remodel it and transform it into an image of the ideal. This is probably what is at the bottom of his notorious doctrine that the rulers of the republic are permitted to tell "lies." The requirement that the recreated past be an image of the ideal, on the other hand, led him to repudiate the amoral "lies" told by the poets about the gods and the heroes.[46]

It would be a mistake to think, however, that there is no conception of historical truth and falsehood in Plato's viewpoint. The very fact that he calls the false stories told by his rulers "lies" indicates that he is cognizant of their falsehood and aware of the kind of truth that they do not possess. And this is not merely a concession to popular thinking, for his own idea that time is a "changing image of eternity," a kind of continuous revelation of eternity, seems to imply a certain notion of historical truth, quite different to be sure from the one that is found in the Greek historians but rather similar to the one that appears later on in Christian theologians like Origen. Events are indeed facts in this kind of thinking and the facts can of course be established by some sort of method, but there is no such thing as a "brute fact," an irrational fact that has no meaning. Instead each event is a "mystery" possessing symbolic significance, disclosing something of the truth of eternity.

The prime instance of an historical fact with eternal significance from Plato's own standpoint was Socrates. It is not that Plato intended to remodel the actual Socrates and transform him into an image of the ideal man but rather that he wished without changing the facts about Socrates to bring to light the transcendent meaning which he thought he could decipher in the facts. If we compare the Socrates who appears in the dialogues of Plato with the Socrates who appears in the writings of Xenophon and the one who appears in the comedies of Aristophanes, we can abstract a common factual denominator while assigning to each witness a personal interpretative numerator.[47] Plato and Aristophanes agree that Socrates' method was supposed to be a kind of midwifery, an attempt to assist others in bringing forth the conceptions already latent in their minds. But where Aristophanes reduces the Socratic method to ridicule, exhibiting one of the younger followers of Socrates having a miscarriage and one of his older followers in bed struggling in vain to give birth to a thought, Plato tries to disclose its ulterior significance, showing the followers of Socrates discovering within themselves a latent knowledge of the eternal archetypes. Plato and Xenophon agree that Socrates bore himself nobly in the fact of his condemnation to death, but where Xenophon ascribes Socrates' willingness to die to a simple desire to avoid the evils of senility, Plato sees in Socrates' detachment from this temporal life a sure hold on the prospect of an eternal life.

Is it possible instead that Socrates' midwifery was actually a method of inducing a person to recall his past, that self-knowledge to Socrates meant knowledge of one's past life, and could it be that his confidence in the face of death was based on belief in the immortality of the past, the assurance that his own past life was a noble life and that no condemnation and no death could ever change the fact? If we wished to put a slogan in Homer's mouth that would correspond to the Socratic dictum "the unexamined life is not worth living,"[48] it would have to be the rather more commonsensical statement "the unhappy life is not worth living." If we wanted then to modify the Homeric maxim so that it would be an appropriate formulation of the view of life that is found in the work of the great Athenian tragedians we would get the statement "the unhappy life can be worth living provided it be a noble life." The tragic poets of the urban republic took their dramatic themes and plots from the stories of heroes and heroines found in Homer and in early tradition but they unconsciously transformed the significance of the legends by introducing the perspective of the immortal past. Socrates, however, transformed things once again by maintaining that the only life that was truly happy was the noble life. No man, according to him, could lead an ignoble life willingly but did so only out of ignorance. If nobility and true happiness are identical, though, there is sufficient motivation for the noble life even if the past is not immortal.

Knowledge is a source of unhappiness rather than of happiness in the tragedies of Aeschylus. Prometheus (the Forethinker) has mercifully taken away from man his foreknowledge of his fate, Aeschylus tells us, and has filled the human heart instead with blind hopes.[49] From the Socratic point of view, on the contrary, knowledge not blind hope would have to be the basis of happiness, and although Socrates did not claim to have foreknowledge of his fate he did claim to have a kind of premonition, a sign that would forbid him when he was about to do something that was not for his own good.[50] From the Aeschylean standpoint it is in the order of things established by Zeus that "learning comes from suffering."[51] The tragic hero like Agamemnon, whose fate it was to be murdered by his own wife, does not know his fate until he suffers it. As man lives his life and his future becomes his past he learns the truth about his destiny and his blind hopes are dissipated. For Socrates the illusions on which men live are to be cleared up by self-examination or by cross-examination; man's blind hopes are dissipated not so much by knowledge of his fate as by knowledge of what is really good for him; and the death he dies does not matter so much as the dispositions with which he dies.

There is an evolution in Sophocles' view of things, it seems, so that in the end it begins to approach that of Socrates. *Oedipus Tyrannus,* the play which Aristotle regarded as the model of tragedy, derived its tragic force from the idea of the unchangeability and immortality of the past. Oedipus learns that he has unwittingly killed his own father and married his own mother. What makes the situation hopeless and what drives him to despair is the fact that his deeds are irreparably done, beyond recall, immortal and unchangeable. The knowledge of what he has done is the source of unrelieved misery whereas the ignorance in which he had lived until his discovery of the truth had been a source of happiness. In the later play *Oedipus at Colonus,* produced posthumously, there is a significant transformation in Sophocles' standpoint on these matters. Oedipus says in the first few lines of the play that his sufferings and his many years and his well-tested nobility have taught him endurance. His self-knowledge has now become to him a source of confidence instead of despair. There is also a defence in this new play of his past deeds, parricide and incest, on the grounds that he did them in ignorance. It was his ignorance that was ultimately the cause of all his misery and knowledge has turned out to be the source of a genuine contentment, free from all illusion.

The viewpoint taken by Euripides was close enough to that of Socrates in popular estimation for Aristophanes to jibe that Euripides had Socrates write his plays for him. Actually in the extant tragedies it often seems that Euripides is testing the idea of the irreparable past. Agathon said "only this is impossible to a god, to render undone what has been done."[52] It is as though Euripides were asking "Is it true that a god cannot render undone what has been done?" Sometimes he seems to answer in the affirmative as when he shows Artemis impotent to undo the death of her beloved Hippolytus or when he has Medea kill her own children in order to drive her husband Jason to despair or when he represents the despair of the Trojan women over the destruction of Troy and the slaughter of all the male inhabitants or when he exhibits the despair of Agave after having killed her son in a Bacchic frenzy. In each of these instances the past is irreparable and the only human response is despair. At other times, however, Euripides toys with the idea that what has been done can be undone as when he has Alcestis brought back alive from the dead by Heracles after having sacrificed her life for her husband or when he has Artemis substitute a hind for Iphigenia as she is sacrificed at Aulis or when he has it that only the wraith of Helen was carried away to Troy while the real Helen was taken by Hermes to Egypt or when he has Helen snatched away to heaven by Apollo as Orestes attempts to murder her. In these instances, though something is not literally done and then undone, the human deed is stultified.

Between the despair of an irreparable past and the stultification of a past that can be undone there lies the Socratic way of salvation. If happiness is to be found in virtue, as Socrates seems to have maintained, then neither the hope nor the despair arising from belief in the immortality of the past has any power to affect it. In fact, genuine happiness is entirely independent of the question of the past's changeability or unchangeability. To be happy in the face of death, as Socrates apparently was, though, one would have to consider virtue itself some kind of hold upon the eternal. Socrates, with all his confidence before the prospect of death, probably had some sense of possessing such a hold, and was not likely to have been animated as Xenophon claimed by a mere desire to avoid the evils of old age. It was for Plato to elucidate this hold, to analyze the knowledge which Socrates tended to equate with virtue, and to describe it as knowledge of the Good. In the perspective of Plato's distinction between time and eternity knowledge of the Good was tantamount to contemplation of eternity itself and was an intimation of immortality for the soul.

NOTES TO CHAPTER FIVE

1. Herodotus, VIII, 62.

2. Cf. H. W. Parke and D. E. W. Wormell, *The Delphic Oracle* (Oxford, 1956), vol. 1, 49 ff.

3. Nietzsche, *Genealogy of Morals*, III, 25.

4. Plutarch, *Lycurgus*, 19; Plato, *Laws*, VI, 778 D; Aristotle, *Politics*, VII, 1330b32 ff.; Alcaeus, frg. 22.

5. Cf. Victor Ehrenberg, *The Greek State* (New York, 1960), 29.

6. Aeschylus, *Persians*, 349.

7. Sophocles, *Oedipus Tyranus*, 56; Thucydides, VII, 77.

8. Herodotus, VII, 143.

9. Thucydides, VII, 77. Later enunciations of the principle are to be found in Demosthenes, XVIII, 299; Dio Cassius, LVI, v, 3; Cicero, *Ad Atticum*, VII, 11.

10. Thucydides, I, 10.

11. Thucydides, II, 13. Cf. Plutarch, *Pericles*, 12 and 13, on the building program.

12. Cf. Apollodorus, *Bibliotheca*, III, 12, 3; *Epitome*, V, 10 ff.

13. *Od.*, VII, 81.

14. Plato, *Laws*, III, 681; Aristotle, *Politics*, I, 1252b (but cf. 1253a).

15. Fustel de Coulanges, *The Ancient City* tr. by Willard Small (Boston, 1901), 12.

16. Cf. Frazer, *The Golden Bough*, Part I (London, 1911), 277 ff. on evidence of such a transition among the Greeks.

17. Cf. Heidegger's essay "Bauen Wohnen Denken" in his *Vorträge und Aufsätze* (Pfullingen, 1954), 145 ff.

18. On living in the heavenly city cf. *Republic*, IX, 592. On Plato's own withdrawal from politics cf. his seventh epistle.

19. The remarks made by Socrates in the first book to Polemarchus seem to be in somewhat the same vein as those to Glaucon, and the ones made to Thrasymachus seem to be in somewhat the same vein as those to Adeimantus.

20. The story is told in the two anonymous *Lives* of Aristophanes.

21. *Republic*, IX, 592 B.

22. *Republic*, V, 452 and 457 (but cf. 451 A).

23. Diogenes Laertius, III, 23.

24. Thucydides, II, 37.

25. *Republic*, II, 368-369.

26. Thucydides, II, 64.

27. Arnold Toynbee, *A Study of History*, vol. VII (London, 1954), 7 ff.

28. For the relevant texts in both directions, eternity and doom, *see* D. A. Malcolm's article "Urbs Aeterna," *Univ. of Birmingham Historical Journal* 3 (1951), 1-15.

29. Thucydides I, 69; II, 8; III, 59; IV, 85, 108; V, 9; VII, 43, 46, 52.

30. Thucydides, II, 41.

31. Thucydides, I, 70 f.

32. Hegel, *The Philosophy of History* (tr. J. Sibree), 104.

33. Thucydides, II, 43.

34. Cf. Herodotus, VII, 104; Aeschylus, *Persians* 241 ff.

35. A. Andrewes, *The Greek Tyrants* (London, 1956), 25.

36. *Ibid.*, 150.

37. *Timaeus*, 37D.

38. Cf. *Republic*, III, 414 C on the "noble lie". For a denunciation of Plato as a totalitarian see Karl Popper, *The Spell of Plato*, vol. 1 of his *Open Society and Its Enemies* (London, 1957).

39. Menexenus, 235.

40. Cf. *Meno* 86 and *Phaedo* 73 in both of which places it is recollection of the archetypes and in both of which it is used as a proof of immortality.

41. On Pythagoras' claim cf. Diogenes Laertius, VIII, 4-5. For Empedocles' assertion cf. H. Diels and W. Kranz, *Die Fragmente der Vorsokratiker*, (Berlin, 1934), 31 B 115 (Cf. 129 on Pythagoras).

42. At the end of the *Republic* (X. 617 D ff.) and at the end of *Timaeus* (90 E ff.)

43. Aristotle, *Rhetoric*, III, 1418a.

44. Parmenides' poem was divided into three parts: The Prologue, The Way of Truth, The Way of Opinion. A third way is mentioned, however, in the part on the Way of Truth (Diels, *op. cit.*, 28 B 2, 7, 8) as being impossible to follow. Plato quotes Parmenides to this effect in the *Sophist* (258D) and deliberately attempts there to follow the third way.

45. Motion is Other than Being and thus involves non-being (*Sophist*, 256 D), namely lapsed time or the past (and also the not-yet-existent future).

46. On the "lies" of rulers cf. *Republic* III, 398 A, 414 C; V, 459 D; and *Laws*, II, 663 E. On the "lies" of poets cf. *Republic*, II, 377; III, 408 B (also X, 597 ff. and *Laws*, XII, 941 B).

47. The comparison here is between Aristophanes' *Clouds*, Plato's *Apology*, *Crito* and *Phaedo*, and Xenophon's *Apology*.

48. Plato, *Apology*, 38 A.

49. Prometheus, 250-253.

50. Cf. Plato, *Euthydemus*, 273 A; *Phaedrus*, 242 C; *Euthyphro*, 3 B; *Apology*, 31 C, 40 A; *Republic*, VI, 496 C. Also cf. Xenophon, *Apology*, 14 ff.

51. Agamemnon, 177 and 250.

52. Cf. Aristotle, *Nicomachean Ethics*, VI, 1139 b 10 f.

CHAPTER SIX

Savior Kings

THERE is a place in Plato's world for a savior, a place which is almost but not quite filled by Socrates. "Until philosophers are kings," Plato said, "or the kings and rulers of this world take up the pursuit of philosophy in earnest, and political power and wisdom meet in one, and the ordinary run of men who pursue either to the exclusion of the other are made to stand aside, cities will have no rest from evil nor, I believe, will the human race."[1] This conviction of Plato's is not the singular opinion and the isolated personal feeling that it is often taken for. It seems rather to be the high crest of a wave of consciousness sweeping over the East and the West, leading first to a spiritual revolution in which there appeared saviors who were thought to be sages and then to a political revolution in which there appeared kings who were thought to be saviors.

These events, especially the spiritual revolution, were so important to subsequent ages that the epoch during which they took place has been called an "axial period" of human history.[2] How they came about as they did, more or less concurrently in the East and in the West, seems to have been as follows. The earliest city-cultures had been spread out from the Tigris-Euphrates valley as far west as the Mediterranean basin and as far east as the Indus valley. Indo-European peoples then invaded all these areas in migratory waves or in conquering armies and brought with them a new conception of life and death epitomized in their practice of cremating instead of burying the dead. Out of the resulting mixture of ideas and customs and out of the vicissitudes of the continuing quest for life there eventually emerged the conviction that the soul was immortal.

Saviors walked the earth in those days. These were men who appeared to have found a way to escape from the evils of the present life and to anticipate the immortal and blessed existence of the dead and, what is more, to share their experience of it with others. To understand and evaluate the overall change which has come to pass in man's spirit as a result of these revolutions, therefore, it is essential to determine just how the afterlife was supposed to be anticipated, how emancipation from the evils of this life was thought to be achieved, and how the experience in which this occurred was believed to be shared.

[1] *Mystical Immortality*

It is ironic that arguments for the immortality of the soul have come to be considered what Kant called "paralogisms," attempts to draw conclusions about an existence which is completely beyond the purview of human experience. To be sure, nothing could seem more obvious than the fact that a man while still alive has no personal acquaintance with the life that is supposed to come after death. This is obvious so long as one does not attempt to cope with the possibility that mystical experience may really be what it ordinarily purports to be, a foretaste of the afterlife. Historically the persuasion that the soul is immortal appears to have resulted not from a kind of thinking which soared beyond the bounds of experience but from a kind of experience which began to be seriously cultivated both in the East and in the West in the centuries preceding the appearance of Jesus Christ. The mystic anticipated, or at least it seemed to him that he anticipated, the afterlife while he still lived in this world, and when he spoke of the afterlife he spoke as it seemed to him from experience.[3]

That mystical experience has purported to be an anticipatory enjoyment of an immortal and blessed afterlife becomes apparent from the attitude commonly adopted in mysticism towards myth. The great archetypal myths, the myth of the eternal return, the myth of dualism, the myth of perpetual life, and the myth of fate all formulate aspects of man's understanding of himself in terms of the quest for life and the effort to overcome death. Once the soul is considered immortal, though, and thought to enjoy something more than a ghostly existence after death in a nether world, the desire for the boundless perpetuation of the present life tends to lose its force. It can actually appear desirable to escape from the situation described in the myths. The mystical concept of salvation, it seems, owes its origin to a wish to be delivered from the evil and the sorrow and the suffering occasioned by man's intemperate will to live. The mystical concept of being, on the other hand, seems to derive from the positive side of the wish for deliverance, the will to live in a higher sense, to live a life that is not merely a life but the afterlife. From the mystical point of view, thus, all the values of the myths are transvaluated, what appeared evil in myth is counted good and what appeared good is counted evil, the joys of life are no longer joyful and the terrors of death are no longer terrible.

The myth of the eternal return instead of pointing the way to further life through periodic rejuvenation or explaining the necessity of death for the sake of new life now seems to reveal an inexorable wheel of transmigration and reincarnation from which the soul must at all costs be delivered. The myth of dualism instead of confronting man with the choice between a life that is good and a knowledge that is evil now seems to confront him with the choice between a life that is evil and a knowledge that is good, for knowledge now seems to be the means of emancipation from the evils of life. The myth of perpetual life instead of symbolizing the goal of the urge to happiness now seems to symbolize the goal of the desire that is the cause of all suffering and that must be renounced if the soul is to be set free from its misery. The myth of fate instead of disclosing the impassable barrier which frustrates all man's efforts to prolong his life now seems to describe a frustration from which man's soul can be liberated provided he abandon his desire to live forever on earth.

The mystical attitude toward myth is clearly exhibited in the late epic literature of the East and the West. The *Bhagavad-Gita,* a poem which was composed probably a century or two before

Christ and inserted into the longest of the ancient Sanskrit epics and which has become the supreme devotional scripture of India, is a comprehensive exposition of the mystical view of life in the form of a dialogue between the hero Arjuna and the incarnate god Krishna. The immortality of the soul is the starting point of the dialogue, Arjuna needing to be persuaded by Krishna that he should not hesitate to shed the blood of kinsmen in battle for the soul is immortal and no one ever wholly dies. The view which this idea leads to is paralleled in the late epic literature of the West, specifically in Vergil's *Aeneid* where the conception of life and death is similarly dominated by the mystical doctrine of the immortality of the soul. The difference between the lot of the dead in Homer and in Vergil is just this that in spite of all the imagery he has borrowed from Homer describing the departed soul as a ghost Vergil seems actually to believe with Plato that the soul is a divine and immortal being.[4]

The experience underlying the doctrine of the immortality of the soul should not be identified with the various literary devices used to cast the doctrine into story form. It is not, for instance, a dream about the land of the dead such as one might be tempted to infer from reading how Aeneas visited the nether world and returned to the land of the living by way of the portal of dreams. Vergil does not seem to have taken dreams of this sort seriously, for he has Aeneas pass through the Gate of ivory whence come dreams that are false rather than the Gate of horn whence come dreams that are true.[5]

Neither is it the reminiscence of one's previous existences, though teachers of reincarnation such as Buddha and Pythagoras were understandably reputed to have been able to remember their former lives. Vergil like Plato has it that souls when they are about to be reincarnated are compelled to drink of the waters of forgetfulness and thus become unable to remember their past incarnations.[6] Krishna tells Arjuna that both of them have gone through many births and that Krishna remembers them but Arjuna does not.[7] In every case the truth seems to be that no one can actually remember his former lives except one who like Krishna or Plato's Er is needed to tell the story.

Nor, finally, is this experience a visual perception of the absolute being which is the origin and goal of every soul, though it is true that Krishna shows Arjuna a spectacular vision of the universal self from which all individual egos arise and Anchises describes for Aeneas the world spirit from which all personal souls derive.[8] There is no attempt to visualize the world spirit in the *Aeneid* and the visualization of the universal self which is offered in the *Bhagavad-Gita* is accompanied by the cautionary remark that this spectacle cannot be seen with one's eyes.

What the experience of immortality seems to be in reality is an experience of enlightenment, the paradigm of which would be the famous awakening of Buddha. The term *buddha* in Sanskrit means "awakened" or "enlightened," and the occasion of Gautama Siddhartha's becoming a Buddha was the juncture at which he achieved the insight subsequently formulated in the Four Truths that all life is subject to suffering, that the desire to live is the cause of repeated existences, that only the annihilation of desire can give release, and that the way of escape is the elimination of selfishness by means of a path which lies between the path of self-torture and the path of self-indulgence.[9] The enlightenment which Gautama experienced, to be sure, was not the simple comprehension one can derive from hearing and understanding the Four Truths. Rather it was the personal knowledge which comes from actually undergoing suffering, from actually following through the path of unselfishness, from actually giving up the desire to live, and from actually tasting the peace arising out of detachment. It was thus an anticipation of *nirvana* ("blowing out"), a foretaste of the emancipated existence which is attained when the flame of the life we live now has been finally blown out.

There is in the *Aeneid* an insight into the enigma of suffering that is comparable in many particulars with that of Buddhism. Ideas similar to the Four Truths appear in the conversation between Aeneas and Anchises in the nether world: Aeneas with his own bitter experience of life considers the departed souls mad for wishing to return to bodily existence; Anchises explains how it is that forgetfulness of their past existence makes it possible for them to desire bodily life once more and how it is this desire that leads to reincarnation; he also explains that some of the dead like himself become sufficiently purified of their earthly fears, desires, griefs, and joys that they are able to abide in Elysium and to escape the necessity of transmigration; and he points out how the need for purification and the possibility of complete purification varies according to the kind of life one has lived on earth.[10] The ideal of *ataraxia* ("undisturbedness") which Vergil has taken over from late Greek philosophy and transformed here by postponing its full realization to the afterlife has become in his hands something remotely resembling the ideal of *nirvana*.

The Four Truths have their counterparts also in the *Bhagavad-Gita*. The opening chapter entitled "The Grief of Arjuna" sets forth the problem of suffering for which the remainder of the dialogue provides the solution, the kind of suffering envisioned being here as in Buddhism the kind from which one can be delivered by detachment, sorrow, namely, rather than physical pain. The diagnosis, that sorrow is due to attachment, and the prognosis, that peace will be attained through detachment, are then understandably similar to those offered by Buddha. The yogas or spiritual disciplines prescribed, moreover, are untechnical enough to be compared with Buddha's description of his middle way as the Eightfold Path of right view, right purpose, right speech, right action, right livelihood, right endeavor, right mindfulness, and right concentration. If the object had been to rid one of physical pain, a more technical sort of yoga would have been called for, the kind of inuring of the body to pain which Buddha rejected as the path of self-torture. As it is, though, the goal is deliverance from unhappiness through the anticipation of an afterlife resembling the Buddhist *nirvana* and called here *brahmanirvana*,[11] "extinction in Brahman" or "the extinction which is Brahman," an absolute existence in which all temporal existence is abolished.

So long as nothing more than rough comparisons like these are drawn, the Four Truths can be made to serve as a general model of the mystical doctrines both of the East and of the West. The teaching on the "practice of death,"[12] for instance, which Plato has Socrates propound in the hour of his death is certainly comparable in a general fashion with the teaching of the Buddha. The highest goal attainable, Socrates teaches, is to escape from this life we lead now in the body and to escape in such a definitive manner that we are no longer obliged to return to bodily life through reincarnation. The way to accomplish this, he says, is not suicide but the life of a philosopher, for the life of a philosopher, when one considers it, appears to be a continual practice of dying. The transcendence of the goal which Socrates proposes is no less than that of Buddha's goal, complete emancipation from the necessity of rebirth into this life, and the detachment required in the practice of dying is no less than that required in the Eightfold Path, complete renunciation of every form of attachment to this life. To travel the path and to attain the goal, moreover, means both to Buddha and to Socrates to travel the path of enlightenment and to attain the goal of wisdom.

A question comes up, though, when one examines the comparison more closely, as to whether the wisdom sought by Socrates is really equivalent to that sought by Buddha. The difference, it is true, will appear greater than it actually is if when one hears the term "philosopher" one is unconsciously led to envision a modern academic and professorial philosopher. When all anachronisms of this sort are set aside, nevertheless, there still seems to be a difference in the "rational" quality of the wisdom sought by the two sages. The difference shows itself in the relative need which is felt of subjecting the supposed wisdom to the test of rational argumentation. Buddha's peace of mind was the warrant of his enlightenment and it would perhaps be droll to imagine his wisdom being submitted to the irrelevancy of a Socratic cross-examination, but Socrates' tranquillity in the face of death after a life of subjecting himself and others to rational scrutiny seems to call for the kind of examination his survivors Xenophon and Plato gave it to determine whether it was proof that he was enlightened or proof that he was deluded. To Plato this meant justifying the practice of death with a rational demonstration of the immortality of the soul.

The demonstration which Plato devised, however, did not meet with wide acceptance, for its cogency depends on the acceptance of his theory of ideas.[13] If the idea, which may be designated neutrally as "what is known," is conceived in Plato's manner to be a transcendent object rather than merely an immanent content of thought, then immortality is guaranteed by the soul's capability of uniting or reuniting itself with the idea through contemplation. The transcendence of the idea, in fact, accounts for everything involved in the practice of death, the misery of man in his present condition, the foolishness of wishing to prolong that situation through one existence after another, the necessity of rising above it, and the method of rising above it. Because the idea is above and beyond man in his actual state there is required of him a kind of ecstasy, a going out of himself, to reach the idea. The fact that man is capable of this ecstasy, though, means that he can be carried out of himself, that his spirit can be transported from time into eternity. This rapture in which his mind or soul is lifted so that it may see eternal objects beyond the range of ordinary human vision is thus the attainment of an eternal life.

If, on the other hand, the idea is conceived in Aristotle's manner to be an immanent content rather than a transcendent object of thought, it is no longer any guarantee of the soul's immortality. Before the idea itself could be said to be eternal, the eternity of the thought in which it is immanent would have to be established. Aristotle's theory of "active mind"[14] is apparently an attempt to do just this, to establish the existence of perpetually active thought in which the idea shall be eternal and in which it shall exist prior to its discovery in the process of human learning. The trouble is that only active mind is therefore immortal, according to Aristotle, not the passive mind with which we do our learning nor the soul as a whole. Like the transcendence of Platonic immortality, nevertheless, the impersonality of Aristotelian immortality is a possible account for the mystic's conviction that eternal life is attainable only through the annihilation of empirical existence and the empirical self. What happens according to Aristotle when mind is set free from its present conditions is comparable with what is supposed to occur in a mystic *parinirvana*. No trace of earthly memory and earthly existence remains but only active mind, impassive, unmixed, immortal, and eternal.

One solution to the dilemma posed by the rival Platonic and Aristotelian conceptions of the idea and of immortality is to combine them as Plotinus did, to postulate the existence both of the transcendent object (the One) and of the immanent content (the Ideas in Mind) and to infer the separate immortality of Mind and Soul.[15] Plotinus is more commonly recognized to have been a mystic than Plato himself since the enlightenment which he taught and experienced was evidently less intellectual and more purely religious. Perhaps the reason for this most intrinsic to his thinking was that in positing both the transcendent object and the immanent content he effectively separated religious enlightenment and intellectual enlightenment, the former attaching to the transcendent object and the latter to the immanent content. Because the One, the transcendent object, was transcendent with respect to Mind and its immanent content of Ideas, the religious enlightenment which arose from the contemplation of the One was placed above the intellectual enlightenment which arose from the contemplation of Mind and the Ideas.

Another solution, that of Kant, is to say that the whole endeavor which was begun by Plato, and which by Kant's time had been going on for many centuries, to work out a satisfactory rational demonstration for the immortality of the soul was a mistake. Kant not only effectively but formally separated intellectual enlightenment from moral and religious enlightenment and assigned the Aristotelian idea, the immanent content, to the former and the Platonic idea, the transcendent object, to the latter.[16] When he asserted, then, that the arguments for the immortality of the soul are necessarily invalid, he was in effect reproducing the Aristotelian objection to the Platonic demonstration. The greatest difficulty with the position of Kant and also with that of Plotinus, besides the ultimate inconsistency of juxtaposing the idea as immanent content with the idea as transcendent object, is the failure to account for an experience of enlightenment which even in Eastern mysticism was not exclusively religious nor exclusively moral but also in a very comprehensive sense intellectual.

It seems possible to combine immanence and transcendence without falling into the implicit contradiction involved in a Kantian or Plotinian division of labor. The way in which this may be done is suggested by Kant himself when he points out that the link between the realm of immanent content and that of transcendent object is the concept of freedom.[17] What Kant understood by "freedom" was free will, and the link which he saw between the two realms was that in the realm of immanent content freedom appears as a possibility, though no more than a possibility, and in the realm of transcendent object it appears as a necessary actuality. If the Kantian concept of essential freedom is replaced by the concept of effective freedom which figures in mysticism, then the two realms which Kant merely juxtaposed begin to coalesce. Freedom from this point of view will not be something which every man possesses but something which every man is called upon to achieve, and the degree of freedom a man achieves will be the degree in which the transcendent becomes immanent in him. The experience of immortality will thus be the experience of freedom and elucidating the experience will mean elucidating the process of liberation.

[2] *Mystical Freedom*

Considering the essential similarity of man's chief wants everywhere and at all times and, on the other hand, the wide difference between the means man has adopted to satisfy them in different ages, Sir James Frazer concludes in *The Golden Bough* that the movement of higher thought has on the whole been from magic through religion to science.[18] If the purpose of magic, religion, and science is to satisfy man's wants, though, and if the three of them differ only with respect to the means employed to reach this end, magic and science invoking man's own powers and religion invoking powers above and beyond him, then it appears that another category must be added, namely mysticism, the object of which is not to satisfy man's wants but to do away with them. Basic drives like the urge to preserve his life and the urge to propagate his race which man seeks to realize when he turns to magic, religion, or science, he seeks to annihilate when he turns to mysticism. To the extent that a man so extinguishes desire as to no longer have need of magic, science, and religion (in the above-mentioned sense), and only to that extent, it seems, does he attain the freedom which is the goal of mysticism.

Until the point of complete freedom is reached, however, he will presumably find himself unable to dispense with one or another of the systems of ensuring the satisfaction of his needs. In the historical rise and development of mysticism, as a matter of fact, such perfect emancipation seems to have been attained only by a few extraordinary individuals like Buddha and Socrates. Buddha, for instance, though he apparently believed in the power of magic, considered magic a temptation to be resisted, and so likewise, renouncing his two million gods, did he consider religion. Socrates, if there is any substance to the charge on which he was condemned to death, that of refusing recognition to the gods recognized by the city, took a somewhat similar attitude toward religion, though he did recognize a kind of divine premonition in his own life, and he also gave up speculation about nature and would have nothing further to do with natural science. Aside from paradigmatic figures of the mystical movement like these, though, we do not find men who were able to carry renunciation so far or to live so independently of all mental comforts but instead we find mysticism ordinarily mixed with some form of magic or religion or science.

What happened when mysticism was mixed with magic can be observed in the development of yoga, the spiritual discipline which Buddha tried and then abandoned in his search for enlightenment.[19] While the goal of yoga in its many forms appears to have been genuine mystical freedom, this freedom was ordinarily sought with the expectation of using it to produce magical effects as though it were the same thing as the "omnipotence of thought" to which the magician lays claim. Buddha himself seems to have been ready to concede that the acquisition of mental powers of an apparently magical nature was unavoidable on the way to mystical freedom, the mystic's emancipation from the world's power giving him a kind of power over the world and its illusions. But to seek mystical freedom or attempt to use it for an ulterior purpose of this kind, Buddha taught, was to effectively deny it to oneself since it is impossible to be genuinely detached from the world and free when one is attached to the possession and exercise of power over the world.

What happened when mysticism was mixed with religion, that is with previously existing religion if we count mysticism "higher religion," is exhibited in the mystery religions.[20] Whether we consider the Eleusinian and Orphic mysteries of Hellenic times which Socrates used to illustrate the mystical "practice of death" or the mysteries of Adonis, Attis, and Osiris of Hellenistic times or those of Mithras which became popular in Roman times, we find in all the mystery religions the common pattern of the initiation rite. The experience into which the participant is initiated, moreover, appears for the most part intended to be something resembling mystical experience. The mystical nature of the goal seems particularly clear in Orphism and Mithraism where the doctrine of transmigration of souls was taught and where moral purification combined with the ritual purification of the mysteries was supposed to assure the soul its final release to the life of the blessed. The attempt to bolster mysticism with religion, though to supplement moral purification with ritual purification, made the value of the mysteries seem largely figurative to Socrates and led him to adjudge to the "true philosopher" the salvation offered in the mysteries to the initiate.

What happened when mysticism was mixed with science can be seen in the evolution of Post-Socratic philosophy, especially in Epicurus and Lucretius. Popular distortions to the contrary notwithstanding, Epicureanism like Skepticism and Stoicism was a way of life aimed at the attainment of ataraxy, the Post-Socratic conception of mystical freedom.[21] While Epicurus and his great follower Lucretius were able to free themselves like Socrates from what they considered the vain hopes and groundless fears engendered by the traditional religion, they were not able like Socrates to do without some substitute for the religious interpretation of nature. What moved the Epicureans against religion was not so much the fact that the gods ministered to desires as the fact that they caused anxiety. To liberate themselves and others from the oppressive fear generated by religion, therefore, Epicurus and Lucretius found it necessary to replace the religious explanation of natural phenomena with a scientific explanation derived from the atomic theory of Democritus. They ended, consequently, like many of their admirers and counterparts in the eighteenth century, with only a relative emancipation, an independence from the anxieties of religion purchased at the cost of a dependence on the consolations of science.

Although Frazer's thesis of a progressive evolution from magic through religion to science and beyond is not a reliable interpretation of the general movement of human thought, the image of a successive emancipation of the human spirit from magic, from religion, and from science might be a fairly accurate representation of the process of liberation which takes place in mysticism. The emancipation from magic occurs with the discovery of universal evil, the starting point of mysticism, whether this takes the form of Buddha's discovery of the universal misery of mankind or that of Socrates' discovery of the universal ignorance of mankind (to him the equivalent of universal misery), for the fact of universal ignorance or misery is clearly incompatible with magical omniscience or omnipotence. The emancipation from religion, that is from the religion of myth, occurs with the subsequent insight into the cause of evil, whether this be Buddha's insight that evil is due to the blindness of our blind will to live or Socrates' insight that it is due to ignorance of our ignorance, because to satisfy as far as possible our will to live and to minister to our unexamined desires and fears is the aim of the religion of myth. The emancipation from science occurs when the blindness causing evil is eliminated, whether this comes about like Buddha's enlightenment through the annihilation of one's blind will or like Socrates' enlightenment through the knowledge of one's ignorance, since the necessity and sufficiency of negative wisdom such as this makes positive science appear unnecessary and insufficient to deliver man from evil.

The discovery of universal evil with which mysticism begins undermines the basic presupposition of magic that there are only particular evils and that each evil has its proper magical remedy. From the standpoint of magic the common afflictions of mankind such as sickness, famine, enemies, and even death itself can all be done away with at will by one who is versed in magic. There is no evil in the world of magic which is inherent in the human condition nor is there any evil which man, properly instructed, does not know how to overcome. Magical power fills all the gaps in man's technological capacity for dealing with his problems and magical lore fills the gaps in the scientific or protoscientific knowledge of nature on which his capacity is based. The discovery of universal misery and ignorance, if it is made, cannot help but bring such a world to an end, because universal misery means that there are evils against which even the most powerful magician is powerless and universal ignorance means that there are remedies of which even the most learned magician is ignorant.

Universal misery as it was conceived by Buddha did not consist so much in the evils themselves against which magic was directed, old age, disease, and death, to name the three which in the story of Buddha's life were supposed to have led him to his discovery, as in the suffering or unhappiness which these evils occasion. The essence of suffering, as he understood it, was in being united with what one dislikes, in being separated from what one likes, in not getting what one wants, liking and wanting youth, health, and life but disliking and getting old age, disease, and death.[22] The discovery that suffering is universal was made, to judge from the ideal of compassion which has been inherited in Buddhism, in an experience of universal compassion. Only in compassion universal as that traditionally ascribed to Buddha does it seem possible, at any rate, to achieve the sympathetic understanding of suffering that will enable one to renounce the struggle for existence, and only in compassion does it seem possible that one who has attained peace within himself will find the inspiration to share his peace with others, to relinquish the full enjoyment of his peace like Plato's philosopher-king or to postpone the full enjoyment of it like the *bodhisattva* in order to save others.[23]

Universal ignorance, the universal misery of mankind as it was conceived by Socrates, was tantamount to universal suffering or unhappiness because it was understood as one's ignorance of what is good and what is evil, not knowing what one is doing, choosing evil thinking that it is good and rejecting good thinking that it is evil, and getting thereby what one doesn't want and missing what one does want. The real evil, Socrates thought, is not dying or being injured by others or going hungry or falling sick, but the ignorance in which we live which makes these things seem evil to us and gives them the power to make us unhappy. Irony, simulated ignorance and willingness to learn from others assumed for the sake of making their ignorance conspicuous by means of adroit questioning, the method by which Socrates brought the fact of universal ignorance to light both for himself and for others seems far removed from the experience of compassion in which the truth of universal misery was brought to light. Yet its unsympathetic quality is not as great as the name *eironeia* ("dissimulation") suggests, for Socrates considered himself wiser than his victims only in that he knew he was ignorant while they were unaware of their ignorance until it was exposed. Although he did wish to bring the ignorance of others to light with his questioning, he was not the *eiron,* the dissembler in his speech, that he was accused of being, but was actually in sympathy with his victims, sharing ignorance with them and wishing them to share his awareness of ignorance.[24]

When he brings universal evil to light in his irony or his compassion the mystic makes nonsense of the magician's divers remedies for the sundry ills of mankind, but when he goes on to diagnose evil and trace it to its cause within man he seems to stultify the skills of the corresponding figure in religion, the shaman.[25] It is true that Buddha was reputed to have a shaman's ability to remember his former lives and Socrates was reputed to have in his premonition something like a shaman's access to the unseen world of gods, demons, and spirits. The contradiction between mysticism and shamanism, however, appears in the fact that mystics and shamans take opposite attitudes toward myth and its ideal of an indefinite extension of life in this world, that a shaman wishes to relive all his past existences in his present experience while a Buddha wishes to abolish the hold of the past on the present and to escape from the cycle of transmigration, that a shaman seeks the protection of spirits against sickness and other menaces to life while a Socrates is thankful that no prompting of his familiar spirit deters him from facing and accepting death.

It would perhaps be possible to account both for the mystic's and the shaman's supposed experience of former lives by saying that the sense of manifold existence is actually a consciousness of the infinite variety of possible lives which constitute the scope of human freedom. One's feeling of being free to choose is a sense of this variety and one's experience of existential decision is a consciousness of having excluded all but one of these possible existences. The will to live, on the other hand, would be the will to live all one's possible lives and it would create dissatisfaction with the exclusion wrought by the choice of one life out of the many. The shaman's effort in remembering former lives would accordingly be tantamount to an attempt to overcome this unfulfillment by tasting all the lives excluded by his actual life. The Buddha's insight, on the contrary, would be the discovery that the will to live all one's possible lives is the basic root of unhappiness.[26]

Maybe the sense of the manifold possibilities of human existence is also the experience underlying the attempt which the shaman makes to communicate with the spirit world, an endeavor which is carried out with the same techniques of ecstasy as his effort to recall his past existences. The laws of the world of spirits do indeed seem to differ from those of the visible world as those of the world of possibilities do from those of the world of actualities. The manner in which the *daimonion* of Socrates prompted him, on the other hand, forbidding him but never giving him positive commands or instructions, implies an intense experience on Socrates' part of the exclusion of possible courses of action other than the one he actually follows and of the exclusion of possible lives other than the one he actually lives.[27] The ignorance of ignorance to which he traces the general ignorance of good and evil, moreover, is similar to the blindness of the will to live all one's possible lives, a failure to see that one's life needs to be examined and that an unexamined life in which one lives by the undiscriminating will to live is not worth living.

If the diagnosis which traces evil to the blindness of man's will thus makes any magico-religious attempt to procure the complete fulfillment of his will appear misguided, the therapy which cures evil with the acknowledgment of that blindness makes any attempt to guide man's will with positive science appear mistaken. What is implied here is not a denial of validity to scientific knowledge but something on the order of Kant's observation that propositions called "practical" in natural science should properly be called "technical" since in science there is no question of determining the will but only of indicating the manifold of a possible action which is adequate to bring about a certain effect, of showing the connection between cause and effect such that whoever chooses the latter must also choose the former.[28] Socrates was mistaken by Aristophanes and others of his contemporaries for a natural philosopher, a figure who in those days seemed to the general public a denier of the nature-religion bent on making his science of nature do for man what religion had done. In reality the mystic, as Socrates said of himself when defending himself against this charge at his trial,[29] is neither opposed to natural science nor concerned with it since it seems to him that science, whatever its value otherwise, is incapable of removing man's ignorance of the good.

Mysticism does not entirely remove it either but only advances man from ignorance of his ignorance to knowledge of his ignorance. This, however, is a truly "practical" gain since it does determine man's will at least so far as to cause him to abandon in Buddha's fashion the will to live. It may seem questionable whether it is psychologically possible to abolish the will to live any more than it is possible to abolish, for instance, the sexual urge, but the real purport of the Buddhist annihilation of desire is probably no more than that of the Socratic acknowledgement of ignorance. This appears likely enough in view of the Buddhist doctrine that desire is conditioned by ignorance and that the annihilation of desire results from the elimination of ignorance.[30] Something similar to the Buddhist elimination of ignorance and annihilation of the will to live seems implied conversely in the Socratic doctrine that knowledge is virtue and that the practice of virtue is the practice of dying. The question that is more difficult to answer is whether the almost superhuman freedom from illusion claimed in both the Socratic and the Buddhist versions of enlightenment is not itself the final and most seductive illusion.

If there is illusion in pure mysticism, it will not be because the paradigmatic figures of the mystical movement left anything undone to free themselves from illusion but it will be, on the contrary, because man cannot be liberated from all illusion or, if he can, because the illusion in which he lives will not permit him to do the liberating himself. The illusion which the man who does everything possible to disillusion himself has to fear is the one Freud came up against at the end of *The Future of an Illusion* after arguing at length man's need to liberate himself from religion, namely the possibility that the intense wish to be free of all illusion may turn everything he does to that purpose into mere wish-fulfillment and render his emancipation illusory. Whether mystical enlightenment can prove itself, as Freud would have freedom from illusion prove itself, by its power to liberate the minds of men through "education to reality" has been an historic problem and a considerably more difficult one than it was for Freud who was not thinking of total emancipation but only of replacing religion as far as possible with science. It does not seem too much to expect, nevertheless, of one who has supposedly reached the Archimedean point of perfect enlightenment that he be able to move the world, and this indeed is what did come to be expected of the ideal king.

[3] *The Mystical King*

The primary aim of *The Golden Bough*, Sir James Frazer said, was to explain the remarkable rule which regulated the succession to the priesthood of Diana at Aricia. It was the custom for the priesthood of that shrine to be given to a runaway slave after he had plucked the Golden Bough, a branch from a certain tree in the grove, and killed in single combat the King of the Wood, the priest who had previously occupied the office. Frazer's explanation, carrying him through a voluminous study of magic and religion in the evolution of kingship, was that the King of the Wood was responsible for the fertility of crops and animals and people, that his divine consort Diana was a fertility goddess, that his magic was liable to failure with the decline of his bodily strength, that his death at the hands of his successor was the remedy for such failure, that his death was thus a boon for fertility like the death of Adonis, Attis, and Osiris, that he was in this way a scapegoat for all the ills of his people, and that his soul was thought to reside in the Golden Bough so that it had to be plucked before he could be killed.

A somewhat different interpretation of Frazer's evidence, along the lines of the interpretation given to early Mesopotamian kingship in the first chapter, is suggested by two facts: first, that Dumuzi or Tammuz, the figure from which Adonis is derived, was supposed to have died, it has now been discovered, in order to take the place of his consort the fertility goddess in the nether world, and second, that the Golden Bough was plucked by Aeneas as a gift to the queen of the dead in order that he might gain entrance thereby to the nether world.[31] These facts point to the possibility that the King of the Wood was put to death in order to obtain the release of his consort, Diana the fertility goddess, from the nether world and that the Golden Bough was a gift to Proserpina, the queen of the dead, given with the purpose of making the king acceptable to her in Diana's stead. This would seem to be a better interpretation of the Golden Bough itself since the use to which the branch was put in the *Aeneid* is the only one that is known other than the one in question, and the killing of the king would seem to be explained at least as well this way as it is Frazer's way.

Whether all the parallels which Frazer adduces to illustrate his own explanation and which constitute the real substance of his work can be reinterpreted in this manner is another question.

One thing that can probably be said with some confidence of most known examples of ritual regicide, though, is that over and above any anxiety about the king losing his magic there is the desire to taste death without actually dying in person. Although the custom of killing the king, if it ever existed there, was not preserved, the meaning of the king's death in Mesopotamia seems to have been essentially this vicarious experience of death, the king sharing in the death experience of the goddess and the people participating in it vicariously in the person of their king.[32] The vicarious experience of death and descent into the nether world was at the same time the evident forerunner of the mystical experience of the afterlife, though it differed from mystical experience proper in that its object was not the anticipation of the afterlife as a relief and an escape from the miseries of the present life but rather the acquisition of the knowledge of life and death, the experience and understanding of life that comes from the experience and understanding of death.

Between this most primitive type of savior king and the kind of savior king that arose out of mysticism proper there is an intermediate type, the autocrat who developed in the evolution away from the basic king-council-assembly form of society and who dominated Asia until the time of Alexander the Great. The early Mesopotamian kings had ruled with the advice of a council and the consent of an assembly but the Babylonian and Assyrian kings of later times were autocrats combining in themselves all the functions which had once been distributed among king, council, and assembly.[33] The first autocrats, those who pertained to the "era of Ishtar" like Sargon of Akkad, still conceived themselves to be human consorts of the goddess Ishtar, the goddess of cities and of war and fertility, as early kings like Gilgamesh had done, and also like these early kings derived from this their claim to hegemony over cities other than their own.[34] In time, though, the possibility of the individual autonomy of cities or the mere hegemony of one over another was no longer allowed and it was claimed instead that the ruler of the hegemonic city was universal monarch of all the land. This conception of the king as it is set forth in the Babylonian creation epic, the *Enuma Elish,* appears to have derived not from the concept of the king which prevailed in cities like Erech where the king was permanent and was called *en* ("lord") as being the human consort of the goddess but from the concept prevailing in cities where a king was chosen only in times of emergency, was called *lugal* ("great man"), and was given emergency dictatorial powers by the council and the assembly.[35]

In the creation epic there is what amounts to a kind of polemic in favor of this new type of savior against the older type dramatized in a struggle between the younger gods led by the autocrat's patron god and the older gods led by the mother of the gods and her consort. The mother of the gods appears in this story as the female monster Tiamat who in the assembly of the older gods called to deal with the disturbance caused them by the upstart younger gods makes the god Kingu her consort, seats him in the council of gods, and indues him with the tablets of fate. The younger gods themselves then assemble and choose Marduk, the patron god of the autocrat, to be their defender and savior, but Marduk agrees to save them only on condition that they give to him permanently all the powers which they had once exercised in their council and assembly. After the issue is thus clearly drawn between the new order in which all powers are united in the autocrat and the old order in which the king had been the consort of the goddess and had ruled with the advice of the council and the consent of the assembly, the battle is fought and Marduk is of course victorious and seizes from his rival the coveted tablets of fate which embody supreme authority over the entire universe. He then proceeds to create the universe out of the body of the dead mother goddess and man out of the blood of her dead consort, and the whole story comes to climax with the building of the city of Babylon.

The vicarious experience of death was continued in the new order but it was given new meaning by its conjunction with a vicarious experience of resurrection from the dead. In the old order there had been a resurrection too, it is true, in that the king's descent into the nether world had brought about the release and resurrection of the goddess. In the new order, however, it was the king himself who rose from the dead, Marduk in the yearly celebration of his victory being represented as having for a time resided in the nether world overcome by his enemies before rising again to conquer them.[36] Perhaps the experience of death was thought to be necessary for the acquisition of the tablets of fate, for these tablets appear to have been the tablets of wisdom which in the old order were in the possession of the king of the dead.[37] The king in the old order did not come into possession of the tablets of fate until he had experienced death and acquired in this manner the knowledge and experience of fate. The king in the new order, however, through his temporary death in the person of his patron god came into possession of the tablets while he was still reigning over the living. When the king came back from the dead, thus, all power had been given to him in heaven and on earth.

With the conquest of the Median and Lydian kingdoms and the Neo-Babylonian empire by Cyrus in the sixth century the Persians, whose society had been organized in the usual king-council-assembly pattern of the Indo-Europeans, entered into the autocratic pattern of society and the Persian king inherited the Babylonian title King of Kings and came to be regarded, as the Babylonian king had been regarded, the rightful ruler of the entire universe.[38] While Cyrus was friendly to the Babylonian religion and probably retained also some of the conceptions which went with the old Iranian religion and the king-council-assembly society, his successors Darius and Xerxes adopted the newer Zoroastrian religion with its dualistic view that Ahuramazda, the lord of light and goodness, wars ceaselessly against Ahriman and the hosts of evil, its belief that Ahuramazda created man to aid him, and its hope that the good kingdom will finally be attained. Xerxes, claiming to rule the whole world in the "shadow" of Ahuramazda, destroyed the great temple of Marduk at Babylon, saying that it was a temple to Ahriman the Evil One, and proclaimed that anyone who wished to be prosperous while alive and blessed when dead should worship Ahuramazda alone.[39] This development, it seems, was a near approximation to the idealized conception of universal monarchy according to which the ruler was supposed to communicate to his subjects the higher truth of mystical enlightenment, a conception which was taking shape at about this time both to the east and to the west of the Persian empire.

To the east the ideal of the universal king, the Chakravartin, had already made its appearance in the common epic literature of India, but the concept appears to have undergone a special evolution in Buddhism where the vocation of the Chakravartin was conceived to be parallel and alternative to that of the Buddha.[40] To communicate the enlightenment of the Buddha was, symbolically, to turn the wheel of Dharma (truth), a function of the "one who is enlightened," the Buddha himself, and a function of the "one who turns the wheel," the Chakravartin. In historical actuality, too, the propagation of Buddhism was due, after the activity of Gautama, the Buddha, to the efforts of King Asoka, an historical approximation to the Chakravartin, who considered it his duty to proclaim the Dharma throughout his empire, though not in the manner of Xerxes prohibiting more primitive ways of life. Asoka had been so distressed by the slaughter and misery involved in his one war of conquest that he renounced conquest by violence and devoted the rest of his life to "conquest by Dharma." With his claims to have made conquests of the latter sort in the whole known world, however, including the Hellenistic kingdoms to the west of India, he showed his unrepenting determination to be a universal monarch, by moral suasion then if not by force of arms.[41]

The ideal which developed in the West out of the Socratic problem of who was to teach virtue, the philosopher king, is comparable to some extent with the ideal of the Chakravartin, though the philosopher king was not at first envisioned as a universal monarch, but only as the ruler of a city.[42] In Socratism the question was whether virtue, given that virtue is knowledge, can be taught and, if it can, who there is who could conceivably teach it. Socrates excused himself from becoming a statesman on the grounds that his premonition forbade it and that if he had attempted to give the kind of advice publicly which he went about giving in private he would never have lived as long as he did. Plato, on the other hand, while remaining a private citizen himself, judged it indispensable that philosophers become kings or kings philosophers if virtue was ever to be effectively taught. Aristotle, denying that virtue was knowledge and affirming that it consisted in a mean determined by the man of practical wisdom, called not for a ruler who should be capable of teaching virtue so much as for one who should be able to determine the mean of virtue for the rest of men. Finally, Alexander the Great, Aristotle's royal pupil, with his ideas on the concord (*homonoia*) that should obtain among all mankind transformed Aristotle's ideal of the ruler into that of a universal king.

It has often been said that when Alexander strove to unite barbarians and Greeks in an all-embracing community he was deliberately ignoring advice given him by Aristotle that he be a leader (*hegemon*) to the Greeks but a master (*despotes*) to the barbarians.[43] The trouble with this notion is that in reality Alexander appears to have followed Aristotle's advice to the letter, making himself Hegemon to the Greeks, Pharaoh to the Egyptians, and Great King to the Persians, his Persian dress and the like being part of the latter role. Aristotle's idea had been that the mean of virtue is not an abstract norm but a concrete one varying from society to society and that each people must be ruled in accordance with its peculiar character, the barbarians like slaves by a master like the Great King and the Greeks like freemen by a leader who would respect the liberty of their urban republics. This is the principle Alexander attempted to follow, ruling each people according to its own laws and customs, and so also did his successors, the Antigonids in Greece, the Ptolemies in Egypt, and the Seleucids in Asia.[44] This is the difference between Alexander and Napoleon, for example, whose idea of unity was to abolish all differences of law and custom and reduce all nations to a single nation.

In an empire such as Alexander's, however, where each people had its own law, the universal monarch was in the position given by Plato and Aristotle to their ideal rulers of being above all law.[45] Plato thought that law was only a general rule unable to allow properly for particular differences among men and circumstances and therefore that the philosopher king should be set above the law and that his rule should take precedence over the rule of law. Aristotle, in turn, believed that a man capable like his ideal ruler of concretely determining the mean of virtue was above all abstract legal standards and was, moreover, like "a god among men." Alexander's request, accordingly, that the cities of Greece recognize his divinity, if he did actually make this request, was probably a demand that he be acknowledged "a god among men" in Aristotle's sense of being above the law, and the legal significance of the deification of his successors was probably similar, each of them being in his own realm a universal monarch set over diverse peoples living according to diverse laws and customs, the Antigonids over Macedonians and diverse urban republics, the Ptolemies over Greeks and Egyptians, and the Seleucids over Greeks, Persians, Babylonians, and other peoples.[46]

Being kings of the Aristotelian type that determined the concrete mean of virtue rather than of the Platonic type that taught virtue, the Hellenistic kings, while they were above all particular laws, had no higher law or truth to proclaim as did Xerxes and Asoka.[47] The nearest thing to the communication of a higher law was Alexander's proclamation of concrete universalism itself, his prayer for and exhortation to concord among all peoples. The deification of Alexander and his successors, to be sure, had something of the effect of a proclamation of higher truth, placing them as it did above all particular laws, and it seems to have gone hand in hand with a religious revolution involving the decline and fall of classical religion and the growth and spread of the semimystical mystery religions. The connection with the decline of classical religion is revealed unwittingly in the theory Euhemerus advanced a couple of decades after Alexander to the effect that the gods of mythology had their origin in kings or heroes deified by those whom they had ruled over or benefited, a theory reducing classical religion to the model of the Hellenistic ruler cult, and the connection with the mystery religions is apparent in the fact that the divinities worshiped in these religions are savior gods like the contemporary deified kings.

A higher law or truth did ultimately make its appearance, however, in the rise of Christianity not long after the disappearance of the Hellenistic kingdoms and the establishment of the Roman principate, and when Christianity was eventually accepted by the Roman Empire in the time of Constantine something comparable to the situation under Xerxes and Asoka did begin to prevail. The fact that a Christian mysticism has developed and has continued to flourish on into modern times will suggest that Christianity is a continuation and perhaps the culmination of the mysticism that went before it in the ancient East and West. The fact that Christ claimed, moreover, that his disciples would know the truth and the truth would make them free (John 8:23) will suggest that Christ's doctrine was meant to be a liberating enlightenment like that of Buddha and Socrates. And the fact that the death of Christ is experienced vicariously in sacraments, that he is believed to have come back from the dead invested with all power in heaven and on earth, and that he is thought to be the Logos enlightening every man coming into the world will suggest a similarity between Christ and each successive type of savior king.

Some fairly salient divergencies exist, nevertheless, between Christianity and the various forms of mysticism which have been under consideration. In spite of the fact that there is a Christian mysticism, the Christian denial of reincarnation, of fate, of dualism, and of immortality apart from God tends to destroy the significance of mysticism as an escape from the present life. In spite of the fact that Christ promised that the truth he taught would make men free, Christ was not supposed to have sought after the liberating enlightenment as did Buddha and Socrates, or to have acquired it through insight into previous failure as Buddha did sitting under the bo tree, contemplating the failure of concentration and asceticism to bring him wisdom, or as Socrates did reflecting on the failure of his attempts to extract real knowledge from the learning of his time. And in spite of the fact that the figure of Christ resembles in some degree each successive type of savior king and notwithstanding the inscription on his cross declaring him a king, Christ was never a king in the political sense that even the Chakravartin and the philosopher king were.

The choice between the two trees in the garden of paradise, the tree of life and the tree of knowledge of good and evil, which in myth is weighted in favor of life and in mysticism is weighted in favor of knowledge, is no longer a choice in Christianity. Knowledge is no longer conceived to be a way of escape from life nor is life conceived any more to be an enslavement to illusion and so there is no further need for a king to save men from life with knowledge. Rather there is a Saviour who with his "I am" statements (which are actually predicate nominative assertions that "It is I")[48] purports to be all that men have been seeking, both knowledge and life. The question which is put to Christianity by mysticism, then, is how man can have knowledge without sacrificing life and how man can have life without sacrificing knowledge.

NOTES TO CHAPTER SIX

1. Republic V, 473.

2. Cf. Karl Jaspers, *The Origin and Goal of History* tr. by Michael Bullock (London, 1953), 1 ff. and 51 ff. Jaspers, however, does not connect the spiritual revolution of which he speaks with the political revolution with which we are linking it here.

3. Kant's criticism of the arguments for immortality as being "paralogisms" falsely extending the use of reason beyond the bounds of experience is to be found in *Critique of Pure Reason* tr. by F. Max Müller (New York, 1961), 216 ff. and especially 244 f. Albert Schweitzer works with a concept of mystical experience as anticipation of the afterlife in *The Mysticism of Paul the Apostle* tr. by William Montgomery (London, 1931).

4. For a general survey of the ideas on immortality in the age to which Vergil belongs cf. Franz Cumont, *After Life in Roman Paganism* (New Haven, 1922). Cf. the later edition of this work in French under the title *Lux Perpetua* (Paris, 1949).

5. Aeneid VI, 893 ff.

6. Ibid., 749 ff. Cf. *Republic* X, 621 C.

7. Bhagavad-Gita 4:5.

8. Aeneid VI, 724 ff. and *Bhagavad-Gita* 11.

9. The classical statement of the Four Truths is the famous Turning of the Wheel of Doctrine discourse (the Dhammakakkappavattana Sutta) translated by T. W. Rhys Davids and Hermann Oldenberg in F. Max Müller, *The Sacred Books of the East,* vol. XIII (Oxford, 1881), 94 ff.

10. Aeneid VI, 718 ff.

11. Bhagavad-Gita 2:72; 5:24, 25, 26. The term *nirvana* by itself occurs in 6:15.

12. Phaedo, 61 ff.

13. The cogency of Plato's various arguments for the immortality of the soul is seriously impaired, it seems, if the link with the theory of ideas is ignored. This link is hardest to ignore in the *Phaedo* where it is expressly formulated (76) but it can be broken there too by separating the various considerations brought forward there into independent arguments. The argument given in the *Republic* that if moral evil does not destroy the soul then nothing can destroy her (X, 608 ff.) should not be separated, it seems, from the doctrine put forward there about the soul's special relation to the Good (VI, 505 ff.). And the argument given in the *Phaedrus* that the soul is self-moving and therefore in perpetual motion (245) should not be separated from the description of the soul's motion in that dialogue as a motion toward the ideas (246 ff.).

14. De Anima III, 430a10 ff.

15. Plotinus' formal discussion of immortality is in *Enneads* IV, 9, but the more revealing thing is the general structure of his system.

16. Thus Kant makes the immortality of the soul a postulate of conscience. Cf. *Critique of Practical Reason* tr. by L. W. Beck (New York, 1956), 3 f. and 126 ff.

17. In the preface to the *Critique of Practical Reason.*

18. In the final conclusion of *The Golden Bough,* Part VII (London, 1913), vol. II, 304.

19. Cf. Mircea Eliade's discussion of the relation of Buddhism to yoga in *Yoga: Immortality and Freedom* tr. by W. R. Trask (New York, 1958), 162 ff.

20. For a general survey of the questions raised by modern scholars on the Hellenic mysteries, the Hellenistic mystery religions, corresponding primitive rites, and corresponding elements in Christianity cf. R. Pettazzoni, "Les Mystères Grecs et les religions à mystère de l'antiquité" in *Cahiers d'histoire mondiale,* II (Paris, 1955), 303 ff. with a very complete bibliography, 661 ff. For the Socratic interpretation of the mysteries cf. especially *Phaedo,* 69 c.

21. For the Epicurean conception of *ataraxia* cf. the epistle of Epicurus to Menoecius in Diogenes Laertius, X, 128. For the Stoic conception cf. Epictetus, *Discourses* II, 2. For the Skeptic conception cf. Sextus Empiricus, *Outlines* I, 12. On natural science contrast the attitude formulated in the epistle of Epicurus to Herodotus on nature and that to Pythocles on celestial phenomena and Lucretius' epic treatise *De Rerum Natura* with the attitude expressed in the statements of Socrates referred to below in note 29.

22. Cf. the traditional formulation of the first of the Four Truths in Müller, *op. cit.,* 95.

23. The ideal of the *bodhisattva* and the various phases in his career are set forth in the Diamond Sutra translated by Edward Conze in *Buddhist Wisdom Books* (London, 1958), 21 ff.

24. See how Socrates explains the enmity he aroused in Athens in *Apology* 20 ff.

25. On shamanism cf. Mircea Eliade, *Le Chamanisme et les techniques archaïques de l'extase* (Paris, 1951).

26. On the will to live as the cause of rebirth and the origin of suffering cf.

the traditional formulation of the second of the Four Truths in Müller, *loc. cit.*

27. On the negative character of Socrates' premonition cf. *Apology*, 31 D, and on the absence of any premonition against death cf. *ibid.*, 40 A. Xenophon, on the other hand, has it that positive commands were given to Socrates by his familiar spirit. Cf. *Memorabilia* I, 1, 4 and IV, 8, 1.

28. *Critique of Practical Reason*, 26, footnote.

29. *Apology* 19 c. Cf. *ibid.*, 26 D and *Phaedo*, 97 ff. Also cf. Xenophon, *Memorabilia* I, 1, 11 ff.

30. Cf. the doctrine of the Chain of Causation in Müller *op. cit.*, 75 ff. On the abolition of the will to live cf. also the traditional formulation of the third of the Four Truths *ibid.*, 95.

31. On Dumuzi-Tammuz cf. Chapter One, Section 2. The texts on the Golden Bough are *Aeneid* VI, 136 ff., 187 ff., 405 ff., and 628 ff. Compare Frazer's account in *The Golden Bough*, Part I (London, 1911), vol. I, 11 and vol. II, 379, and Part VII (London, 1913), vol. II, 279 ff.

32. Cf. Chapter One, Section 2.

33. Cf. Chapter Three, Sections 2 and 3 and references there in notes 22 and 43.

34. On Ishtar's love for Sargon cf. the Legend of Sargon in Pritchard, *op. cit.*, 119. On Sargon and the "era of Ishtar" cf. the Sargon Chronicle, *ibid.*, 266 where the wrath of Marduk, the god of the later era, is also mentioned.

35. The *Enuma Elish* is translated by E. A. Speiser in Pritchard, *op. cit.*, 60 ff. On the difference between the *en* and the *lugal* cf. Frankfort, *The Birth of Civilization in the Ancient Near East,* 69 f.

36. Cf. Frankfort, *Kingship and the Gods,* 317 f. and 321 ff.

37. On the tablet of wisdom cf. Chapter One, note 15, and on the tablets of fate cf. Chapter Three, note 20.

38. For a composite picture of Iranian kingship cf. Geo. Widengren in *The Sacral Kingship* (Supplement to *Numen* IV) (Leiden, 1959), 242 ff. The title "king of kings" had already been given to Ashurbanipal (cf. Pritchard, *op. cit.*, 297) and the titles "king of the world" and "king of the four rims" were regular ones for Assyrian kings (cf. *ibid.*, 275, 276, 281, 289, 297).

39. Compare the inscription of Xerxes given in Pritchard, *op. cit.*, 316 f. with that of Cyrus given *ibid.*, 315 f.

40. On the Chakravartin cf. J. Auboyer in *The Sacral Kingship*, 186 f. and also her book *Le trône et son symbolisme dans l'Inde ancienne* (Paris, 1949), 112 ff.

41. Cf. the translation by N. A. Nikam and Richard McKeon, *The Edicts of Asoka* (Chicago, 1958). The idea of "conquest by Dharma" and the references to the Hellenistic kingdoms are in Rock Edict XIII (*ibid.*, 27 ff.). Asoka's tolerance appears in Rock Edicts VII and XII (*ibid.*, 51 f.), but see the manner in which he questions the value of rites and ceremonials in Rock Edict IX (*ibid.*, 46 f.).

42. The question whether virtue can be taught is discussed especially in *Protagoras* and *Meno,* and the question as to who could conceivably teach it is treated especially in *Meno*. On Socrates' reasons for not becoming a statesman cf. *Apology* 31 C. Plato's famous statement on philosophers and kings is in *Republic* V, 473. Cf. *Laws* XII, 964 where it is argued that the magistrates must be the teachers of virtue in the state.

Aristotle's conception of the ideal ruler seems to become clear if we compare his definition of virtue as consisting in a mean determined by the man of *phronesis* (*Nicomachean Ethics* II, 1106b36 ff.) with his discussion of legislative *phronesis* (*ibid.*, VI, 1141b24 ff.) and his declaration that *phronesis* is the proper virtue of the ruler (*Politics*, III, 1277b25) .

Alexander the Great's ideas on the unity that should exist among all mankind are treated by Sir W. W. Tarn in *Alexander the Great* (Cambridge, 1948), vol. II. Appendix 25 "Brotherhood and Unity." In Appendix 24 "Alexander's Supposed Plans and the World Kingdom" Tarn seems to overstate the case against Alexander having any design of world conquest. Actually it seems that with Alexander we have the emergence in the West of the idea of the universal monarch.

43. This view goes back to Plutarch, *De Alexandri Virtute aut Fortuna* I, 329 B. cf. Tarn *op. cit.*, 437 ff. For Aristotle's view cf. *Politics* III, 1285a17 ff.

44. For a general discussion of the nature of the Hellenistic kingdoms and of Hellenistic law cf. Ehrenberg, *op. cit.*, Part II "The Hellenistic State."

45. Plato's position is formulated in the *Statesman*, 293 ff. Aristotle's position is formulated in *Politics* III, 1284a3 ff.

46. Cf. Tarn, *op. cit.*, Appendix 22 "Alexander's Deification." It seems that the deification of Alexander's successors too can be interpreted this way as setting them above the particular laws which obtained in their realms. For a survey of the various interpretations of deification and an extensive bibliography of the relevant literature Cf. L. Cerfaux and J. Tondriau, *Le Culte des souverains* (Tournai, 1957).

47. For a comparison of the inscriptions of Asoka and the ideal of the Hellenistic king cf. A.-J. Festugière in *Recherches de science religieuse* XXXIX (1951) , 31 ff.

48. *Cf.* Rudolph Bultmann, *Theology of the New Testament*, vol. II (London, 1955), 63 ff.

CHAPTER SEVEN

The City of God

THE "transvaluation of values,"[1] as Nietzsche called it, which Christianity wrought upon paganism and which Nietzsche wanted to reverse again in modern times, and which he thought had almost been successfully reversed in the Renaissance, has been the subject of sharp controversy and polemic down the centuries. The pagans, for instance, who had argued that the downfall of Rome was caused by Christianity and who were answered by Augustine in the *City of God* were echoed more than thirteen hundred years later by Edward Gibbon who in the *Decline and Fall of the Roman Empire* revived the pagan accusation in the name of the eighteenth century ideal of enlightenment.

There is an interesting paradox, however, latent in the reasonings and argumentations of some of the more earnest adversaries of Christianity from the time of Celsus to that of Nietzsche. It is that the main indictment leveled against Christianity has been its reputed hostility to life or to knowledge or, more vaguely, to the world, while the main argument raised against the existence of the Christian God has been the existence of evil in the world. The feeling for evil in the world which one finds in the opponents of Christianity, a feeling so strong that it excludes the very idea of the world being created and governed by an all-good God, seems to argue a certain hostility toward the world, an unconscious hostility perhaps, and a profound disapproval of the way things are which seems at least comparable with the hatred of the world which is being imputed to Christians. This inconsistency gives one to believe that there is serious need to ascertain apart from all polemic the nature of the Christian transvaluation before it can be properly attacked or defended.

A way in which this might be done is suggested by the procedure which Plato adopts in the last and largest of his works, the *Laws*, where, notwithstanding what he said previously about the philosopher king being above the law, he endeavors to formulate his vision of the city entirely in terms of law and the rule of law. What seems particularly striking about this final dialogue of Plato's is that he conceives the rule of law to be the farthest remove from the rule of man and the nearest approximation to the rule of God which is humanly attainable and that he describes the ideal city now as the city of God.[2] One cannot help thinking here of the relationship between the rule of Roman law and the Christian city of God. A considerable evolution came about in Roman law before and after the conversion of the Roman Empire to Christianity and there may be in this development the key at least to the worldly significance of the transvaluation of values wrought by Christianity.

[1] *The Universal City*

A man who is forty years old, if he has any understanding at all, Marcus Aurelius thought, has seen by reason of the uniformity which prevails all that has been and all that will be.[3] This view which the philosopher emperor repeats in various ways, saying for instance that to have contemplated human life for forty years is the same as to have contemplated it for ten thousand years, is a solution to the problem of death, a modest one indeed but nevertheless a solution, for it means that a man who has lived the usual human life has run the gamut of human experience and therefore is deprived of nothing by death. Human life being everywhere and at all times essentially the same, a man who has lived forty years, according to this standpoint, will have seen and experienced all there is to see and experience and, if he has any understanding at all, he will recognize this, but if he is somewhat deficient in understanding he will perhaps think that death is a frustration and that by dying he is going to miss something that he might otherwise have enjoyed.

Whether life is really as uniform as this may appear somewhat questionable. It has been said that the inductive method, the method of determining the future probability of an event from its past frequency, is based on the assumption that the future will be like the past and that this assumption is neither self-evident nor susceptible itself of inductive proof.[4] If the uniformity of nature is thus doubtful, the uniformity of human life may seem doubly doubtful by comparison. In view of the pragmatic success of the inductive method, however, the fact that induction seems to suppose that this uniformity exists or, more accurately perhaps, that the degree of uniformity determines the type of inductive method applicable and that a complete absence of uniformity would rule out the method entirely may lend the assumption a certain solidity. The applicability of the inductive method to human affairs, an essential premise of the modern statistical sciences of human behavior, depends at any rate on the uniformity of human life, and the use of the ordinary type of induction in which future probability is completely determined by past frequency supposes that the uniformity is perfect.

If the uniformity of life, though plausible, is thus no more than an assumption, and if it constitutes a positive solution to the problem of death, a solution according to which man can consider his quest for life somehow satisfied, then perhaps it may be justifiable to speak of it as a "myth." Although it is not the sort of myth that could have built the Roman Empire, it is the kind that could make eminent sense out of life once the *Pax Romana* had been firmly established. Since the principal conquests of the Romans were made under the republic and the emperors were satisfied for the most part with holding what had already been acquired, the inspiration which built the Roman Empire should probably be sought in the political mythology of the republic. It seems reasonable to anticipate, however, that the political revolution which occurred when Augustus established the principate should have been prepared, accompanied, and followed by changes in the Roman myth and in the Roman outlook on life.

As a matter of fact, a development of this kind does appear to be traceable in the evolution of Roman law, especially in the gradual transformation of Roman law wrought by what was called the *ius gentium.*

Originally Roman law was *ius civile,* law applicable to Roman citizens and in some degree to allies of Rome to whom rights of trade and intermarriage had been extended. At this stage it consisted of the written and unwritten traditions and customs of the Roman people, the peculiar precedents which had been established by their practice or by their explicit agreement, the immortal and normative past of their republic. Although each deed when done was done forever, the past was regarded as being continually created by new deeds so that the law constituted by the past was continually evolving. Among the immortal deeds there were not only the deeds of peace but also those of war, the latter being declared in advance, ratified when done, and celebrated if successful with triumphs and ovations. Very likely it was this immortal character of deeds, especially that of deeds of war, that inspired the citizen armies of Rome much as it had inspired the citizen armies of Athens and Sparta and that built the Roman empire much as it had built the more temporary Athenian empire and Spartan hegemony.[5]

The greater permanency of the Roman Empire, however, gave rise to an evolution of law which was not paralleled at Athens and Sparta. It became necessary with the expansion of Rome for the law to deal more and more frequently with cases in which one or both parties were foreigners. This led to the gradual development of a body of law called the *ius gentium* distinct from the native Roman traditions embodied in the *ius civile* and believed to consist of the common traditions of all nations. In practice it amounted to the rules which Roman magistrates thought foreigners could be expected to observe in their intercourse with Romans and with one another.[6] The introduction of the new kind of law, though it was kept distinct from the older kind, had the effect of gradually modifying and simplifying the law for Romans, eliminating the many peculiar formalities and observances that had been prescribed by the native Roman tradition.

The process appears to have been accompanied on a deeper level by a weakening of the authority of the Roman past in favor of the authority of what was considered the common past of all mankind such that ultimately the idea of the immortal past lost its concreteness and with that its significance as a solution to the problem of death.

The weakening of the authority of the Roman past can be observed in the successive extensions of Roman citizenship and thus of the *ius civile* to non-Roman peoples in the declining years of the republic and in the time of the principate, from the extension of full citizenship to all Italians which Rome was compelled to grant in the last century of the republic's existence in order to end the Social War to the ultimate extension of Roman citizenship to all freeborn inhabitants of the Roman Empire which the Emperor Caracalla granted, it may be, in order to increase the revenue from taxation. Each further extension of the franchise was at once an extension of Roman law and a thinning of the significance of Roman citizenship, and each further addition of non-Roman peoples to the domain of Roman law was at once a contribution to the Roman unification of mankind and a lessening of the significance of the native Roman past. There was a need to stretch the concept of the Roman past so as to include the past of other peoples as Vergil did in the *Aeneid* where the Roman past is made to include the past of all the Italian peoples.

While the old solution to the problem of death contained in the notion of the immortal past was losing its hold on the minds of the Romans, however, a new solution was taking shape around the very ideas and forces which were undermining the old one. In the last century of the republic, through the influence of Greek philosophy, the *ius gentium* came to be identified with the *ius naturale*,[7] the natural law which was supposed to be dictated by reason, and the city of Rome itself came to be identified with the Cosmopolis,[8] the universal city in the supposition that all the world is a city and all men its citizens. Though being a cosmopolitan had probably meant to the Cynics who originated the idea little more than being above the laws of any particular city in the world, to the Stoics who came afterward it meant living according to the natural law by which the whole world is governed.[9] When the Roman Empire had reached out toward all the boundaries of the known world, therefore, it was easy for Roman jurists and Greek historians and, for that matter, people who had little or no acquaintance with Stoicism to think that Rome, although it was a particular city with its own particular law, was also the universal city with its universal law.

The universal validity of the Roman law of nations identified in this manner with the law of nature implied that Roman rule should prevail at all times and all places, that as Vergil said in the *Aeneid*, a work composed in the first years of the principate, Jupiter had set no limits of place or time upon the destiny of the Romans but had given them boundless empire.[10] A man as intelligent as Vergil could actually believe this in spite of what he knew about the Roman Empire having had a beginning in time and also what he knew about it not reaching to the very ends of the earth, for these limitations were all part and parcel of the admitted fact that Rome was a particular city among other particular cities and that its citizens lived by a particular law among other particular laws. The civil law of Rome embodied a way of life which admittedly applied only to those who did as Romans did (in Vergil's day this meant all freeborn Italians), but the Roman law of nations embodied, so it was thought, the common ways of all mankind, the law of nature which applied to all men at all places and all times, This union of a particular way with the common way, of a particular people with all peoples, whether or not it was conceived explicitly in terms of a union of two kinds of law, seemed to confer on that particular way and that particular people a universality to which no other way or people could lay claim. Thus, as Vergil said in the lines which are often thought to contain the central thought of the *Aeneid*, where other peoples excelled in this or that art or science, the Roman people excelled in the art of ruling and were meant to impose peace on the world, "to spare the submissive and to battle the arrogant."[11]

The solution to the problem of death in such a conception is the far-reaching uniformity that must obtain in human life if all men belong in principle to one great community and all their lives are capable of being regulated by a common law. It is the solution of Marcus Aurelius' forty-year-old man who has seen everything that has been and everything that will be, whose forty years of experience, given the uniformity of human life, are as good as ten thousand. Although each people was acknowledged to have its own peculiar institutions and therefore human life was admitted to vary from place to place and from time to time, it was thought that the common institutions of all cities and peoples were proof that there is a common human nature and a common natural law and that the differences are insignificant when set beside the likenesses. Specifically in terms of law, of the three conventional divisions of private law, the law of persons, the law of things, and the law of procedures, an overriding uniformity in the first two was thought to exist among the various peoples of the human race so that one could speak of a natural law of persons and a natural law of things, and a modification of the law of procedures, in spite of its inevitable peculiarity in each people, was thought to be effected by natural principles of equity.

The law of persons according to which all human beings were either free or slaves and according to which slavery was a condition such that the master had power of life and death over the slave and that whatever a slave acquired was acquired for the master was uniform among all peoples, it was believed, though it was conceded that only among the Roman people did this situation also exist within the family such that a father had this kind of power over his son and a husband could have it over his wife.[12] The law of things, according to which some things belonged to one person and others to another and still others to no one and according to which there were certain basic modes of acquiring ownership of things and certain kinds of obligation which human beings contract with one another in regard to things, was also uniform among all peoples, it was thought, though here likewise it was granted that only among the Roman people did some special methods of acquiring ownership exist such as by possession for a certain time, by cession in the form of a lawsuit, and by a kind of ceremonial transfer.[13]

When Roman citizenship was finally extended to all subjects of the Roman Empire, however, and the peculiar characteristics of the Roman civil law of persons, things, and procedures became features of the common law of the whole Roman world, it became difficult to believe any longer that the mere fact of a law being observed by all or most of the human races makes that law natural to man. If the private law admittedly native to Rome could become universal law for all mankind or at least for all peoples under Roman authority, the law of persons, things, and procedures already observed by all those various peoples might well be as purely conventional and as little natural as the native Roman law. At all events, whether it was the imposition of Roman ways upon these peoples that brought their common ways into question or whether it was doubt about the natural validity of their common customs that made the attempt to spread Roman customs possible or whether both processes ran concurrently and mutually influenced one another, the significance of the *ius gentium* did change and it ceased to be identified with the *ius naturale* at about the time when the *ius civile* became the law for all free inhabitants of the Roman Empire.[14]

The natural law now came to be limited to the law that is in force not only among men but also among animals, the law regulating activities which are common to men and animals such as the union of male and female and the rearing of the young, and though the institutions of slavery and property were still considered common to all races of man, they were no longer considered natural to man. Originally all men had been free, it was now believed, and this had been man's natural state, and it had been only as a result of war and captivity that the institution of slavery had been introduced. Originally too the earth and everything on it had belonged to no one in particular, it was thought, and only afterward had the institution of private property been established. Thus there entered into Roman law the idea that man existed originally in a state of nature in which he was subject to no law except that to which all animals are subject, an idea which has had an exceptionally long life, having reappeared in the medieval revival of Roman law and then in the modern theories of the origin of society through social contract.

The distinction between the actual human condition and the state of nature reflects, it seems, not merely a change of professional opinion in the circle of Roman jurists but a change of attitude widespread throughout the Roman world. Undermining as it did the assumption that human life is fundamentally uniform, it undermined what seems to have been the basic solution to the problem of death in Roman imperial society and thus was not a distinction which jurists could make with impunity. It not only set the present condition of mankind off against a prehistoric situation but by reducing the present state of affairs to a set of conventions it made an infinite variety of human conditions conceivable. Life in existing society, if human life could not be assumed to be always and everywhere the same, was no index of what life might be in other possible human societies and the ordinary span of human life was not enough time to run the gamut of human experience. Death was now a frustration for which society could provide no remedy and men began to look elsewhere, to religions like Mithraism and Christianity, for a way to overcome it.[15]

[2] *God and the Gods*

In classical Greek and Roman civilization as in most of the ancient civilizations the gods had been divided into two groups: the gods above and the gods below, the gods above being the gods of the living and the gods below being the gods of the dead.[16] The fundamental terms of the problem of death, it appears, had been set by this division of the gods so that no solution to the problem was admissible in which the gods of the dead did not receive their due. None of the solutions, accordingly, which had actually been accepted in classical society before Christianity, neither the doctrine that the past is immortal nor the doctrine that life is uniform, involved any attempt to save man from the gods of the dead, but each of them amounted to a way of satisfying man's quest for life with the limited span of time granted to him among the gods of the living. When Christianity was accepted, therefore, with its teaching that there is no god but the God of the living and that to this God, as Christ had argued against the Sadducees,[17] the dead are alive, the problem of death did not acquire a new solution but the very terms of the problem were changed.

A desire to reverse this change and to restore the original terms of the problem of death perhaps more than anything else has led to the modern denial of the God of the living, a denial which at first was formulated in the flat statement "there is no God" but which has subsequently found expression in the more pointed assertion "God is dead." The removal of the Christian God has indeed the effect of restoring the old dichotomy between the living and the dead in the manner requisite for restoring the old terms of the problem of death. Maybe it would not be too fanciful to suggest that the assertion "God is dead" taken negatively is a direct denial of the living God affirmed in Christianity and taken positively is almost a kind of reaffirmation of the gods of the dead which have been denied in Christianity and a kind of reduction of the Christian God to the status of God of the dead. To make the reversal complete, it has actually been maintained that in the wake of the realization that God is dead human thinking must reorientate itself in terms of *das Geviert*,[18] the foursome: heaven, earth, gods, and mortals, a reorientation which would revive not only the old terms of the problem of death but even the old gods of the living.

What happened to *das Geviert* in Christianity is revealed in the imagery used in the New Testament and the early creeds to describe the work of Christ. The drama of salvation opens with the incarnation symbolized in the descent of Christ from heaven to earth, then there is the death of Christ symbolized in his descent from earth into hell (hell being understood here as the land of the dead), then there is the Resurrection symbolized in the ascent of Christ from hell to earth, and finally there is the exaltation of Christ symbolized in his ascent from earth into heaven. The point of the descent and ascent symbolism seems to be that Christ has broken down all the barriers that were erected between heaven, earth, and hell, and that after Christ the gates of heaven are open so that mortals on earth can no longer be set off against the immortals who dwell in heaven and the gates of hell are open so that the dead in hell can no longer be set off against the living who dwell on earth. Thus in the modern attempt to restore *das Geviert* as the framework of human thinking it has been urged that these barriers must be erected again, that man must realize once more that he is mortal and that he lives on earth, under heaven, and in the presence of the gods.

What appears to have been found objectionable about the Christian idea of the living God is that it so changed the terms of the problem of death that death ceased to be a soluble problem at all and became an enigma and a mystery, the obverse of the mystery of eternal life. To know the "why" of death, one might say, is to know the "how" of eternal life. If it were true, for example, that man is mortal because his present life is ever becoming a past life, then to know this would be to know that he can be immortal insofar as the past itself is immortal and unchangeable. Or if it were true that man is mortal because there is a gamut of experience which he has to run, then to know this would be to know that he can be immortal, as though he were to live everywhere and always, insofar as human life is uniform at all places and times. If, however, there is a living God to whom all including the dead themselves are alive, then it will be somewhat presumptuous for man to think that he knows why he is mortal or how he can be immortal, for the "how" of eternal life and the "why" of death will be known only to this God to whom the dead are alive and will remain unknown to man until such time as God reveals the mystery and in revealing it reveals himself to man.

Since human societies had always been built upon solutions to the problem of death, the reception of an idea of God such as this, according to which death is not a problem that man can solve, created a rather unprecedented situation. As long as the gods were divided into the gods of the living and the gods of the dead it had been possible to conceive the rule of law as the rule of the gods, the gods of the living that is, and to contrast it with the rule of man. The obvious limitations to which the power of the law was subject by the inescapable fact of death were simply the limitations which were placed upon the authority of the gods of the living, it had been thought, and did not prove that the law's power was purely human. It had been readily acknowledged, therefore, that the law had no authority over the dead, so much so that among the Greeks any attempt to carry authority beyond the limit of death like the one dramatized in the *Antigone* of Sophocles where a ruler tries to prevent a private individual from burying the dead had been considered an abuse and an encroachment upon the realm of the nether gods, and among the Romans, while it had been considered the prerogative of public authority to consecrate a place to the gods of the living, it had been considered the prerogative of the private individual to consecrate a place to the gods of the dead.[19]

When it was denied, then, that there are gods of the dead and affirmed that there is no god but the God of the living, a significant change was necessarily introduced into the whole conception of the rule of law, far more significant than the mere substitution of one pantheon for another which took place when the Romans assimilated their own gods to the gods of the Greeks. Two opposing courses of action apparently presented themselves. One was to reconceive society on the principle that the rule of law instead of being the rule of the old gods of the living is the rule of the new God of the living to whom the very dead are alive and thus to remove the limits which had previously existed on the authority of the law over the private individual on account of the individual's relation to the gods of the dead. The other was to reconceive society on the principle that the law being limited by the fact of death is in itself human rather than divine since if it were divine the dead would be alive to it and within its power and thus to place new and greater limits upon the authority of the law over the private individual on account of the individual's relation to the God of the living.

The dilemma seems to have been resolved substantially by following the first course of action in the realm of public law and following the second in the realm of private law. By receiving the idea that the rule of law is the rule of God into the sphere of public and constitutional law it was possible to reaffirm the eternity of the Roman Empire insofar as the empire could be said to be the rule of the eternal God.[20] Formerly, to be sure, the empire had been conceived to be the rule of the immortal gods and, if it had not been for the fact that the gods of the living were considered incapable of saving the living from the gods of the dead, this would have been enough to make the empire immortal. As it was, that the empire under the gods be immortal it had been necessary to postulate some form of immortality intrinsic to human life such as the immortality of the past or the uniformity of life. So when this sort of thing became discredited, the empire's eternity became discredited along with it. When the old gods of the living were replaced by the God to whom the dead are alive, however, and the empire came to be conceived as the rule of this God, then it began to seem that this alone without the support of any human solution to the problem of death was enough to prevent the gates of hell (hell being understood here too as the land of the dead) from prevailing against it.

It had also been necessary, as long as the gods were divided into gods of the living and gods of the dead, to deify dead emperors in order to maintain the validity of their acts after death.[21] This had come to appear more and more imperative as the idea of the immortality of the past lost influence and was succeeded as a solution to the problem of death by the idea of the uniformity of life. If he had not been deified and thus placed among the gods of the living, the dead emperor's acts would have become merely the acts of a dead man who had nothing further to do with the living. When the existence and power of the gods of the dead were denied, though, and the gods of the living were replaced by the Christian God to whom the dead are alive, the need for deification after death was for all practical purposes eliminated. It was no longer important that the emperor be counted one of the gods of the living if the dead themselves could be counted alive. Although the custom of referring to dead emperors as *divi* was continued, therefore, the custom of having them actually deified by the Senate fell after a while into disuse.[22]

The validity of the emperor's acts, nevertheless, while it could thus be maintained in terms of the Christian God, inevitably became less absolute when it ceased to rest on the emperor's personal divinity. The imperial enactments continued to be called "divine responses"[23] as though the emperor were an oracle, of God now rather than of the gods, and the imperial laws were still said to be destined to endure forever, but the fact that the emperors were no longer thought to be living gods in themselves made it possible in spite of all this to regard the civil law which they upheld as essentially human and mutable. As a sign of how little the traditional terminology had come to mean, there are instances of laws and rescripts being called "divine imperial responses" in the very decrees in which they were abrogated.[24] Eventually the Emperor Justinian was to formulate explicitly the principle that the civil law is mutable and has in practice frequently been changed while the natural law, being the work of God himself, is immutable. The constitution and the public law of the Roman Empire Justinian apparently considered divine, for he has it that the empire was constituted by God and that it will last forever, but the private law he evidently considered human except insofar as it embodied natural law.[25]

It was not hard for a Christian to believe that the public law was divine, consisting as it did of the laws concerning rites, the laws concerning priests, and the laws concerning magistrates.[26] When Christianity became the established religion of the Roman Empire, the rites of the old Roman religion were forbidden and the laws recognizing the gods and organizing their worship were replaced by laws upholding the creed and regulating the practice of the Christian religion. The laws defining the functions and privileges of the pagan priests, in turn, were abolished and replaced by laws determining the rights and duties of the Christian clergy. If the Christian could not accept the old public law on these matters as divine, therefore, he could certainly accept the new. As for the laws dealing with magistrates, the doctrine had already been set forth in the New Testament, and set forth with an eye to Roman magistrates in the days of the pagan empire, that all authority is from God.[27]

Another Christian view of the public law was possible, how-

ever, and was actually adopted, especially by Augustine in the
City of God, and was to prevail in the West after the breakdown
of the Roman Empire there, while the view that the public law
is divine continued to be maintained in the East as long as the
Roman Empire there continued to exist. Augustine's attitude
toward the public law seems to have been somewhat similar to
what Justinian's attitude was to be toward the private law, the
belief that the law is human except insofar as it embodies divine
law to some extent in its content.[28] According to this the rule
of Roman law could not be equated with the rule of God and the
Roman Empire could not be claimed to be necessarily eternal.[29]
It was a fairly reasonable viewpoint to take when Augustine took
it, after Alaric had tested the humanity and mortality of the
Roman Empire by sacking the city of Rome. This event, in fact,
was the occasion which led Augustine to elaborate his point of
view, to explain how such a thing could have happened and to
answer pagan critics who blamed it on Christianity.[30] The position which Augustine came to adopt began to seem still more
sensible a few decades after his death when the Roman Empire
in the West collapsed completely.

Conceiving the public law to be essentially human, Augustine
had to distinguish between the rule of law and the rule of God.
This he did using the image of the two cities, the heavenly city
and the earthly city, an imagery which was particularly con-
genial in his day coming as it did after Constantine had founded
Constantinople and left the Roman Empire with two capitals and
after Theodosius had died and his sons had divided the empire
into two, the Western Roman Empire with its capital at Rome
and the Eastern Roman Empire with its capital at Constantinople. Augustine seems to have thought it significant that the old
capital at Rome had been the seat of paganism and idolatry
whereas the new capital at Constantinople had witnessed no
religion except the worship of the true God.[31] It was not that
he identified Constantinople or the Eastern Empire with the
heavenly city and Rome or the Western Empire with the earthly
city. The two cities were not the two capitals, for Augustine was
thinking primarily of the city as community rather than of the

city as place, of the *civitas* rather than of the *urbs,* nor were they
the two empires, for both empires to Augustine were embodiments of the rule of human law rather than of the rule of God.
It was only that the polarity of the Roman world at this time
prepared the imagination for the tale of two cities which he had
to tell.

Perhaps the nearest thing there is to a precedent for the kind
of transvaluation of Roman values which inspired Augustine's
tale is Plato's transvaluation of Greek values. The likenesses and
differences between the two can be ascertained by comparing the
critique of the earthly city carried out in the first half of the *City
of God* with that carried out in the *Republic* and the *Laws.*
In the dialogues which form the sequel to the *Republic* and
which are designed to exhibit the republic in action there is
even a precedent for the actual tale of the two cities told in the
second half of the *City of God,* the origins and prehistory being
recounted in the *Timaeus,* the mythical history in the unfinished
Critias, and no telling what in the projected but never written
Hermocrates which was to follow.[32] Some of the points of comparison and contrast result from the similarity and divergency
of the Roman and the Greek commonwealth, but some result
from the affinity and disparity of Christianity and Platonism,
particularly from the respective ideas of the heavenly city which
set the standard for the critique of the earthly city and which
determine the plot for the tale of the two cities.

Plato's doctrine that the soul is immortal was not a solution
to the problem of death which made it possible for man to satisfy
his quest for life while still alive like the doctrine that the past
is immortal or the doctrine that life is uniform, but by making
the lot of the dead appear attractive it tended to end the effort to
solve the problem of death and thus had something of the effect
of the idea of the living God. That the traditional terms of the
problem of death were actually abolished in Platonism is strongly
suggested by the fact that the division between the gods above
and the gods below, though Plato retained it in his reformation
of Greek law, was really eliminated in his theory of the gods
according to which the gods are the immortal souls of the

celestial bodies.[33] The concept of the immortal soul seems to
have affected the whole notion of the heavenly city such that
Plato came to conceive it as a city of spirits, the immortal souls
of men and the immortal souls of the celestial bodies, united
under the rule of the transcendent Good, a notion which was
to reappear in a Christian Platonist like Leibniz as that of a city
of spirits united under the rule of the Christian God.[34]

There is some question, though, as to whether the Platonic
city of spirits is not ultimately a necropolis. Men who are alive
can belong to it only in spirit, it seems, and to the degree to
which they engage in the "practice of dying," the practice of
detachment from this bodily life and attachment to the future
existence of the separated soul.[35] The gods who belong to it,
as Plato conceived them, while they might appear to be a reduction of the gods below to the gods above in that they are thought
to inhabit the celestial bodies, would appear to be a reduction
of the gods of the living to the gods of the dead in that they too
like the men who belong to it are thought to be essentially souls.
Augustine, it is interesting to observe, when he was trying to
prove in the first five books of the *City of God* that the Roman
gods were incapable of helping the living, was able to follow a
procedure quite similar to that which Plato had followed in
criticizing the Greek gods, as though he and Plato were in agreement in rejecting the popular pagan notion of the gods of the
living.[36] When he went on in the succeeding five books, however, to argue that the gods were also incapable of helping the
dead, he found it necessary to criticize the gods of Plato, as
though Plato's gods were essentially gods of the dead.[37]

The tale of the two cities as it was told by Plato, since his
heavenly city was a city of spirits, is not the story of the heavenly
city and the earthly city but the story of two earthly cities, one
of which approaches and the other of which recedes from the
heavenly city. It is a story with a moral, the moral being the
happy state of a city which conforms to the heavenly city and
the evil state of one which deviates from it, and so it has no
need of being historically true. The tale Plato told, to be sure,
was based on the true story of the resistance put up by Athens

against the Persian invasion of Europe, but he transformed the story to suit the purpose of the moral lesson he wished to teach. It became the story of Athens and Atlantis, how both of them were founded by the gods when the world was still new, how Athens remained true to its divine origin and how Atlantis, on the contrary, declined and fell away from its original state, how Atlantis attempted to bring the whole world under its sway and how Athens alone had the strength to resist, and how both met their end by being swallowed up in the great flood which thereupon engulfed the world.

The tale of the two cities as it is told by Augustine, on the other hand, is not the story of two earthly cities but the story of the earthly city and the heavenly city, and so it is not for him as it was for Plato a mere fable told to illustrate the truth about the heavenly city but it is the telling of that truth itself. The Christian idea of the God of the living prevented him from making the earthly city the city of the living and the heavenly city the city of the dead, and so he did not think like Plato that the heavenly city exists in the land of the living only insofar as an earthly city conforms to it or approximates its condition. Instead it was his conviction that the heavenly city will be fully established on earth when the dead rise again, that it has already begun to exist here, in fact, since Christ rose from the dead, that before Christ it existed among the living by way of anticipation and prefiguration in the form of the chosen people described in the Old Testament, and that after Christ it exists among the living by way of union with the risen Christ in the form of the church described in the New Testament.[38]

Whether it is conceived as a city of the living or as a city of the dead, however, the heavenly city, when it is set apart from the earthly city, leaves the earthly city altogether helpless in the face of death. It is to be expected when such a separation occurs in the minds of men that a fresh effort will be made to provide the earthly city with a solution to the problem of death. Plato seems to have realized this, for if he was content in the *Republic* to criticize the traditional gods and to propose a notion of the transcendent Good and of the immortal soul which would stultify the problem of death, he was careful in the *Laws* where he was trying to devise a concrete and workable reformation of Greek law to retain the traditional gods and the traditional division of the gods into gods of the living and gods of the dead.[39] He apparently realized that the earthly city, however true it might be that it was only an approximation and an imitation of the heavenly city, would probably not be able to live with such an understanding of itself but would need to regard itself as the city of the gods. He seems to have thought it sufficient that the law-giver himself recognize the truth and that there be a council of wise men in the city, the famous "nocturnal council,"[40] who would keep critical understanding of this sort alive.

Augustine, by contrast, does not seem to have been fully aware of the difficulties in which the earthly city would find itself if a view like his, discriminating radically between the earthly city and the heavenly city, should win acceptance. No doubt Augustine's city of God was more like the kingdom of God which had been proclaimed by Christ than was the empire of God into which the Christian emperors had endeavored to transform the Roman Empire. And no doubt his view on the mortality and transience of the earthly city was vindicated completely by the decline and fall of the Roman Empire in the West. Still it was almost inevitable that as soon as the effort was made to rebuild the earthly city the attempt would also be made to construe it as the city of God and to provide it with an answer to death. Augustine left the Christian church in the West prepared to criticize as a new manifestation of the sinful will to power each fresh attempt of the earthly city to divinize itself but unprepared to offer any positive hope or plan for rebuilding the earthly city in a manner consistent with Christianity. It has only been gradually over the course of centuries as the church has struggled against one attempt after another to immortalize the earthly city that it has begun to become apparent that the critical under-standing of the earthly city propounded by Augustine can be translated into a constructive plan for an earthly society in which man, by renouncing every attempt to divinize and immortalize society, can achieve a freedom never attained in any previous society.[41]

NOTES TO CHAPTER SEVEN

1. This expression was the title of a projected work of which Nietzsche finished only the first part (*The Antichrist*). It directly refers to his own transvaluation of Christian values, but it is clear that he wishes to reverse what he considers to be the Christian transvaluation of pagan values.

2. The city of "God" in a general sense without implying that there is only one God just as one might speak of the city of "Man" without implying that there is only one man. Observe that the first sentence in the *Laws* is the question put by the Athenian to the Cretan and the Spartan as to whether a god or a man is the author of the laws of Crete and of Sparta.

3. *Meditations, XI*, 1. Cf. *ibid.*, II, 14; IV, 32; VI, 37; VII, 1; 49; XII, 24; 36. Cf. Lucretius, *De Rerum Natura*, II, 978, "eadem sunt omnia semper."

4. On this issue which was raised by Hume and revived by Russell cf. Rudolph Carnap, *The Continuum of Inductive Methods* (Chicago, 1952) who holds that there is an infinity of possible inductive methods differing according to the degree of uniformity assumed to exist in the world.

5. Cf. Chapter Five, Section 3. For references on the eternity of Rome cf. article cited *ibid.*, note 28.

6. For a standard history of Roman law cf. H. F. Jolowicz, *Historical Introduction to the Study of Roman Law* (Cambridge, 1939). On the identification of *ius gentium* and *ius naturale* cf. *ibid.*, 100 ff. Note, however, that Jolowicz (*ibid.*, 105) considers unimportant the later separation of *ius gentium* and *ius naturale* referred to below in note 14.

7. Cf. Gaius, *Institutes*, I, 1 and the quotation from Gaius in Justinian *Digest*, XLI, 1, 1 (where the *ius gentium* is said to be as old as the human race). Cf. also Cicero, *De Officiis*, III, 5, 22f.

8. On the tendency to identify Rome with the Cosmopolis cf. H. A. Wolfson, *Philo* (Cambridge, Mass., 1948), II, 419 ff.

9. On the Cosmopolis cf. Cicero, *De Officiis*, I, 16, 50; Seneca, *De Otio*, IV, 31; Philo Judaeus, *De Josepho*, VI, 28 ff.; *Apostolic Constitutions*, VII, 34, 3; Pseudo-Aristotle, *De Mundo*, 5 and 6; Dio of Prusa, *Borysthenic Oration* (36) and *First Oration on Kingship*, 42; Epictetus, *Discourses*, I, 9, 1 ff; II, 10, 3f.; Marcus Aurelius, *Meditations*, IV, 4; 23; VI, 44; X, 15; also VIII, 9 and XII, 36.

10. *Aeneid*, I, 278 f.

11. *Aeneid*, VI, 847 ff.

12. On the *ius gentium* in the law of persons cf. Gaius, *Institutes*, I, 52; 78; 80; 83-86; 89; 156; 158; 189.

13. On the *ius gentium* in the law of things cf. Gaius, *ibid.*, II, 65-79; III, 92; 119; 132; 154. (On equity in the law of procedures cf. *ibid.*, IV, 115).

14. The distinction between the *ius gentium* and the *ius naturale* appears in Ulpian as quoted in Justinian, *Institutes*, I, 2 and *Digest*, I, 1.

15. The mystery religions, accordingly, reached the zenith of their influence during this period. Cf. Cumont, *The Oriental Religions in Roman Paganism*

(Chicago, 1911) for a general discussion of the success of such religions among the Romans.

16. This division of the gods appears in Roman law as can be seen in Gaius, *Institutes*, II, 4 where the distinction is made between *res sacrae* consecrated to the gods above and *res religiosae* consecrated to the gods below. It appears in Greek law as can be seen in Plato, *Laws*, IV, 717 A; VIII, 828 D; XII, 958 C. It had already appeared in the earliest civilizations as can be seen from the Babylonian creation epic (Pritchard, *op. cit.*, 68) where the story is told of how the gods came to be divided in this way.

17. Mt. 22: 32 f.; Mk. 12: 36 f.; Lk. 20: 37 ff. Cf. the discussion of this idea in Chapter Two, Section 2 where it is compared with an older solution to the problem of death, the appropriation of the dead by the living.

18. This appears in Heidegger's essays "Bauen Wohnen Denken" and "Das Ding" in his *Vorträge und Aufsätze* (Pfullingen, 1954). Cf. Vincent Vycinas, *Earth and Gods* (The Hague, 1961).

19. Gaius, *Institutes*, II, 5 and 6.

20. For assertions by Christian emperors that the empire is eternal cf. Valentinian, *Novels*, 24 and Theodosius II, *Novels, passim* (on the eternity of laws) in Clyde Pharr, *The Theodosian Code* (Princeton, 1952).

21. For a general history of the deification of Roman emperors cf. the work of Cerfaux and Tondriau referred to in Chapter Six, note 46.

22. For the same reason the Christian emperors, without endangering their authority, could dispense with the worship of their images (*Theodosian Code*, XV, 4), a practice which had apparently been meant to anticipate while they were still living and reigning the formal deification which was to take place after they had died.

23. Cf. Pharr's index to the *Theodosian Code* under "oracle" (*op. cit.*, 629 f.). For statements that the laws are destined to endure forever cf. *ibid.*, Theodosius II, *Novels, passim.*

24. Cf. *Theodosian Code*, XVI, 5, 51. Also *ibid.*, VIII, 4, 26; XI, 21, 3; XIII, 11, 12; XVI, 10, 8; Theodosius II, *Novels*, VI, 1; VIII, 1.

25. That civil law is mutable whereas natural law, being the work of "divine providence," is immutable cf. Justinian, *Institutes*, II, 11. That the empire is constituted by God cf. Justinian, *Novels*, LXXIII, 1. That the empire is eternal cf. *ibid.*, VI, epilogue.

26. This is Ulpian's description of the contents of public law, quoted in Justinian, *Digest*, I, 1, 1. The public law under the Christian emperors seems, in the light of this description, to have been what appeared in the first and last books of the *Theodosian Code* and in the first book of the *Justinian Code*.

27. Romans 13: 1 ff.

28. Augustine does not discuss the public law under that name, *ius publicum*, but he builds his criticism of pagan Rome on the description of Roman institutions given in Varro's *Antiquities*, and the topics dealt with by Varro as Augustine lists them in the *City of God*, VI, 3, correspond exactly to the topics which, according to Ulpian's definition, are the subject matter of public law.

29. Augustine formulates clearly in *Sermon* 105, 9 f. the rejection of Rome's eternity which is implicit throughout the *City of God*.

30. Because he had to answer the pagan accusation that the fall of Rome was due to the establishment of Christianity, Augustine could not very well criticize the public law under the Christian emperors as he did the public law under the pagan emperors and the republic. Yet in order to explain the fall of Rome he had to assume that Rome remained altogether human and mortal even after the reception of Christianity. Thus he praises the Christian emperors, *City of God*, V, 24 ff., and yet not as vicars of God on earth but as being citizens of the heavenly city in spite of the great power they possessed in the earthly city.

31. Ibid., V, 25.

32. That *Hermocrates* was projected appears in *Critias*, 108. That the dialogues *Timaeus, Critias,* and *Hermocrates* were designed to exhibit the republic in action appears in *Timaeus*, 19.

33. On the division of the gods cf. texts cited in note 16. On the gods as souls cf. *Laws*, X, 899.

34. Monadology, 85 ff. *Discourse on Metaphysics*, 36.

35. On belonging to the heavenly city while one is still alive cf. *Republic*, IX, 592 (cf. *supra*, Chapter Five, Section 2). On the practice of dying cf. *Phaedo*, 61 ff. (cf. *supra*, Chapter Six, Section 1).

36. Augustine shows his awareness of the argument in *op. cit.*, II, 14 and VIII, 6 and 13 (where he also shows that he knows and agrees with Plato's two principles of theology, that a god must be good and must be unchanging, cf. *Republic*, II, 379 ff.).

37. Ibid., VIII, 12 ff. Most of Augustine's criticisms, though, are directed at the Neo-platonists rather than at Plato.

38. Augustine has it that Christ is the founder of the city of God (*ibid.*, XXII, 6; etc.) and therefore that before Christ it did not exist on earth except by way of anticipation and prefiguration (*ibid.*, XV, 2; 8; 20) and that even after Christ it does not exist on earth except as a stranger and a wanderer until the dead rise again and it is fully established (*ibid.*, XV, 1).

39. Cf. texts cited in note 33.

40. Cf. *Laws*, X, 908 A; 909 A; XII, 951; 961; 968. Cf. the discussion of the nocturnal council in G. R. Morrow, *Plato's Cretan City* (Princeton, 1960), 500 ff.

41. Augustine is often understood to have meant by the earthly city the city of the wicked and by the heavenly city the city of the good. Many of the statements he makes about the two cities, if they are isolated from the general context of his tale of the two cities, do indeed seem to support such an interpretation. If, however, the whole tale is taken into account, such an interpretation will appear greatly over-simplified. What is sinful about the earthly city in Augustine's eyes is its attempt to divinize itself or, as he puts it, the will to power (*ibid.*, V, 12 ff.; XIX, 15), the love of self unto the contempt of God (*ibid.*, XIV, 28) which leads the earthly city to create its own gods rather than recognize the true God (*ibid.*, XVIII, 54; XXII, 6). Although it is true that Augustine never contemplated the possibility of the earthly city renouncing this attempt to divinize itself, still the possibility is not logically excluded as it would be if the earthly city were formally defined as the city of the wicked. It is on this possibility that the idea of translating the critical view of the earthly city into a constructive plan is predicated.

CHAPTER EIGHT

The King Never Dies

THERE is an interesting discrepancy between the Bible and the Koran in the description of the garden of paradise and of the sin which caused man to be expelled from it.[1] According to the Bible there are two trees in the garden, the tree of life and the tree of knowledge of good and evil, and man's sin consisted in eating the fruit of the tree of knowledge. According to the Koran, on the contrary, there is only one tree, the tree of life or "the tree of immortality and an everlasting kingdom," and man's sin, conformably with this, consisted in eating the fruit of the tree of life.

According to Dante's *Divine Comedy*, surprisingly, there is as in the Koran only one tree in the garden of paradise, the tree which occasioned man's fall.[2] Whether this tree is the tree of knowledge or the tree of life is not clear, but to judge from the complicated allegory about the relations of the church and the empire which is constructed around it the tree has a connection with an earthly kingdom that is supposed to be in some sense eternal. If man will only cease to violate the tree and begin to respect its sacredness, Dante seems to think, the universal kingdom on earth will be his to enjoy. Thus man has two goals according to the *Divine Comedy*, an earthly paradise to which as in Islamism he must return through an earthly kingdom or empire and a heavenly paradise to which as in Christianity he must attain through a heavenly kingdom or church.

The idea that man has two goals rather than one was a portentous one, and Dante was by no means alone in maintaining it. He seems, in fact, to represent in this an endeavor which was quite universal in the Middle Ages to combine Christianity with something else, not with Islamism indeed, but with a philosophy of life and death which would answer to man's earthly aspirations. That philosophy was the one that was inherent in the hierarchical type of society which prevailed in the Middle Ages; it was the political myth of that society, its answer to death and its response to man's innate quest for life.

Dante stands toward the end of the effective existence of the medieval empire somewhat as Shakespeare stands toward the end of the effective existence of the medieval kingdom. Between them they sum up both the ideals of the hierarchical society and its sense of its inadequacy to the reality of human existence, Dante perhaps more the ideals and Shakespeare more the inadequacy to reality. "Dante and Shakespeare,' it has been said, "divide the modern world between them; there is no third."[3] Actually it seems that they divide between them the modern world's immediate predecessor, and by summing up its attempt to be a world and its simultaneous attempt to recognize another world, and the shortcomings of its endeavor in both respects, they lead to an understanding of the modern world which probably could not be extracted from a simple study of the modern world in itself.

[1] *Monarchy and Comedy*

Dante called the epic poem in which he described his imaginary journey through hell, purgatory, and heaven a "comedy," the *Divine Comedy*, apparently because like a comedy the journey had a happy ending.[4] The happy ending of Dante's journey, however, appears to have been twofold, first the reaching of the terrestrial paradise which is recounted in the last cantos of the part on purgatory and then the reaching of the celestial paradise which is recounted in the part on heaven. In his treatise *On Monarchy* he explained what the distinction between the terrestrial and the celestial paradise meant to him, how man has two goals, happiness on earth and happiness in heaven, and how earthly happiness is symbolized by the earthly paradise and heavenly happiness by the heavenly paradise.[5] It is the business of the Roman emperor, the monarch, to direct mankind in the pursuit of earthly happiness, Dante thought, while it is the business of the Roman pontiff, the Pope, to direct mankind in the pursuit of heavenly happiness. Thus Dante proposed to resolve the problem which had vexed medieval Christendom almost from the beginning, the conflict of the Roman Catholic Church and the Holy Roman Empire.

The society supposed by Dante differs from modern society in the most fundamental way in which one society can differ from another, namely in the prevailing attitude toward life and death. It has been said that in a modern society where equality is an ideal there is a kind of race against death, a restlessness amid the greatest prosperity, due partially to a taste for physical gratifications which finds the limited span of human life too short to allow for its full satisfaction, and partially to a social condition in which neither laws nor customs retain any person in his place and a near equality of conditions which increases competition for the more desirable places in society and which renders all remaining inequalities intolerable.[6] Actually the modern equalitarian society seems to have its own answer to death but it is true that this answer is quite different from the kind of answer that can be offered by an hierarchical society such as Dante envisions in which there are laws and customs to retain each person in his place and in which conditions are so unequal that there is not such intense competition for the more desirable positions and in which there is no ideal of equality to make inequalities intolerable but, if anything, the contrary ideal of inequality or hierarchical order.

If someone living in the last days of the Roman Empire had attempted to predict the course which events would take in the following millenium, he would have had some difficulty foreseeing the rise of the Holy Roman Empire and its future rivalry with the church. It is true that the structure of society in late Roman times was becoming more and more hierarchical and that the structure of the new society when it arose was also hierarchical and that this seems to have been the basis for the struggle within it. The hierarchy of late Roman society, though, appears to have been an enforced and compulsory affair, each man having a special and hereditary place in society which he was obliged to fill as a public duty and from which he could not escape without becoming liable to punishment. The hierarchy of medieval society, on the contrary, appears to have been rather the opposite sort of thing, each man having a special place in society which he was permitted to occupy and often to pass on to his heirs provided that he and they promised faithfully to carry out the duties of that station and provided that he and they did not become guilty afterward of a serious breach of the promise.

It was not simply that the material burdens of each station, high and low, in late Roman society were heavier—the material obligations attached to a much prized station in medieval society could be very heavy too—but rather that a distinctive place in late Roman society did not mean the immortality that a distinctive place in medieval society was to mean. In a relatively equalitarian society such as Roman society had been after the extension of Roman citizenship to all freeborn inhabitants of the Roman Empire, there is no such thing as perpetuating one's identity on earth by perpetuating one's distinctive place in society, for in an equalitarian society any citizen can theoretically be substituted for any other and no one therefore really has a permanent place. When such a society is forced by economic circumstances to become a hierarchical society, as late Roman society was, there will inevitably be a certain amount of compulsion required, binding the various citizens and their descendants to the special tasks which must be performed if the society is to survive.[7] The constraint of having to become a hierarchical society in this manner without at the same time possessing the political myth of a hierarchical society may, in fact, have made for the Roman Empire's downfall.

After the fall of the Roman Empire, though, a gradual change came about in the common attitude toward existence in an hierarchical society which appears to have made for the rise of a new empire as much as the original attitude made for the fall of the old one. The old hierarchical structure of Roman society slowly dissolved in the West following the breakdown of Roman political power and it was slowly replaced by a system of personal relationships which was such that a person's relationship to the world in the new society, specifically his relationship to the land, was based upon his relationship to other persons to whom he was lord or vassal.[8] As this state of affairs became more and more prevalent it became easy to believe that a person's identity consisted entirely of his personal relationships. The problem of perpetuating personal identity thus became ultimately a matter of preserving this complex of relationships, of perpetuating a special place in a society in which everyone had a special place. Immortality of a kind was assured if the hierarchical structure of the new society could be stabilized and, in particular, if everyone could be sure of having a successor.

It was probably the desire for continuity that led to the insistence that the new society was a Roman empire.[9] When Charlemagne was crowned Emperor of the West at Rome in 800, though continuity was not yet assured, there was already a special place for each man in society and there may already have been some general desire to assure the continuity of society. Such a desire, apart from any consideration of the personal designs of the emperor or of the Pope who crowned him, would have made this event welcome. As the continuity of each position in society did become assured, moreover, the tendency to affirm the continuity of the society itself by calling it a Roman empire, the Holy Roman Empire, became pronounced. It was possible for a given emperor like Henry II to react against the Italy-centered policies of his predecessor by adopting the motto "renovation of the kingdom of the Franks" as against his predecessor's motto "renovation of the Roman Empire," but it is significant that the empire nevertheless had to be a renovation of something, if not of the Roman Empire then of the Kingdom of the Franks.

Along with the claim to be successors of the Roman emperors, the rulers of the Holy Roman Empire also adopted the title "vicar of God" or "vicar of Christ" which had been given to Roman emperors in the latter days of the empire when the rule of

Roman law tended to be regarded as tantamount to the rule of the Christian God.[10] In the East where the rule of Roman law had been maintained and where the tendency to equate it with the rule of the Christian God had been not merely maintained but carried still further it had become customary to say that the Byzantine emperors reigned with God or that God reigned with them. In the West, to judge from the scandal taken at the Eastern manner of speaking,[11] the claim to be vicar of God or vicar of Christ was evidently not felt to be as presumptuous as the claim to reign with God and thus was not thought to be an equivalent assertion. The Western manner of speaking about kings and emperors, on the contrary, seems to have been connected with the continuity problem in that an interregnum would usually be referred to as a period when God or Christ reigned,[12] the implication apparently being that the hierarchical order of things still prevailed as long as God or Christ continued to reign and that it was not entirely disrupted by a lapse in the succession of kings or emperors who, after all, were only the vicars of God or of Christ.

However modest the claim of the Holy Roman emperors to be the vicars of God may have appeared by comparison with that of the Byzantine emperors to reign with God, though, the claim was eventually challenged by the popes. The investiture controversy in which the challenge and the answer to the challenge first took shape was not a mere struggle for power between the empire and the papacy,[13] for what was ultimately at issue, it seems, was the hierarchical society's solution to the problem of death. On the one side, that of the empire, there was a feeling that the hierarchical society was simply Christian society, that it was Christendom, and therefore that the answer to death provided by the hierarchical society was a Christian answer to death. On the other side, that of the papacy, there appears to have been a feeling that the ideal of immortality through the continuation of one's distinctive place and identity in society was not really Christian and that it could serve quite well as the ideal of a society that was thoroughly pagan. The feeling of the papacy found expression in a new emphasis given to clerical celibacy, a practice which amounted to a renunciation of the continuity offered by the hierarchical society and thus to a witness against that society's attempt to answer death.

This critical reaction against the hierarchical myth accompanied or was accompanied by the rise of a mysticism in which the quest for life purporting to be satisfied in the myth was renounced. An hierarchical mysticism had developed already among the Neoplatonists in the days of the Roman Empire and its language and spirit had become well known to medieval thinkers, especially through the writings of Dionysius the Areopagite, his *Mystical Theology, Divine Names, Celestial Hierarchy,* and *Ecclesiastical Hierarchy.* This influence was reinforced later on by the writings of the Arabian followers of Aristotle, particularly Avicenna and Averroes, whose Aristotelianism was strongly marked with Neoplatonism. In spite of these influences, though, there is a consistent pattern traceable in the more learned of the medieval mystics from John Scotus Erigena to Thomas Aquinas according to which Neoplatonic mysticism is transformed into something entirely new and different, a development which is not surprising or unexpected given that mysticism in the middle ages was set off against a myth which had not existed in the heyday of the Neoplatonists. Where a Neoplatonist mystic like Plotinus will consider the hierarchical order of the world a kind of ladder which one must use to attain the contemplation of the One, a mystical theologian like Thomas will consider it more of a scaffolding which one must dispense with to enjoy the immediate presence of God.

Both Plotinus and Thomas, when they interpret man's spiritual and intellectual experience, try to reconcile the Platonic view that the idea is the transcendent object of understanding with the Aristotelian view that the idea is the immanent content of understanding.[14] The reconciliation proposed by Plotinus is to admit a lower and a higher level of understanding, the idea being immanent content on the lower level (that of Mind) and transcendent object on the higher level (that of the One). The reconciliation proposed by Thomas, on the other hand, is apparently to say that what is immanent content to divine understanding is

transcendent object to human understanding.[15] In Thomas' view
there is a hierarchy of minds running from the human mind
up to the divine mind, each mind being characterized by its own
immanent content, but the hierarchy is in some sense abolished
when the immanent content of the divine mind becomes by God's
grace the transcendent object of the angelic minds and the human
mind. In Plotinus' view, on the contrary, the level of transcendent object is one of the levels in the hierarchy and so is the
level of immanent content so that the hierarchy is only ascended,
never transcended.

In Thomas' view too, nevertheless, the hierarchy of minds,
though it is ultimately abolished in that angelic minds and
human minds are equal, so to speak, before God the transcendent
object, still subsists in that each mind has its own level of immanent content. For this reason Thomas had to ascribe a double
goal to every created mind, the transcendent goal to be attained
in the vision of God and the immanent goal to be attained on
its own level.[16] This gave the handle to a thinker like Dante
who wished to reaffirm the hierarchical myth of the Holy Roman
Empire alongside the hierarchical mysticism which seemed to be
undermining it in favor of the Church. Carrying the double goal
doctrine of Thomas a step further, Dante maintained that man
has not simply a proximate goal and an ultimate goal as Thomas
had taught but two ultimate goals,[17] the one being the collective
fulfillment of the mind on earth described in the beginning of
the treatise *On Monarchy* and the other being the individual
fulfillment of the mind in heaven described in the last canto of
the *Divine Comedy*. The earthly goal was admittedly proximate
and provisional as far as the individual is concerned, but it was
ultimate and final, according to Dante's viewpoint, as far as the
collectivity is concerned.

Translating the essence of the hierarchical myth into the language of Aristotle, Dante said that the proper function of man
in this world is to actualize the total potentiality of the human
mind.[18] This, he thought, is man's role in the hierarchical order
of the universe and it implies that there is a special role for each
individual man within the whole community of mankind existing

at any one time. Since no one man by himself is able to bring the entire potential of the mind into operation, the combined activity of the whole race is required, one man actualizing the potential in one respect and another in another until in the end the entire mental capacity of mankind is realized. Dante evidently did not envision a progressive evolution of human knowledge in which total understanding would be attained at some time of fulfillment in the future. Instead total understanding was to exist, according to his way of thinking, at all times so that at any given moment in human history the human race would be in possession of the whole treasure of possible human knowledge. This apparently meant an abiding hierarchical society in which each rank and position was defined by the special skill or learning required to hold it and in which every form of knowledge was represented from the lowliest of the useful arts to the most sublime of the fine arts, from the most practical of the applied sciences to the most speculative of the pure sciences, from the most particular form of private prudence to the most universal form of political wisdom.

Thomas, though he too conceived the goal of man to be the actuation of the total potentiality of the mind, does not seem to have considered the possibility of a collective actuation on earth such as Dante envisaged. Rather he thought that man has an innate desire to know which cannot rest content with anything less than the beatific vision of God, and he took pains to demonstrate that the individual mind cannot be satisfied with the kind of knowledge which man can attain in this life on earth and that at best such knowledge is a shadow and a participation of the sort of knowledge that man innately seeks.[19] The nearest Thomas came to considering the perspective adopted by Dante was in his disputes with contemporary Averroists who maintained that immortality is to be had only through participation in the universal mind. To them he endeavored to prove that there is no universal mind common to all men but that each man has his own and that immortality must therefore be personal.[20] Very likely he thought that he had disposed in this way of any notion of collective enlightenment and collective immortality since if there is no collective mind but only individual minds there will be no one mind that will be actuated by the sum total of human knowledge at any given time.

Dante, while agreeing with Thomas that there is no collective mind but only individual minds, thought nevertheless that the knowledge distributed among these minds could be regarded as forming a unity and a totality, a hierarchy corresponding to the hierarchy of the society he knew in which each role called for a special wisdom and each generation was apprenticed to a preceding generation. What is more, he seems to have thought that there was a kind of eternity in this, the kind of eternity which Thomas ascribed to the vision of God, that of a mental existence that is "all at once," *tota simul,* for the sum of human knowledge like the vision of God is a sort of omniscience existing complete at any given moment of time.[21] On the other hand, agreeing that there are only individual minds, Dante had to agree that the individual mind is not completely actuated by the particular attainments that go with a particular role in society and therefore that the vision of God is necessary if the whole potentiality of the individual mind is ever to be realized.

This unfortunate drawback, that in spite of the "all at once" quality of collective existence the existence of the individual remained incomplete, was to prove the eventual undoing of the hierarchical society and its myth. Human concern was still sufficiently directed toward the afterlife in Dante's time for human existence to seem a comic rather than a tragic existence in spite of the implicit tension between the mortality of the individual and the immortality of the collectivity. Afterward, though, that tension increased or was felt more vividly and a hundred years after Dante it began to give rise to such phenomena as the dance of death. In another hundred years or so the tension had developed and attention had focused on death as a problem for this earth to such an extent that, for these perhaps among other reasons, there was at length a rebirth of tragedy. When human existence ceased to seem the divine comedy envisioned by Dante, however, and began to seem the purely human tragedy envisioned by Shakespeare, the years of the hierarchical society were numbered, and the search for a new solution to the problem of death was sure to begin.

[2] *Monarchy and Tragedy*

Shakespeare based most of his historical plays on what he has Richard II call "sad stories of the death of kings" wherein it is told "how some have been deposed, some slain in war, some haunted by the ghosts they have deposed, some poisoned by their wives, some sleeping killed, all murdered."[22] King John was poisoned, Richard II was deposed, Henry IV was haunted by the ghost he had deposed, Henry VI was deposed, and Richard III was haunted by the ghosts he had deposed and was slain in war. The wonder and irony Shakespeare saw in such stories was apparently the paradox that the immortal crown should circle a mortal head, that "within the hollow crown that rounds the mortal temples of a king keeps Death his court."[23] To Shakespeare a king was almost the same as his kingdom and could be called by its name, the English king "England," the French king "France," so that if any man were more than mortal it would be the king, the man who could conceivably claim for himself the very immortality of the kingdom. When King John dies, however, Shakespeare has Lord Salisbury say "But now a king, now thus" and Prince Henry say "What surety of the world, what hope, what stay, when this was now a king, and now is clay?"[24]

Thoughtful men of all times and places, it is true, have meditated upon the fact of death and upon its inescapability, and yet death was viewed differently by men living in the hierarchical society of Shakespeare's time than it is by men living in a modern equalitarian society. To those who lived in the hierarchical society, a society in which inequality was not merely a fact but actually a principle, death appeared as the great equalizer. This is the theme of the late medieval dance of death, a symbolic dance either performed or else represented in pictures and poems in which the various personages of the hierarchical society, pope, emperor, king, queen, bishop, knight, commoner, serf, are shown dancing with their own future corpses or with the skeletal figure of Death himself who leads them to their graves.[25] To those who live in a modern equalitarian society, a society in which inequality is no longer recognized as a principle, though it continues to exist as a fact, death no longer has this function of reducing everyone to the same level and reminding one and all that they are human. This is perhaps the reason why the late medieval sense of the macabre strikes modern feelings as morbid.

The special preoccupation with the death of kings, however, which is to be found in Shakespeare reveals a stage in the development of the hierarchical society which comes after that revealed in the fifteenth century dance of death. This later stage is the period of absolute monarchy which could be said to have begun in England with the accession of the Tudors and in France with the accession of the Bourbons, a period in which the collective existence of the hierarchical society became concentrated and epitomized in the king and the contrast between the mortality of the individual and the immortality of society tended to be summed up in the contrast between the king's mortal "body natural" and his immortal "body politic."[26] To be sure, the kings whose deaths are dramatized by Shakespeare are mostly Plantagenets, kings who belong to the earlier period when the king was simply the most important of the various figures in a highly differentiated society. But these Plantagenets tend to become as important as Tudors in the history plays of Shakespeare and their deaths tend to acquire all the irony and paradox that belong to the death of absolute monarchs.

Four phases may perhaps be distinguished in the evolution of kings and kingdoms in Western Europe,[27] the first of which would be the phase of the tribal kingdom when the king was set off against the tribal council and assembly. Although at this early time the death of kings was not yet the paradox it was to become in the days of absolute monarchy, it seems to have been already something in the nature of a special problem and it seems to have had something to do with the conversion of the Teutonic peoples to Christianity. Conversion almost always began in the

king's court and violent opposition to Christianity was offered
only among peoples like the Old Saxons who had no kings or
else, as happened in Norway, in defiance of the king's authority.
What led kings and their courts to accept Christianity is suggested by the story which Bede tells of the discussion held by
King Edwin and his councilors as to whether or not the king
should embrace the new religion.[28] One of the councilors argued
for Christianity from the contrast between God and the gods,
proposing that God might be more capable of rewarding his
worshippers than were the gods, but another argued for it from
the shortness of man's lifetime and his ignorance of what goes
before and what comes after his life on earth, proposing that
Christianity might offer something more definite and reliable on
such matters. This second councilor's argument combined with
the fact that in the years preceding their conversion to Christianity the various Teutonic peoples had abandoned the practice
of cremation in favor of the practice of inhumation[29] suggests
that Christianity may have been seen by these early kings and
their councils as a solution to a problem about death and the
shortness of human life.

What happened in the subsequent phase in the evolution of
the kingdom, the phase of the feudal kingdom, together with
parallels from other societies which started from a king-council-
assembly structure, indicates that the original problem may well
have been the indefinite prolongation of life. In this second phase,
at any rate, the quest for life which had been in evidence in pre-
Christian societies like the one reflected in the *Epic of Gilgamesh*
was in evidence again and was now given a specifically Christian
cast. The cycles of romance which date from this period, the
Charlemagne cycle, the Arthurian cycle, the cycle of Rome and
Alexander, and the Germanic cycle, all exhibit in one degree or
another the pervading idea of quest, and the Alexander cycle
even shows the quest for life in its old pagan form according
to which the hero seeks and finds at the ends of the earth the
well of perpetual life. The Arthurian cycle shows the quest in a
form more characteristic of an age of faith, namely as the quest
for the Holy Grail,[30] a quest carried out in romance which is

paralleled by a quest carried out in historical reality at this time in the Crusades, the quest for the Holy Sepulchre.

Whatever Christian or pagan symbol was used to represent its object in romance or in actual adventure, though, the ordinary quest for life in feudal society seems to have taken the more prosaic form of what was called in feudal law the "quest for a lord," the seeking of a new lord to which every freeman was entitled so long as he had done his duty to his existing lord.[31] For to seek a lord, whether he was thought to be only a human lord or thought to take the place of the divine Lord, was to seek a personal identity for oneself as that lord's vassal, an identity which was of one's own choosing and which therefore one would wish to perpetuate. To have one's quest for life satisfied, accordingly, was to be satisfied with one's existing lord and with one's existing identity and with its perpetuation through the perpetuation of society. At the same time, however, the satisfaction of the quest in this way could be inimical to the further extension of the quest itself. In fact, when the class lines of the feudal kingdom were drawn more sharply in the thirteenth century and the "estates of the realm," clergy, nobility, and commons, were more fully and finally defined, the possibilities of the quest for a lord were correspondingly reduced, the quest for life took on a somewhat different aspect, and the kingdom itself entered upon a third phase in its evolution, becoming what might be called an "estate kingdom."

Considering the way the period of the estates formally began in England, with the signing of Magna Charta forced upon King John by the English barons, one might be led to conclude that the estate kingdom was characterized by a reduction of the king's power. Considering the way the period formally began in France, on the other hand, with the convocation of the States General for the first time by King Philip to support him in his struggle with the Pope, one might be led to conclude rather that the estate kingdom was characterized by a reinforcement of the king's power. In reality it seems to have been characterized by a reduction of personal significance and a reinforcement of impersonal status at all levels of society from king to commoner. The dichotomy between a man's impersonal significance and his personal insignificance is perhaps what finds expression in the sense of the macabre which emerges in the latter part of this period and appears in the two-story tombs, for instance, wherein the deceased is represented above as alive and dressed in the symbols of his status and below as dead and stripped to his naked and private corpse.[32] When the king's power was eventually enlarged at the end of this period and the kingdom entered upon the fourth phase in its evolution, the phase of absolute monarchy, consequently, it was not the personal significance of the king that was enhanced but rather his impersonal status, and so his personal mortality became that much more of a private catastrophe.

A rebirth of tragedy as a dramatic form took place at this fitting time, or at least the tragic drama of this time tended to be regarded as a rebirth of classical tragedy. Actually it was almost inevitable that the tragic drama of the absolute monarchy, no matter how much it was meant to be a renaissance of classical tragedy, should differ essentially from the tragic drama of the urban republic. There was, of course, this much common ground, that instead of living happily ever after the heroes and heroines of both classical and renaissance tragedy lived a life that had all the finality of death itself. What made such an existence tragic to the Greeks, however, seems ultimately to have been the fact that it could not be undone, that not even the gods, as Agathon said, could undo the deed once it was done.[33] When Shakespeare had Lady Macbeth say "what's done cannot be undone," on the other hand, he was having her reassure herself that the dead could not come back to life and take their revenge, that "Banquo's buried; he cannot come out on's grave."[34] Indeed what made human life appear tragic to men of Shakespeare's time seems to have been the fact that once lost it could not be regained, that once the light of human life was put out, as Shakespeare had Othello say, it could never be rekindled.[35]

If Othello had been the hero of a Greek tragedy, his misfortune would probably have been the fact that no matter how sincerely convinced he was of his wife's guilt when he killed her he could never afterward change the reality of his deed which was to have killed a wife who was faithful and innocent. As it was, when he learned that his wife had been innocent, he could ask others to treat his "unlucky deeds" as the deeds of "one that loved not wisely but too well" but then killed himself because he could never find "that Promethean heat" which could rekindle the light of her life.[36]

If Macbeth had been the hero of a Greek tragedy, he probably would not have finally succeeded in hardening his heart against the memory of his past deeds and overcoming his fear of his victims' ghosts but Furies would have been unleashed against him and would have pursued him and driven him to madness. As it was, when he had consummated all the murderous deeds necessary to attain absolute power, he found life a time too short to enjoy it, a "brief candle," a "walking shadow," a "tale told by an idiot, full of sound and fury, signifying nothing."[37]

If Hamlet had been the hero of a Greek tragedy, his dilemma would probably have been that like Orestes he was bound to avenge one unpardonable deed, the murder of his father, with another unpardonable deed, the murder of his mother (a deed which Shakespeare's Hamlet was forbidden to do by his father's ghost) and the murder of her paramour. As it was, when Hamlet contemplated the fate of the king his father, "the question" for him, more than to do or not to do the deed necessary to avenge his father and become king himself, was "to be or not to be," reflecting as he did in the beginning "how weary, stale, flat, and unprofitable seem to me all the uses of this world" and in the end "to what base uses we may return" when we are dead and buried.[38]

If King Lear had been the hero of a Greek tragedy, he probably would have avoided madness and instead learned endurance like Oedipus at Colonus from his sufferings, his many years, and his well-tried nobility. As it was, when he resigned his "absolute power" to his daughters, he found himself reduced to being an old man, a sick man, a dead man, a "ruined piece of nature" from which the only lesson to be learned was that "this great world shall so wear out to nought."[39]

The nearest thing to a notion of tragedy of this kind to be found in classical culture, if questions of dramatic form are left aside, seems to be the sense of tragedy that appears in the Homeric epics, the more unrelieved and unmitigated sense of man's mortality which prevailed among the Greeks before the rise of the urban republic with its worldview according to which the past is immutable and deeds once done are immortal. In the *Iliad* and the *Odyssey* the mortality of men is set off in stark contrast with the immortality of the gods and there is as yet no clear thought of a man's life possessing some kind of intrinsic immortality of its own unless it be the chance of its living on in the memory of mankind. In Shakespearean tragedy, in *Troilus and Cressida* to take an example where the story material coincides to some extent with that of the *Iliad*, the mortality of men is set off in equally sharp relief, and where the story material once carried the idea that man's life is a series of immortal deeds, as in those plays of Shakespeare which were based on Plutarch's *Lives,* the immortal past is reduced once more to immortal fame and survival in human memory.

The foil for the mortality of men in Shakespeare, nevertheless, is not the immortality of the gods as it is in Homer, though Shakespeare uses traditional formulas about the "immortal gods," so much as human greatness and especially the greatness of kings. "Twin-born with greatness," says Henry V describing the condition of the king, "subject to the breath of every fool . . . What have kings that privates have not too, save ceremony? . . . And what art thou, thou idle ceremony? What kind of god art thou, that sufferest more of mortal griefs than do thy worshippers? . . . Art thou aught else but place, degree, and form?"[40] The "greatness" of which Shakespeare speaks here and elsewhere is evidently not personal greatness, but, as he has Henry say, "place, degree, and form." It was, of course, just these things, place, degree, and form, that were immortal according to the political myth of the hierarchical society. Their immortality, though, could be made by a dramatist not only to overshadow the mortality of the individual person but oppositely to highlight it, and the individual's mortality could be made not only to highlight the immortality of place, degree, and form, but also to overshadow it.

The kings who are dispossessed in Shakespeare's plays, King Lear, Richard II, Henry VI, all exemplify the contrast between mortality and greatness. Henry VI, it is true, is so filled with the thought of the afterlife that he is quite content to be simply a man and to be relieved of the burden of kingship,[41] but Richard II and Lear both discourse upon the deceptive appearance of immortality with which their former greatness clothed them and upon the naked mortality which is revealed when they are stripped of royalty. King Lear, fantastically dressed with flowers, recalls in his madness that when he reigned "they told me I was everything" and comments "'tis a lie, I am not ague-proof," and when Gloucester asks to kiss his hand Lear answers "Let me wipe it first; it smells of mortality."[42] Richard II, sitting upon the ground, contemplating the prospect of being deposed, meditates upon the death of kings and upon the "solemn reverence" shown them as though they were immortal gods and tells his friends "you have mistook me all this while: I live with bread like you, feel want, taste grief, need friends: subjected thus, how can you say to me I am a king?"[43] Both Lear and Richard could have said what Shakespeare has Cleopatra's attendant say, "The soul and body rive not more in parting than greatness going off," or what he has Wolsey say, "Farewell! A long farewell, to all my greatness! This is the state of man . . ."[44]

The kings who use violence and fraud in Shakespeare's plays to attain or secure their power, King John, Henry IV, Richard III, Macbeth, also show up the antinomy of greatness and mortality, not by being deprived of their greatness and reduced to their mortality but by failing to overcome their mortality with their greatness. King John disclaims all responsibility for his nephew's death saying "We cannot hold mortality's strong hand" while his accusers say he is guilty of "foul play; and 'tis shame that greatness should so grossly offer it," but in the end John's inability to hold mortality's strong hand is ironically proved in his own "ending of mortality" and all are amazed to see that "this was now a king, and now is clay."[45] Henry IV in a pathetic death-bed scene asks that his crown be placed upon his pillow, and when his son Hal seeing him asleep thinks that he sleeps with the sleep of death, "a sleep that from this golden rigol hath divorced so many English kings," and tries on the crown himself, Henry awakens and reproves him saying "Thou seekest the greatness that will overwhelm thee."[46] Richard III, pretending not to seek that greatness, says "I would rather hide me from my greatness. . . . than in my greatness covet to be hid," but when he has perpetrated all the murders necessary to secure it he is overwhelmed by it and is told by a nightmare procession of his victims to "despair and die."[47] Macbeth in the beginning speaks confidently to his wife as his "dearest partner in greatness" and tells her of "what greatness is promised thee" by the weird sisters who have prophesied that Macbeth will be king, but when the prophecy has come true and all the murders needed to fulfill it have been committed Macbeth learns that his enemies are gathered to overthrow him and that his wife is already dead apparently by suicide, and then he sees how he is defeated by time and mortality, how "Tomorrow and tomorrow and tomorrow creeps in this petty pace from day to day to the last syllable of recorded time; and all our yesterdays have lighted fools the way to dusty death."[48]

If the foil to mortality in Shakespeare's histories and tragedies is thus what he terms "greatness," the foil to greatness in his comedies and romances appears conversely to be what he terms "mortality." What he has Puck say, "Lord, what fools these mortals be!" or what he has Vincentio say, "No might nor greatness in mortality can censure 'scape" may be the intended theme of the comedies.[49] This seems, at any rate, to be the role of the jester in Shakespeare's plays, especially of King Lear's "all-licensed fool,"[50] to see to it that no greatness in mortality does escape censure. The clowns in *Hamlet* significantly are grave-diggers, and Hamlet, contemplating the skull of "poor Yorick" the jester, is led to reflect that Alexander the Great and Julius Caesar died and turned to dust and that their dust may have been used at last to stop a bung-hole.[51] A clown brings Cleopatra the asp with which she is to kill herself and while she is doing what Caesar feared, defeating the Romans "in her greatness by some mortal stroke," that is killing herself while she is still queen, the clown wishes her "the joy of the worm."[52] And Touchstone, the jester in *As You Like It,* is quoted in lines that mimic Macbeth's "Tomorrow and tomorrow": "Call me not a fool," he says, "till heaven hath sent me fortune" and then bringing out a sundial says "It is ten o'clock; thus we may see how the world wags: 'tis but an hour ago since it was nine, and after one hour more 'twill be eleven; and so, from hour to hour we ripe and ripe, and then from hour to hour we rot and rot, and thereby hangs a tale."[53]

Thereby hangs a tale indeed, but the tale told in Shakespearean comedy, for all that the comedies and romances usually have the unhappy beginnings and happy endings which Dante and the classical dramatists expected comedy to have, is no more the tale told in Dantean comedy than is the tale told in Shakespearean tragedy. Place, degree, and form, what Shakespeare sums up in the term "greatness," is not set off by Dante against mortality so much as against another system of place, degree, and form, that of the other world. The world of the afterlife, as Dante conceives it, has an hierarchical structure exactly as does the world of this life, only one's position in the one hierarchy does not determine one's position in the other but a person who is high in the hierarchy of this world, a pope or an emperor, may well be near the bottom of the hierarchy of hell in the world of the afterlife. While both Dante and Shakespeare might thus serve to encourage the man who sets his heart upon the life to come, Shakespeare would tend to discourage much more than Dante the man who sets his heart upon the present life, for the foil to the greatness of this life in Shakespeare is not the greatness of another life but the mortality of this life itself. To men who set their heart upon this life the contrast between greatness and mortality could become intolerable, as it seems to have become soon after Shakespeare's time, so intolerable that given the impossibility of eliminating mortality it should become necessary to eliminate greatness.

NOTES TO CHAPTER EIGHT

1. Compare Genesis 2:9 with Koran 20:118 (in Fleugel's edition) (20:120 in the official Egyptian edition). Also cf. Koran 7:19 (7:20).

2. The tree is described in Purgatorio, XXXII and XXXIII. Some commentators have it that the tree mentioned in XXII, 131 ff. is connected with the tree of life just as the one in XXIV, 116 f. is connected with the tree of knowledge. But this is rather doubtful. Also note that Dante never calls the tree in XXXII and XXXIII the "tree of knowledge." For a general discussion of Islamic precedents for Dante's earthly paradise cf. M. Asin Palacios, *Islam and the Divine Comedy* (New York, 1926), 121 ff.

3. T. S. Eliot, *Selected Essays* (New York, 1932), 225.

4. This is the explanation of the title which Dante gives in his epistle to Can Grande della Scala (Epistle X, 10).

5. De Monarchia, III, 16 (according to Witte's numbering of the chapters).

6. Alexis de Tocqueville, *Democracy in America*, vol. II (New York, 1959), 144 ff.

7. The great witness to this situation in the late empire is the *Theodosian Code*. For discussion and references cf. the edition by Clyde Pharr cited in the previous chapter, especially the introduction by C. D. Williams and Book XII, 1, on decurions.

8. For a general treatment cf. Marc Bloch, *Feudal Society* (Chicago, 1961).

9. Observe how Dante spends the whole second book of the *De Monarchia* trying to prove that the empire must be a Roman empire.

10. On the titles *vicarius Dei* and *vicarius Christi* cf. M. Maccarrone in *The Sacral Kingship*, 581 ff.

11. Cf. the *Libri Carolini*, I, 1 (Migne, *Patrologia Latina*, XCVIII, 1005 ff.).

12. Cf. E. H. Kantorowicz, *The King's Two Bodies* (Princeton, 1957), 334 ff.

13. G. Tellenbach in *Church, State, and Christian Society* (Oxford, 1959) develops the general thesis that "the investiture contest was a struggle for the right order in society."

14. Thomas shows his awareness of the problem in the *Summa Contra Gentiles*, II, 98 where he states it and leaves it apparently unresolved. On Plotinus' solution cf. Chapter Six, Section 1.

15. This is almost a definition of "participation" as Thomas seems to understand it. Cf. my article "St. Thomas' Theology of Participation" in *Theological Studies*, XVIII (1957), 487 ff.

16. Summa Theologiae, I, 23, 1; I-II, 3, 6; 5, 5; 62, 1.

17. Dante actually uses the phrase *duo ultima* in *De Monarchia*, III, 16.

18. Ibid., I, 3.

19. Summa Contra Gentiles, III, 48; *Summa Theologiae*, I, 12, 1; I-II, 3, 8.

20. Cf. his treatise *De Unitate Intellectus Contra Averroistas*. Also cf. *Summa Contra Gentiles*, II, 73 and *Summa Theologiae*, I, 76, 2.

21. On Thomas' notion of eternity my article cited above (note 15), 489 f. esp. note 8. Dante uses the terms *tota simul* and *semper* to describe the collective actuation of the mind on earth in *De Monarchia*, I, 3. It is interesting to observe that Thomas wrote two treatises against the Averroists, one on the collective mind and the other on the eternal world.

22. Richard II, 3, 2, 156 ff.

23. Ibid., 160 ff.

24. King John, 5, 7, 66 and 68 f.

25. Cf. J. M. Clark, *The Dance of Death* (Glasgow, 1950) and J. Huizinga's chapter on "The Vision of Death" in his *Waning of the Middle Ages* (New York, 1954), 138 ff.

26. This is the main theme of Kantorowicz's study, *The King's Two Bodies*, cited above. The more universal theme on which this is a variation is directly treated in his chapter entitled "The King Never Dies," *ibid.*, 314 ff.

27. W. J. Shepard in the *Encyclopedia of the Social Sciences*, VII, 11 ff. distinguishes six phases in the evolution of government in England: the tribal state, the feudal state, the estates state, the absolute state, the parliamentary state, and the democratic state. My four phases here are the first four of his six.

28. Bede, *Historia Ecclesiastica*, II, 13. On the conversion of the Teutons to Christianity cf. the summarizing remarks of H. M. Chadwick in *The Heroic Age*, 393 and 410 and 414.

29. Cf. Chadwick, *op. cit.*, 410.

30. In Wolfram von Eschenbach's *Parzifal*, 469, the Holy Grail is actually described as the means of indefinitely prolonging life.

31. On the "quest for a lord" cf. Bloch, *op. cit.*, 184 f.

32. Cf. Kantorowicz, *op. cit.*, 419 ff.

33. Agathon's line is quoted by Aristotle, *Nicomachean Ethics*, VI, 1139б10 f. For the theory of Greek tragedy supposed in this section cf. Chapter Five, Section 4.

34. Macbeth, 5, 2, 74 and 69 f.

35. Othello, 5, 2, 7 ff.

36. Ibid., 12 ("Promethean heat") and 340 ff. ("unlucky deeds" etc.).

37. Macbeth, 5, 5, 17 ff.

38. Hamlet, 3, 1, 56 ("to be"); 1, 2, 133 f. ("uses of this world"); 5, 1, 222 ("base uses").

39. King Lear, 5, 3, 302 ("absolute power" resigned back to dying Lear by Albany); 4, 6, 137 f. ("ruined piece of nature" etc.).

40. Henry V, 4, 1, 254 ff.

41. Henry VI, III, 3, 1, 13 ff. and 56 ff.

42. King Lear, 4, 6, 107 f. and 136 f.

43. Richard II, 3, 2, 174 ff.

44. Antony and Cleopatra, 4, 11, 5 f.; *Henry VIII*, 3, 2, 351 ff.

45. King John, 4, 2, 82 ("mortality's strong hand"); 4, 2, 94 ("greatness"); 5, 7, 5 ("ending of mortality"); 5, 6, 69 ("king" and "clay").

46. Henry IV, II, 4, 5, 34 ff. and 96.

47. Richard III, 3, 7, 160 and 162 ("greatness"); 5, 3, 121 ff. ("despair and die").

48. Macbeth, 1, 5, 12 ff. ("greatness"); 5, 5, 19 ff. ("tomorrow").

49. Midsummer Night's Dream, 3, 2, 115 (Puck); *Measure for Measure*, 3, 2, 196 (Vincentio).

50. King Lear, 1, 4, 223.

51. Hamlet, 5, 1, 201 ff.

52. Antony and Cleopatra, 5, 1, 64 f. ("in her greatness"); 5, 2, 260 and 280 ("the joy of the worm").

53. As You Like It, 2, 7, 19 ff. (Jacques quoting Touchstone).

CHAPTER NINE

The King Is Dead

WHEN Hobbes called the body politic the "mortal God"[1] he was signaling the beginning of a new era in the history of political myth. His intention in using this turn of phrase was, as he said, to find a more reverent title for the commonwealth than Leviathan, the name he used as the title of his book on it. But someone acquainted with the language of the Tudor lawyers who used to say that the king, though mortal in his body natural, was immortal in his body politic might be as surprised and impressed by the adjective "mortal" as by the noun "God."

The mortal God appears to have been as much a Christian image in its origin as the immortal body politic had been, and it is probably not altogether true to say, as has been said, that "temporal Christianity" came to an end when Charles I was executed in England or when Louis XVI was executed in France,[2] God being killed then in his human incarnation. God, after all, was killed in his original human incarnation and deicide is thus a Christian symbol. Charles I and Louis XVI to the extent that both of them saw themselves led to execution in the image of Christ,[3] the mortal God, were as modern in their thinking as were their executioners. The old myth had been that the king had two bodies, his body natural in which he was mortal like the earthly Christ and his body politic in which he was immortal like the risen and glorified Christ. The idea that the king in his body politic too was mortal like the earthly Christ was rather in accord with the ideas of the revolution against kingship, in fact was the initial form of the new political myth.

To be sure, the revolutionaries who executed Charles I and even those who executed Louis XVI, though they believed the king mortal in his body politic, were not as willing to believe that they were killing God as were their opponents and as were later revolutionaries. The image of the mortal God, nevertheless, has haunted all the great modern revolutions. And it has become the very image of man himself with the ideal of "free death"[4] exemplified sometimes in atheistic visions of the superman, sometimes in strange new visions of Christ himself, the Christ who said "No one takes my life from me, but I lay it down of myself" (John 10:18). To interpret the attitude toward life and death embodied in such symbolism, it seems, would be to unravel all the antinomies in modern man's irreligious religion and his religious irreligion.

[1] *The Death of God*

If there are gods, Marcus Aurelius had told himself in the course of his *Meditations,* there is no reason to dread the thought of death, for surely the gods will not involve a man in evil, but if there are no gods, there is still no reason to dread the thought of death, for "what is it to me to live in a world empty of gods or empty of providence?"[5] Some seventeen hundred years later Nietzsche was arguing that the world actually is empty of gods and empty of providence and that life in such a world can nevertheless be worth living. "God is dead," he repeated again and again, "and we have killed him," and "everyone who is born after us, for the sake of this deed," the killing of God, "will be part of a higher history than all history heretofore."[6] "If there were gods," Nietzsche argued, "how could I bear not to be a god? Hence there are no gods."[7] The intolerable contrast between immortal gods and mortal men is eliminated in the modern world, but this does not mean that the modern world is empty of all gods and thus, as Marcus Aurelius would have said, unfit for human habitation. There are still mortal gods. For "must we not ourselves become gods simply to seem worthy of it,"[6] this deed of killing God, and must not God himself be mortal in some sense for us to be capable of killing him?

The history of this enigmatic sentence "God is dead" is the

history at once of modern myth and of modern mysticism. Behind the myth of the dead God which took shape in the eighteenth and nineteenth century there is the mysticism of the hidden God which had taken shape already in the sixteenth and seventeenth century. The idea of the hidden God was, of course, a traditional one, going back to the statement in Isaiah 45:15, "Truly thou art a God who hidest thyself," or as it is in the Vulgate, "Truly thou art a hidden God," and the paradigm of the experience of the hidden God was Christ's own suffering on the cross, the experience which issued into the cry, "My God, my God, why hast thou forsaken me?"[8] The sense of being forsaken by God or the participation in Christ's feeling of abandonment, the state which St. John of the Cross called the "dark night of the soul," became for a mystic like St. John of the Cross the touchstone of genuine religious experience.[9] And the idea of the hidden God, the concept which to Pascal was the notion of what he also termed a "lost God," became for a thinker like Pascal the touchstone of genuine religious doctrine.[10]

There is an ambiguity in the experience of being forsaken by God, however, which perhaps explains how it could be not only the experience underlying the mysticism of the hidden God but also that underlying the myth of the dead God. The ambiguity, whether abandonment is to be taken as a religious or as an irreligious experience, was resolved differently in the three great religious traditions which diverged in the sixteenth century. In the Catholic tradition the ambiguity was resolved into the uncertainty of the one who undergoes the experience as to whether he is sharing in the abandonment felt by Christ on the cross or sharing in the loss of God felt by the damned in hell.[11] In the Lutheran and Calvinist traditions the ambiguity was resolved into the paradox of a cross on which the Christ, since he had to undergo the full penalty of sin in order to deliver us from it, will have experienced the loss of God which is experienced by the damned.[12] But the two Protestant traditions diverged fundamentally on the question as to whether Christians should share in Christ's experience.

Luther, thinking of his own sufferings and terrors of conscience, was inclined to believe that Christians were called upon at least in the hour of their death to participate in Christ's experience and that at any rate the only genuine understanding of Christianity was what he called the "theology of the cross," the viewpoint of one who recognizes the crucified and hidden God alone.[13] The alternative viewpoint, what he called the "theology of glory" and defined as the viewpoint of one who would find God manifest in all things, manifest we might say in the hierarchical order of things, was in his eyes a misunderstanding of Christianity. God hides himself, according to Luther, in the suffering and crucified Christ and there alone where he hides himself is he to be found. This means that God is not to be found manifest in the hierarchical society or in the works prescribed by the laws of that society or in the rewards promised to those who perform the works but that he is to be found hidden in the very things which are assumed to be evil by society and from which it promises deliverance, namely suffering and death.

Calvin, by contrast with Luther, believed that God was a manifest God, manifest not indeed in an hierarchical order or an hierarchical society but in each individual's life, manifest as the merciful God in the lives of the elect and as the wrathful God in the lives of the reprobate. What Calvin understood by the manifestness of God to the reprobate or to the unbelievers, however, is somewhat similar to what Luther understood by the hiddenness of God. There are two kinds of suffering, according to Calvin, the suffering of the elect, those who are to be saved, who experience God as the father who chastises those whom he loves, and the suffering of the reprobate, those who are to be damned, who experience God already in this life as the judge who punishes those whom he hates with the tortures of hell.[14] Christ himself, and here Calvin at least agreed with Luther if he did not actually go further, will have suffered on the cross the tortures of the damned, but the whole point of Christ's undergoing this, and here Calvin differed fundamentally with Luther, will have been to release the elect from all liability to such an experience.

In all three of the religious traditions the "kenosis" described in Philippians 2:7, God's "emptying" of himself on becoming man, humbling himself even to the point of undergoing death, was set against what Shakespeare was to call the "greatness" of "place, degree, and form" in the hierarchical society. The opposition to the myth of the hierarchical society was the more radical in the Protestant traditions in that the conception of the kenosis was the more extreme, Christ being thought to have emptied himself so far as to experience the loss of God that is experienced in hell. The participation in the experience of the kenosis, the sense of being oneself forsaken by God, was perhaps in any case the fundamental spiritual experience of modern times. The possibilty of the experience being in some sense an irreligious experience, however, the uncertainty ascribed to it in Catholicism, the ambivalence ascribed to it in Lutheranism, and the definite irreligiousness ascribed to it in Calvinism, was the possibility of its becoming the basis of a new myth, a countermyth, itself as much opposed to genuine Christianity as was the old myth which it would replace.

That possibility became an actuality in the philosophy of Hegel where the kenosis did actually become an answer to death as purely human as the answer which had been offered by the hierarchical society. The use of the present tense instead of the past tense in the statement "God is dead"[15] which Hegel found in a Lutheran hymn, a use which made it seem as though Christ were not risen from the dead, became emphatic when the statement was repeated by Hegel, for Hegel thought that a resurrection of Christ's human individuality would be a kind of anticlimax to the drama of his sufferings and death. The use of the term "God," moreover, instead of "Christ" in the sentence, a use which made it seem as though Christ had died in his divine nature as well as in his human nature, also became emphatic, for Hegel thought that the significance of the kenosis as God's emptying of himself would be nullified by a preservation of Christ's divinity in the destruction of his humanity. If one wished to rise to the comprehension of "infinite grief" and "absolute suffering," Hegel believed, one had to dispense with the palliatives and to experience in all its starkness the "Golgotha of absolute spirit."

What Hegel meant by the "Golgotha of absolute spirit" was

what he thought to be the profoundest spiritual experience of modern man, an experience which he believed was felt and expressed inadequately in the modern religious movement, the Reformation, and in the modern irreligious movement, the Enlightenment.[16] The experience, it seems, was the consciousness of the absoluteness of the human spirit, the experience of complete independence, of universal and unrestricted autonomy. In terms of God it was the human spirit's consciousness of being left to itself, of being altogether forsaken by God, and of being abandoned to suffering and death. The experience will have been expressed by the Reformation, in Luther's theology of the cross, with the symbol of God's death, only this symbol will have been deprived of much of its significance by the continuing faith in Christ's resurrection from the dead. The experience will have been expressed by the Enlightenment, for example in Voltaire's *Candide* where the suffering and death in the world are used to explode the notion that "all is for the best in the best of all possible worlds," with the symbol of God's absence from the world, only this symbol too will have been deprived of much of its significance by an abstract deism according to which God will never have been experientially present to man in the first place. In their purity, though, these symbols, God's death and God's absence, will have revealed clearly the real nature of the spiritual experience and, from Hegel's viewpoint, they will have uncovered the latent unanimity of the Reformation and the Enlightenment.

How the experience of autonomy answered the problem of death appears in its contrast with what Hegel considered imperfect forms of consciousness, the consciousness of the master and the consciousness of the slave. The master does not experience complete autonomy because he needs recognition from the slave in order to be sure of his own reality as a master. The slave, on the other hand, does not experience complete autonomy because out of fear of death he lives in dependence on the master. The slave's consciousness, nevertheless, is surprisingly nearer, according to Hegel, to the experience of autonomy than is the master's because the slave does not need recognition from another human being in order to be sure of his reality. The only threat to the slave's reality is death itself which, Hegel says, is the "sovereign master"[17] beyond all human masters and is the motive for the slave's submission to a human master. To attain complete autonomy, therefore, one must not only dispense with recognition by other human beings as does the slave but one must overcome the fear of death itself. This overcoming occurs when one faces death squarely, without hope of staving it off and even without hope of resurrection from it, in other words when one tastes the utter despair and complete abandonment which belong to the experience of God's death. When one travels to the end of what Hegel calls the "highway of despair,"[18] one faces death in this way, one experiences complete autonomy and death ceases to be the sovereign master.

Because he did not identify God with death as the sovereign master, Hegel did not require that the human spirit assert itself against God in order to become absolute but simply that it give up the hope of being delivered from death by God, the hope for deliverance being the implicit acknowledgment of death's actual sovereignty. If God, however, considered as the arbiter of man's fate, were to be identified with death and God's sovereignty with death's sovereignty, then to attain autonomy and overcome death the human spirit would have to positively assert itself against God. Such an identification of God with death, the sovereign master, seems to have been what underlay Nietzsche's rebellion against Christianity, his denunciation of the Christian preachers of God as "preachers of death," and his accusation that the "eternal life" they proclaimed was nothing but death.[19] When he repeated Hegel's statement "God is dead," he meant it to be a great affirmation of life as though he had said something like the old antiphon "death was dead when Life was dead on the tree,"[20] only something less paradoxical and more truistic like "death was dead when Death was dead" or simply "Death is dead."

Hegel's despair and Nietzsche's rebellion have this in common, nevertheless, that both end in an assertion of human autonomy calculated to solve the problem posed by the sovereignty of death. The solution, moreover, has in both Hegel and Nietzsche mythological overtones resembling those of earlier answers to death and tending to confer on the dead God an existence comparable with that of the old gods of the dead. Despair of God and reliance instead upon the human spirit tends to make the autonomous spirit the successor of the dead God, a spirit prefigured by the spirit of the dead Osiris in the living Horus, while rebellion against God as death the sovereign master tends to keep the caricature of God alive in the rebellious consciousness as a figure resembling Hades, the god of the dead or death in person, of whom Homer said "men hate him most of all the gods."[21] How indispensable the continued existence of the dead God is to the myth that God is dead appears in how much Nietzsche has to say in his *Zarathustra* about God and the death of God and how little Hegel has to say about the absolute spirit when he has finished describing in his *Phenomenology* the transition from the experience of God to the experience of autonomy or how little he has to say about the absolute idea when he has finished describing in his *Logic* the corresponding transition from the idea of the Good to the absolute idea. The experience of autonomy would indeed be difficult to sustain if there were nothing to despair of or nothing to rebel against, if the dead God were ever to be forgotten like a dead language, if, in short, the myth that God is dead were to come true.

[2] *The Sovereignty of Death*

The sentence "God is dead" is paralleled by the sentence "the world is dead" which occurs in Donne's poem "An Anatomy of the World."[22] This poem, one of the most sombre in the English language, was the first half of Donne's chief work "The Anniversaries" occasioned by the death of a woman he admired and has as its theme the mortality of the world as manifested in her mortality. Although this sort of theme was not treated so elaborately elsewhere, it was not an extraordinary one in Donne's time. Shakespeare, for example, when he has King Lear speak of his mortality has Gloucester exclaim "O ruined piece of nature!

This great world shall so wear out to nought."[23] There seems to have been, in fact, a pervading feeling of the world's mortality at this time when the hierarchical order of things was being called into question. This sickness of the world of which Donne speaks, the impossibility of health, the shortness of life, the smallness of stature, the decay of nature, the disformity of the world's parts, the disorder in the world, the weakness in the want of correspondence of heaven and earth, all point to the dubiousness of the hierarchical order that had been thought to prevail in nature and among men.

Death had begun to appear as the nemesis of the hierarchical organization of mankind already in the fifteenth century with the dance of death, the double tombs, and suchlike images of death as the great equalizer, the irresistible force which knows no distinctions of rank. Soon afterward it began to appear also as the nemesis of the hierarchical order of nature when the old worldview according to which the heavenly bodies were immortal and incorruptible started to give way to a new worldview according to which they were as mortal and corruptible as earthly bodies. By the time Shakespeare was talking about the world wearing out to nought and Donne was saying "the world is dead" both processes were far advanced, the changing attitude toward society no doubt helping and favoring the change of perspective on the universe. What was developing, it seems, was the idea to which Hegel was later to give expression, that death is the sovereign master of the world. In the dance of death the apparent rulers of the earth, prince and king and emperor, were dragged away by death, and in the new systems of the world the apparent rulers of the sky, sun and moon and stars, were declared subject to death. The implied conclusion was that death was the real ruler of the sky and the real ruler of the earth.

Before this conclusion was drawn, however, the conclusion was drawn that the real ruler was God. The statement that God is the sovereign master of the world could of course, taken in itself, be simply an expression of traditional Christianity or of one of the other monotheistic religions, Judaism and Islamism, but made as it was in the days of absolute monarchy in the sixteenth and seventeenth centuries it inevitably carried a somewhat distinctive connotation. Calvin's teaching, the chief influence on this score, dealt with the sovereignty of God as mainly and mostly as Christ's teaching (in the "synoptic gospels," Matthew, Mark, and Luke) had dealt with the kingdom of God. There was a characteristic difference, though, between Calvin's language about the reign of God and the language of the Gospels, a difference which Calvin himself recognized although he saw in it no real contradiction.[24] The kingdom of God or the reign of God which had been the theme of Christ's teaching had been something for which one could hope and pray, "Thy kingdom come," whereas the sovereignty of God which was the theme of Calvin's teaching was a universal sovereignty which, as he conceived it, was verified in what had been called in the New Testament the "reign of sin unto death" or the "reign of death" as well as in what had been called the "reign of grace through justice unto eternal life."[25]

In the "reign of grace through justice unto eternal life" Calvin saw the reign of God's mercy, the reign of God or kingdom of God which had been proclaimed by Christ, while in the "reign of sin unto death" and especially in the "reign of death" he saw the reign of God's wrath. The kingdom of God which Christ had proclaimed was thus one of two unequal and opposite manifestations of what Calvin conceived to be the sovereignty of God. Calvin, nevertheless, in seeing and formulating things this way was a theological innovator, if we compare his ideas on predestination and reprobation with those of Augustine, only to the extent that he was a "supralapsarian," that is insofar as he maintained that "God not only foresaw the fall of the first man, and in him the ruin of his posterity; but also at his own pleasure arranged it,"[26] and he limited his teaching to this effect by a refusal to call God the author of sin, an attribution which he considered a blasphemy. Where his originality lay most importantly, it seems, was not so much in asserting God's universal sovereignty as in proclaiming it and making it his message. This had the effect of turning the universal sovereignty of God into tidings, not indeed "glad tidings" as the kingdom of God had been but rather fearsome tidings, and yet, so Calvin thought, salutary tidings for the society of his time.

The risk to Christianity inherent in this was that the response of men to Christianity might be directed rather to the tidings of God's universal sovereignty than to the tidings of God's kingdom, that men might try to respond to God's power and will to mete out eternal life and eternal death rather than to God's call to eternal life. Thus the believer, instead of simply accepting the divine invitation and building his hope on the belief that he has a savior, might find himself in the situation described in Bunyan's *Grace Abounding*, the situation of a man who holds fast to the truth of God's universal sovereignty but who swings back and forth between hope and despair of his own salvation and searches desperately for some means of determining whether he is among those who are destined to be saved. The unbeliever, on the other hand, instead of refusing the invitation to salvation and rejecting the idea of a God who would offer it, might find himself in the position ascribed by Milton in *Paradise Lost* to Satan, the position of one who rebels hopelessly against the invincible power of the sovereign master of the world, against God's power of life and death or, having denied the existence of God and of the power to save from death, against the power of death.

If the power of God to mete out eternal life and eternal death is reduced, as Hobbes reduced it in *Leviathan*, to something comparable with the power of life and death possessed by human authorities, eternal life being understood as an indefinitely prolonged earthly life to be enjoyed after the resurrection and eternal death or the "second death" (Apocalypse 20:14) being understood literally as a second and final death in the physical sense to be undergone after the resurrection, then belief and unbelief of this sort can be directed, as Hobbes wanted belief directed, toward human authority. "It is impossible a commonwealth should stand," Hobbes said, "where any other than the sovereign hath a power of giving greater rewards than life, and of inflicting greater punishments than death."[27] That Hobbes should have wanted to reduce first of all human authority itself to the power of life and death wielded by government is understandable, for by his time the feeling that death was the real ruler of the world had grown to the point that the apparent rulers, whether kings or parliaments or lords protectors, seemed merely apparent except insofar as they had power to mete out death. The feeling that death was the real ruler would also explain why he should have wanted to reduce God's power also to the power of life and death or to an extension of it. Once these reductions were made, however, there remained only one real power in the world, that of life and death, so that the concentration of this power into the hands of one man or a body of men by the mutual agreement of men, the formation of a commonwealth, could be conceived by Hobbes to be without exaggeration the making of a "mortal God."

By directing what he thought to be a Calvinist faith in universal sovereignty towards his mortal God, Hobbes tried to make rebellion against the mortal God seem as desperate an act as rebellion against the immortal God. Calvin, though, rejecting what he called the "fiction of absolute power,"[28] had made it clear that the sovereignty of God which he proclaimed was not an arbitrary power but a power that was always used rightfully and reasonably even if the rightful reasons were secret counsels of God and were not made known to men. Locke then, speaking also from a Calvinist background but taking a view in his *Reasonableness of Christianity* somewhat similar to that of Hobbes about the power of God to mete out eternal life and eternal death being only an extension of the power of life and death possessed by human beings ("Could any one be supposed by a law that says 'For felony thou shalt die' not that he should lose his life but be kept alive in perpetual exquisite torments?"),[29] was able to argue that "political power" which he defined as "the right of making laws with penalties of death and consequently all less penalties"[30] was not an absolute or arbitrary power but a power which had a rightful use and that it was only the rightful power of life and death which men agreed to concentrate when they created a civil government. If wrongful power were to be used, therefore, or rightful power neglected and the offending government were to be overthrown, men will not have rebelled against rightful power but will have appealed to universal sovereignty, Locke says "appealed to heaven," in order to resume "supreme power" and "continue the legislative in themselves or place it in a new form, or new hands, as they think good."[31]

The rightful use of the power of life and death as Locke conceived it was its use to protect property, the dominion of man over the world being man's likeness to God (Genesis 1:28) and property being each man's personal share in that dominion and likeness.[32] With the growing feeling that death was the real ruler of the world, however, it was natural that the dominion over the world and the likeness to God the supreme ruler should seem to consist rather in the power of life and death itself. This had already been the view of Hobbes and it became in a new form the view of Rousseau. Sovereignty, according to Rousseau as according to Hobbes, was power to dispose of the individual's very person, not to speak of his goods, so that "when the prince says to him: 'It is expedient for the State that you should die,' he ought to die."[33] Yet though the individual as "subject" was completely subject to this power, he was not merely subject to it as Hobbes thought, but as "citizen" he was, according to Rousseau, a participant in sovereignty, for sovereignty was "nothing less than the exercise of the general will."[34] Men, in other words, were not only to create the mortal God but they were to be the mortal God which they created.

As for the mortality of the mortal God, Rousseau believed that the sovereign was mortal and that the "death of the body politic" occurred when the exercise of the general will ceased, but this was only the exercise that ceased whereas he believed that in itself "the general will is indestructible."[35] This general will which Rousseau considered both infallible and indestructible and the exercise of which he defined as sovereignty was evidently an earthly approximation of the will of the sovereign God in which he had believed before he abandoned Calvinism and then Catholicism and was even a closer approximation to the will of the God in which he afterward believed, the God whose supreme justice claimed vengeance only in this life.[36] What was needed to make the general will actually take the place of the divine will, since it was already infallible and indestructible, was to make it irresistible. This further step was taken by Hegel who criticized Rousseau's conception as being "abstract" rather than "concrete"[37] and who replaced Rousseau's idea of general will as the common interest which is opposed to conflicting private interests with the idea of a universal will or purpose which is actually accomplished through the mutual conflict of particular wills or purposes.

This "universal will" was not something apart from the human will but was what Hegel called "the absolutely rational element in the will,"[38] the will to absolute freedom or autonomy which he considered latent in every one of the various purposes of men and ever triumphant through the interplay of cross-purposes in that the irrational elements in opposing purposes necessarily cancel one another out. Having formulated explicitly the problem of death with which Hobbes, Locke, Rousseau, and their contemporaries had been concerned, namely that death is the sovereign master of the world, Hegel was able with this conception of autonomy and the universal will to autonomy to articulate fully the solution to the problem for which Hobbes and Rousseau, at any rate, seemed to have been groping. The Christian paradigm of the problem was to be found in Calvin's idea of God as the sovereign master of the world, and the Christian paradigm of the solution was to be found in Luther's idea that to "despair utterly of one's own ability" and to place all one's faith in the power of God was to make God's power one's own power, to make God's freedom one's own freedom, to acquire a "truly omnipotent power," to be "omnipotent with God."[39] The problem of death for Hegel, accordingly, was that death was the sovereign master of the world, and the solution was to despair of all deliverance from death and to yield oneself completely to its power thereby making its exigency one's own will and its sovereignty one's own autonomy.

Hegel's realization that autonomy is what modern man values most was shared by Marx, though Marx did not share Hegel's understanding of the manner in which autonomy is an answer to death. If indeed the power of life and death were reducible not merely in its rightful use, as Locke conceived it, but in its actual historical use to the protection of property, then it could be considered, as Marx wished to consider it, merely instrumental to the power of property.[40] If, furthermore, man were called upon to alienate himself completely to the power of property, as Hobbes wanted him alienated to the power of life and death, and if he could hope that total autonomy would be the outcome of total alienation to the power of property, as Rousseau and Hegel promised for total alienation to the power of life and death, then the will to autonomy could be considered, as Marx considered it, a historical force making for the establishment of a "classless society" in which the power of life and death would become inoperative.[41] Unfortunately the terrorism which has been characteristic of revolutions since the French Revolution makes it appear, in spite of Hegel, that the concrete will to power is as terrible as the abstract will to power and, in spite of Marx, that the historical will to power is not the mere will to power of property but the will to power of life and death.

[3] *Freedom from the Past*

With the sentences "God is dead" and "the world is dead" one might compare the sentence "the state is dead" which occurs in Rousseau's *Social Contract*.[42] Each of these sentences, before becoming an expression of the autonomy experienced in modern society, was a declaration of independence from the hierarchical society of the past. The sentence "God is dead" was originally meant to suggest that the true God was not manifest in the structure of the hierarchical society and the hierarchical order of nature which was its context but was hidden in the crucified Christ. The sentence "the world is dead" was originally meant to suggest that the immortality of place, degree, and form constituting the hierarchical society and the immortality of earthly species and of heavenly bodies constituting the hierarchical order of nature was illusory. And the sentence "the state is dead" was originally meant to suggest that the laws of the hierarchical society were not universal laws and that lawmaking in that society was not the work of the general will nor in the common interest but that because of the prevailing principle of inequality the exercise of the general will had for all practical purposes ceased.

All three of these sentences seem to have some validity as criticism of the hierarchical myth and in that capacity seem to offer some justification for the revolutions against the hierarchical society: "God is dead" the religious revolution, "the world is dead" the intellectual revolution, and "the state is dead" the political revolution. All three, however, or their equivalents have also come to stand for the new myth of autonomy and in that capacity have become liable to the same kind of criticism as that to which the hierarchical myth has been subjected. The religious revolution has become liable to such criticism insofar as it has led to a religion of autonomous conscience and ultimately to the kind of exaltation of the autonomous spirit (the "absolute spirit") carried through by Hegel in his *Phenomenology*. The intellectual revolution has become liable to a similar criticism insofar as it has led to a philosophy of autonomous reason and ultimately to the kind of exaltation of the autonomous idea (the "absolute idea") carried through by Hegel in his *Logic*. The political revolution, though, has become more directly liable to this sort of criticism than either the religious or the intellectual revolution in that it has led to the establishment of autonomy as a full-fledged political myth on an evident par with the old hierarchical myth.

What autonomy can mean as a political myth and a political reality was exhibited first in the Puritan revolution which took place in seventeenth century England. The Puritan ideal of autonomy was derived from the ideal of Christian liberty envisioned by Luther and Calvin, the ideal, as Luther conceived it, of sharing in God's omnipotence or, as Calvin conceived it, of sharing in God's sovereignty. Given the existence then of absolute monarchy in which kings claimed absolute power as a divine right, it was not unnatural, though Luther and Calvin had repudiated any such translation, that the ideal of sharing in God's omnipotence or in God's sovereignty should be translated into an ideal of sharing in the absolute power which had been arrogated by kings. Against the divine right of kings, accordingly, the Puritans asserted the divine right of the people or of the "people of God," and against the absolute power of kings they asserted the absolute power or "liberty" of the people.[43] The ideal thus translated into political terms was subsequently realized to the extent that the absolute power which had been wielded by the Stuart kings was wrested from Charles I and wielded for a time instead by the commons of the English parliament.

The Stuart as distinct from the Tudor concept of absolute monarchy comes to light in a work called the *Eikon Basilike* or the *King's Book*, "a portraiture of his sacred majesty in his solitude and sufferings," a justification of Charles I which appeared ten days after his execution and which excited much sympathy for him and for the restoration of the monarchy. The argument of the book was that "sovereignty" was the "right" of the king and that it was incapable of "alienation" either by act of the king or by the act of others and therefore that the king could never be rightfully judged or condemned.[44] The Puritan answer was formulated in a work called the *Eikonoklastes* written by Milton who became in the Puritan regime one of the secretaries of the council of state. Milton's argument, as it had been also in his *Tenure of Kings*, was that sovereignty was the right of the people and that it could not be alienated by any oath of allegiance to the king and therefore that the king could be tried and executed by the people or by their parliament. What was at issue on both sides, it seems, was not merely a legality but an ideal, the ideal of inalienable sovereignty, which differed drastically from the Tudor ideal of the immortal body politic in that immortality of the body politic was immortality both of king and people, whereas inalienable sovereignty was sovereignty either of the king or of the people but not of both and therefore was inevitably an object of contention and a cause of revolutions and restorations.

Unlike the Puritan Revolution of 1649 and the Stuart Restoration of 1660, the Whig Revolution of 1688 and the American

Revolution of 1775 were aimed rather at the limitation of political power than at the acquisition of absolute power. The limiting
principle, if we may judge from the ideas of Locke who attempted after the fact to justify the Whig revolutionaries of
England and whose language was used later on by the Whig
revolutionaries of America, was the right of property. The power
of life and death was to be used only for the protection of
property and not for any other purposes, and especially not
for encroaching upon property rights. Locke's concept of property, however, included not merely goods but life and liberty,
primarily life and liberty, in fact, these being conceived as self-
possession and being regarded, by contrast with goods, as inalienable. The concept of the inalienability of life and liberty
appears explicitly in the American Declaration of Independence
where it is said "that all men are created equal, that they are
endowed by their Creator with certain unalienable rights, that
among these are life, liberty, and the pursuit of happiness, that
to secure these rights governments are instituted among men."[45]

Alienation and autonomy being opposites, inalienability is
always a form of autonomy, but it makes a great deal of difference
whether it is the right to life or whether it is the right over life,
in other words sovereignty, that is inalienable. As Locke and the
Whigs conceived it, inalienable liberty is the inability to enslave
oneself to another in such a way as to give the other absolute
power of life and death over oneself.[46] Inalienable life, according
to them, is not an inability to risk one's life or to lay down one's
life for a just cause, as Rousseau erroneously supposed when he
attempted to refute the idea, but the inability to give another or
even to arrogate to oneself an absolute power of life and death
over oneself. Inalienable liberty, therefore, is the same thing as
inalienable life or is a facet of it. Inalienable life, moreover,
is an answer to death, a divine answer insofar as men "are endowed by their Creator with certain unalienable rights" but a
human answer insofar as "to secure these rights governments are
instituted among men." The answer to death implied is that
although one's life can be taken away and will some day be
lost one's right to life can never be taken away. The quest for

life, conceived as the "pursuit of happiness" and counted itself also as an inalienable right, is satisfied from this point of view not by an unlosable life but by an unlosable right to life and by the protection of that right.

The expression "inalienable rights" was also used in the declarations of rights which were made during the French Revolution in 1789 and in 1793, but the application of the adjective "inalienable" to the noun "sovereignty" which occurs in the latter of these two declarations suggests that the understanding of inalienability was not the same as it was in the Declaration of Independence.[47] Few of the French revolutionaries would have gone so far as to maintain with Rousseau that sovereignty alone was inalienable, but the radical group, the Jacobins, may well have regarded inalienable rights to liberty, equality, and fraternity as being reducible to inalienable sovereignty, the "sovereignty of the people." When it began in 1789 the French Revolution appeared to be aimed at the limitation of political power, the transformation of the absolute monarchy into a constitutional monarchy, and in this guise it found expression in the Declaration of the Rights of Man and Citizen and in the change of the king's title from "Louis, by the grace of God, King of France and Navarre" to "Louis, by the grace of God and the constitutional law of the State, King of the French."[48] When in 1792, however, the monarchy was abolished and the king was put to death, the aim of the revolution appeared to have become the acquisition of the absolute power which the king had formerly wielded and the intentions of the revolutionaries found expression in a proclamation of popular sovereignty.

What the Jacobin revolutionaries conceived sovereignty to be became plain in the "reign of terror" which ensued and which went on from 1793 to 1794. It was the absolute power of life and death and, though its exercise was intended to be only temporary, the restrictions which were to be eventually imposed upon it when terrorism had ceased to be necessary were intended to be merely self-imposed rather than inherent limitations. "If the resort of popular government in time of peace is virtue," Robespierre explained, "the resort of popular government in time of revolution is both virtue and terror," terror being an "emanation of virtue."[49] The meaning of a virtue which has terror for its emanation is absolute power, not indeed absolute power in the hands of a tyrant but absolute power in the hands of the people in that the "force of reason" and the "force of the people," according to the Jacobin motto, are one and the same thing. How far the desires of a man who wanted to participate in such power could go is revealed in the words of Saint-Just written when he was almost ready to despair of becoming a member of the revolutionary assembly in Paris: "My resolution is made, meanwhile. If Brutus does not kill others, he will kill himself."[50]

Desires like this to have life at one's disposal appear also in the history of terrorism and nihilism in Russia during the nineteenth and early twentieth century[51] and a belief in the people's sovereignty over life appears in the Bolshevik Revolution of 1917 and in the "Red terror" which lasted from 1918 to 1921. There was agitation in 1905 and in 1917, it is true, for the abolition of the death penalty, and the first legislative act of the Bolsheviks upon attaining power in November 1917 was to abolish the death penalty in its entirety. This law, though Lenin considered it "madness," a "mistake," and an "inadmissible weakness," and would have liked to revoke it immediately,[52] was passed in good faith and was in accord with the ultimate aims of the Bolshevik revolution. One who believes in popular sovereignty as a solution to the problems of life and death usually hopes that the power of life and death once it is in the hands of the people will no longer be exercised, or at least that the day will come when it will not be necessary to exercise it any more. This cessation was called in the Marxist terminology used by the Bolsheviks the "withering away of the state."

If Lenin disapproved of the abolition of the death penalty in 1917, it was not because he did not believe that the state would ever wither away but because he thought that the active exercise of the people's sovereignty over life, in Marxist terminology the "dictatorship of the proletariat," was necessary for the time being. The meaning of the dictatorship of the proletariat in the Bolshevik Revolution like the meaning of the divine right of the

people in the Puritan Revolution and of the sovereignty of the
people in the Jacobin Revolution is to be sought not only in the
ideological language used by the revolutionaries but in the historical nature of the absolute power which the revolutionaries
wished to take from the absolute monarch and to bestow upon
the people. Kautsky, the literary continuator of Marx and Engels,
was probably right when he objected that the terrorism used by
the Bolsheviks was not in accordance with Marx's conception of
the dictatorship of the proletariat.[53] Lenin and Trotsky, on the
other hand, though they meant to be orthodox Marxists, were
speaking for the Bolshevik Revolution as a historical reality
in Russia when they defended the necessity of terrorism. The
absolute power which had been exercised by the Tsars and which
the Bolsheviks had acquired through the revolution was not the
economic power of capital envisioned by Marx but the absolute
power of life and death.

The people's sovereignty over life and the citizen's right to life
seem in effect to be alternative and mutually exclusive solutions
to the same problem, the problem which Hegel was to formulate
when he said that death is the sovereign master. The political
embodiment of the problem was the absolute power of life and
death possessed by the absolute monarchs of Eastern and Western
Europe, and the political embodiments of the solutions are the
revolutionary societies which have come into existence in Europe
and America, some of them representing the popular acquisition
of absolute power and others the popular limitation of political
power. The inalienable sovereignty over life and the inalienable
right to life, while contrasting in this manner, are both forms of
autonomy or inalienability, the alienation excluded in both cases
being the alienation which exists under absolute monarchy where
men are subject to an absolute power of life and death. The
solution, however, which instead of limiting the power of life
and death would place it unlimited in the hands of the people
must be construed as posing the problem all over again in a new
form unless being in the hands of the people means that the
power will cease to be exercised and that the state will cease to
exist in the future.

[4] *Openness to the Future*

"The future," Albert Camus said, "is the only transcendent value for men without God."[54] That there is still a transcendent value for men who would be autonomous, however, means that autonomy does not satisfy them completely and that there is a basis in their experience for a critique of autonomy. Nietzsche, sensing this, attempted to eliminate the transcendent value of the future by affirming the eternal recurrence of all events and thereby identifying the future with the past, but he was aware that this doctrine, however necessary it might be for a consistent and complete ideal of autonomy, would never be accepted by modern man. He could only look forward to the coming of a type of man who would be truly autonomous, the "superman" or "overman" (*Übermensch*), a man who would will to recur eternally, a man who could look back over the events of his life and say "once more."[55] Meanwhile, looking forward to the future in this manner, Nietzsche showed that he himself still experienced the future as a transcendent value and that he had not been able to assimilate personally his doctrine of eternal recurrence though he saw its logical necessity for an autonomy that would be perfect.

If autonomy is the modern myth, the experience of the transcendent value of the future is the modern mysticism and is the basis for the criticism of the modern myth. The great critic of autonomy, though his criticism of the modern myth is not as thoroughgoing as Plato's criticism of the Greek myth or Augustine's criticism of the Roman myth, has been Kant. Autonomous reason is criticized in Kant's *Critique of Pure Reason* and autonomous conscience is criticized in his *Critique of Practical Reason* and in both the ultimate basis of the criticism is the experience of transcendent value. Kant published his critiques in the years immediately preceding the French Revolution and thus before autonomy had become an important political reality on the continent of Europe. His criticism of autonomy, as a result, moves upon purely religious and intellectual planes and lacks the historical and political dimensions which are to be found in the critical thinking of Plato and Augustine. Incomplete as they are for this and other reasons, his insights into the religious and intellectual foundations of autonomy and into the experience of transcendent value nevertheless suggest the lines of the more radical sort of criticism that is in order since autonomy has become political and especially now since the attempt has 'been made in totalitarianism to suppress all transcendent value.

Because Kant more than any other was responsible for introducing the terms "autonomy" and "autonomous" into the technical vocabulary of modern philosophy and because he was at pains to show how much autonomy could be ascribed to reason and conscience, he could easily be taken, and is often taken, for the author rather than the critic of autonomy. That he was the critic rather than the author can be ascertained by comparing him with his rationalist predecessors and successors. He was concerned to prove against his predecessors, especially Wolff, that the intelligibility of things to human reason is not the foundation of their possibility but that human reason is autonomous only with respect to phenomena, things as they appear to us, and not with respect to noumena, things as they are in themselves. His successors, when they denied the distinction between noumena and phenomena and when Hegel in particular asserted that "the rational alone is real," were maintaining against Kant the absolute autonomy of reason and were upholding the thesis that human reason is the measure of all reality.

The autonomy of reason, as Kant understood it, was, in accord with the etymology *autos* "self" and *nomos* "law," the normative or legislative function of reason, the activity of reason imposing order upon things rather than having order imposed upon it by things. Since a man uses one and the same faculty of reason to understand the divers and sundry things that make up his world, an order that consists in uniformity will appear to be something that his reason has imposed upon things, whereas an order that consists in variety will appear to be something that things have imposed upon his reason. The hierarchical order of things postulated in medieval worldviews consisted in variety and on that account appeared to be something imposed upon human reason by things themselves. As this type of order was gradually discredited, however, and gradually replaced with the rise of modern science by an order consisting in uniformity the impression was created that things had to conform to human reason rather than human reason to things. Thus Kant has it that the rise and progress of science was the result of reason learning from nature no longer as a pupil learns from a teacher, accepting whatever the teacher chooses to say, but as a judge learns from a witness, compelling the witness to answer the questions which he proposes to him.[56]

The critique of autonomous reason, as it was carried out by Kant, amounted to showing how reason can exercise autonomy only over things as they appear to us, not over things as they are in themselves. The new uniformistic worldviews which in the seventeenth and eighteenth century were called "systems of the world" became untenable, according to Kant, as soon as they were taken for systems of things as they are in themselves rather than as systems of things as they appear to us. Newton's system of the world, the most important example, if space and time were to be taken for the "sensorium of God"[57] as Newton himself wanted them taken, would have to be considered a system of things as they appear to God, that is, a system of things as they are in themselves. If, on the contrary, space and time were to be taken for our own sensorium, then Newton's system would have to be considered simply a system of things as they appear to us. Kant endeavored to show that space and time are actually our own sensorium, not our sense organs or our sensory apparatus, to be sure, but the forms of our sensory intuition, the general subjective conditions of our sense perceptions.[58]

This doctrine of the subjectivity of space and time seems to be akin to the post-Newtonian doctrine of the relativity of space and time (perhaps to be conceived as a doctrine of the intersubjectivity of space and time) and seems to have really been what Kant believed it to be, a new Copernican Revolution in thought.[59] There is some parallel, in fact, with all three of the revolutions in thought which Freud was afterward to regard as the great blows to man's self-love,[60] the Copernican, the Darwin-

ian, and the Freudian, for each one of them involved at least a
partial critique of reason's autonomy along these lines. In the
Copernican view there was at least the realization that the
Ptolemaic system was simply a system of things as they appear
to an observer on earth, though there was not a correspondingly
clear realization that the Copernican system itself was not a
system of things as they are in themselves but only a system of
things as they would appear to an hypothetical observer on the
sun. In the Lamarckian and Darwinian views there was at least
the realization that the Linnean system was simply a classifica-
tion of species as they appear to observers in the present, though
there was not a correspondingly clear realization that the
Lamarckian and Darwinian theories themselves were not accounts of the ultimate origin of species rivaling the doctrine of
creation but only accounts of the origins of species as they would
have appeared to hypothetical observers in the past. In the
Freudian view there was at least the realization that former
psychologies were simply systems of things as they appear in
consciousness, though there was not a correspondingly clear
realization that Freudian psychology itself was not a system of
things as they are independently of consciousness but only a
system of things as they appear when what is ordinarily unconscious becomes conscious.

In the Kantian view itself, if we may turn the comparison
around full circle, there was at least the realization that reason
exercises autonomy only over things as they appear to us, though
there was not a correspondingly clear realization that the Kantian
system was not a system of the possibilities of reason in itself but
only a system of the possibilities of reason as they had been revealed in its actual exercise of autonomy. Kant realized that the
self and the world in itself are ideals by which reason can measure
the shortcomings of its achievements in imposing order upon the
phenomena of internal and external experience and that God
is an ideal by which reason can measure the limitations of its
possibilities as a mind imposing order. What he did not realize,
it seems, is something which is suggested by the subsequent history of science, namely, that the achievements of autonomous

reason are never more than provisional and that its possibilities are to approximate its ideals indefinitely, and therefore that the ideals of reason are more definite than its possibilities and more definitive than its achievements.

Kant believed instead that the results of the science of his day were final and that his own list of reason's possibilities was complete, and so he came to consider the ideals of reason merely hypothetical except insofar as they became ideals of the will and thereby ends in themselves. The subsequent history of science, a history of periodic revision, creates the impression rather that if anything it is the ideals of reason, the norms which preside over the revisions, that are certain and finally reliable, not the tentative results and the incomplete lists of possibilities. If Kant did not realize that the ideals were to be approximated indefinitely as ideals of reason, however, he did realize that they were to be approximated indefinitely as ideals of the will. An infinite future would be required, he maintained,[61] to attain perfect conformity to the ideals of the will, to overcome desire so completely as to be able to treat the self, the world of selves or free persons, and God purely as ends in themselves.

The autonomy of conscience, the ability of reason to impose its ideals upon the will, is limited therefore, according to Kant, by the transcendence or futurity of the ideals. Since he saw this futurity in the ideals only as ideals of the will and not as ideals of reason, he attempted to base religion on conscience rather than on revelation and envisioned the history of Christianity in his *Religion within the Limits of Reason* as a gradual advance from a religion of revelation to a religion of conscience. There was in his thinking, in spite of this, a basis for making sense of the notion of revelation, namely, the idea which he expounds in his *Critique of Judgement* that reason is able not only to impose uniform order upon phenomena but also to recognize its ideals, the noumena, in the phenomena, specifically to recognize beauty and purpose. The idea of the noumena being recognizable in the phenomena in its widest application becomes the idea that nature and history are revelation and in its highest application becomes the idea that God is recognizable in Christ. As it was, Kant was content to limit the pretensions of a religion of autonomous conscience such as Rousseau's by a doctrine of the will's inability to conform perfectly to the ideals imposed on it by conscience,[62] a surrogate of the doctrine of man's helplessness apart from Christ.

The religion of autonomous conscience, however, possessed a political significance with which Kant did not much concern himself. Political autonomy had been understood from the first to be autonomy of conscience: the Puritans could not submit to the king, they had argued, because this would have been to subordinate to him their consciences, and the king in turn could not submit to the parliament, Charles I had argued, because this would have been to subordinate to them his conscience.[63] The Jacobins could not agree to accept even a merely constitutional monarch, they argued, because moral freedom, as Rousseau had said, was "obedience to a law which we prescribe to ourselves"[64] and was therefore something which could not exist where the sovereignty of the people was limited. Louis XVI in turn could not agree to be merely a constitutional monarch, though he accepted rather unwillingly the constitution of 1791, because this, he argued, took away his ability to prevent evil in his kingdom and to do the good that was in his heart, his freedom to carry out the basic dictates of his conscience as king.[65]

If the struggle between royal absolutism and popular absolutism resolved in this manner into a struggle between autonomous consciences, a struggle to see whose conscience should be what Milton called the "master conscience"[66] in the kingdom, then a critique of autonomous conscience would necessarily be also a critique of political autonomy. Kant's critique of autonomous conscience was a criticism of Rousseau's "obedience to a law which we prescribe to ourselves," and since moral liberty so defined existed, according to Rousseau, only in civil society, could not help being, in spite of Kant's unconcern with its political significance, an implicit criticism of Rousseau's conception of sovereignty. The point of the critique, moreover, that the ideals of the will require an infinite future for their attainment was to some extent discovered anyway by the moderates in the revolu-

tionary movements, by the Whigs and the Girondins, who sensed
the need of an indefinite future for the achievement of their
aims and placed their best hopes in posterity rather than in the
present.[67] The futurity of the ideals was for Kant, however, the
proof of the immortality of the human spirit, the proof that the
human spirit does have an infinite future ahead of it, a future
which by contrast with mere posterity means that death will never
be fully answered through autonomy.

The reply to the mysticism of posterity and to the mysticism of
the immortal spirit was to identify the future with death so that
openness of the spirit toward the future should become openness
toward death and should thus collapse once more into autonomy.
The reply was offered not only in the form of a new and more
uncompromising absolutism of the spirit, that of Hegelianism,
but in the form of a new and more uncompromising political
absolutism, that of totalitarianism. It has been said that when the
two chief forms of totalitarianism, Hitlerism and Stalinism, met
on the battlefield in the Second World War, right-wing Hegelianism met left-wing Hegelianism.[68] The kinship of both forms of
totalitarianism with Hegelianism, though, seems to go deeper
than the borrowing of Hegelian language and seems to be founded
not on something borrowed from the Hegelians but on something
shared with them, an attitude toward death. There was in Hitlerism an openness toward death which clothed itself in the symbolism of the old Teutonic myth of the "twilight of the gods," the
Ragnarök of the Eddas or the *Götterdämmerung* of Wagner's
Ring cycle, a use of pagan symbolism where Hegel had used the
Christian symbolism of the death of God but a symbolism which
was effective enough to inspire the suicide of Hitler and his
associates in their moment of final defeat in 1945. And there was
in Stalinism an openness toward death less dramatically clothed
in symbolism but nonetheless real enough to inspire the public
self-accusation and what seem to have been the truly voluntary
deaths of the victims of the Stalinist terror which lasted from
1936 to 1939.

Totalitarianism, if the standpoint taken here is correct, consists essentially in an attitude toward death, an attitude fore-

shadowed in Saint-Just's exclamation "If Brutus does not kill others, he will kill himself" and inspired ultimately by a desire to have life at one's disposal. To have life at one's disposal, however, solves the problem posed by one's alienation to death only by making one a killer and thus posing the problem of death in a new form. The revulsion which has in fact been aroused by totalitarianism may be greater than that aroused by the earlier Jacobin and Bolshevik reigns of terror and may be sufficient to set man in search of a solution to the problem of death which will render reigns of terror politically impossible, a myth like that of inalienable life or perhaps an entirely new myth. Meanwhile the terms of the problem to which totalitarianism and earlier reigns of terror answered are being abolished as modern mysticism develops in the direction of what has come to be called "eschatology." The futurity of God, the world, and the self, according to Kant's thinking, is their immortality, but their futurity recognized in the phenomena of their mortality is their resurrection.

NOTES TO CHAPTER NINE

1. Leviathan, 17.

2. Albert Camus, *The Rebel* (New York, 1956), 121.

3. On Louis XVI cf. Camus, *loc. cit.* Charles I was imaged this way in the *Eikon Basilike* or *The King's Book*, "The Portraiture of his Sacred Majesty in his Solitudes and Sufferings," which was written in his name and which appeared ten days after his execution.

4. Cf. Nietzsche, *Thus Spake Zarathustra*, I, 21, "On Free Death."

5. Meditations, II, 11.

6. The Gay Science, 125.

7. Thus Spake Zarathustra, II, 2.

8. Matthew 27:46, Mark 15:34. From Psalm 22:1.

9. Cf. E. Allison Peers, *The Complete Works of St. John of the Cross* (London, 1953), mainly *The Dark Night of the Soul* (in vol. I, 325 ff.), also *The Spiritual Canticle*, 1 (on the hidden God) (vol. II, 187 ff.), and *The Ascent of Mount Carmel*, II, 8 (on Christ's abandonment on the cross) (vol. I, 87).

10. Cf. *Pensées* (Brunschvicg's numbering), 441 (the "lost God"); 585 (the hidden God and true religion); 242; 288; 428; and 548 f.

11. For the Catholic doctrine on the uncertainty of one's justification cf. The Council of Trent, Session VI, chapter 9 in H. Denzinger, C. Bannwart, J. B. Umberg, *Enchiridion Symbolorum* (Barcelona, 1948) #802 (p. 289). Cf.

also *ibid.*, chapter 12 (#805, p. 291) on the uncertainty of one's predestination. Compare St. John of the Cross in *The Dark Night of the Soul*, II, 5 and 6 (Peers, vol. I, 383 ff.) on how the soul undergoing the dark night feels that God is against it and that it has set itself against God.

12. Cf. Luther's commentary on Psalm 22: 1 in *Opera* (Jena, 1566), II, 227 ff., and Calvin's *Institutes of the Christian Religion*, II, 16, 10 ff.

13. On the two theologies, the "theology of the cross" and the "theology of glory," cf. the *Heidelberg Disputation*, 19 ff. and *Explanations of the Ninety-five Theses*, 58 in Jaroslav Pelikan and Helmut T. Lehman, *Luther's Works*, vol. XXXI (Philadelphia, 1957), 52 ff. and 225 ff. For Luther's thinking about the experiences of the dying and for the connection he sees between these and his own experiences cf. *Explanations of the Ninety-five Theses*, 14 and especially 15 (*ibid.*, 128 ff.). Also note how in his commentary on Psalm 22 (cited in note 12) he treats the doctrine of Christ's abandonment on the cross as "solid food" for the strong who have suffered greatly not "milk" for the weak in faith who have suffered little.

14. *Op. cit.*, III, 4, 32 ff. on Christ's sufferings cf. *loc. cit.* in note 12.

15. Hegel, *The Phenomenology of Mind* tr. by J. B. Baillie (London, 1961), 753 and 782. Cf. *ibid.*, 808 (the last page) on the "Golgotha of absolute spirit." Cf. *The Spirit of Christianity and Its Fate* in Hegel, *Early Theological Writings* tr. by T. M. Knox (Chicago, 1948), 291 ff. on the resurrection of Jesus as anticlimax, and references *ibid.*, 38 f., by Richard Kroner to "infinite grief" and "absolute suffering."

16. Cf. *The Phenomenology of Mind*, 561 ff. (on the Enlightenment as a movement against superstition), 590 ff. (on the truth of the Enlightenment), and 750 ff. (on revealed religion, i.e. on the Christianity of the Reformation). Cf. also Hegel's *Philosophy of History* tr. by J. Sibree (New York, 1956), 412 ff. (on the Reformation and the Enlightenment).

17. *The Phenomenology of Mind*, 237.

18. *Ibid.*, 135.

19. *Thus Spake Zarathustra*, I, 9. Cf. what he says *ibid.*, 21, advocating "free death."

20. The first antiphon of first Vespers on the feasts of the Holy Cross (May 3 and September 14).

21. *Il.*, IX, 159.

22. "To the Praise of the Dead," 1 and 7; "The First Anniversary," 56 and 63.

23. *King Lear*, 4, 6, 138 f.

24. Cf. Calvin's explanation of "Thy kingdom come" and "Thy will be done" in *op. cit.*, III, 20, 42 and 43, where he makes it clear that the kingdom is not the universal sovereignty and that the will is not the secret will which is always done.

25. Cf. Romans 5:14 ("death reigned from Adam to Moses") and 5:21 ("as sin reigned unto death so grace should reign through justice unto eternal life"). Cf. also I Corinthians 15:26 on death as the "last enemy."

26. *Op. cit.*, III, 23, 7. Cf. what Calvin says on the "instrumentality of the wicked employed by God while he continues free from every taint," *ibid.*, I, 18.

27. *Op. cit.*, 38.

28. *Op. cit.*, III, 23, 2. Also *ibid.*, I, 17, 2.

29. The Works of John Locke (London, 1824), vol. VI, 6.

30. Second Treatise on Civil Government, 1.

31. Ibid., 19. On the appeal to heaven cf. also *ibid.,* 3; 14; and 16.

32. Ibid., 7 (preservation of property as the purpose of this power); 5 (dominion of man over world). On the latter point cf. the argument of his *First Treatise on Civil Government* (against Filmer).

33. Rousseau, Social Contract, II, 5.

34. Ibid., I, 6 (citizen and subject); II, 1 (sovereignty as exercise of the general will).

35. Ibid., III, 11 (death of the body politic); IV, 1 (general will indestructible); II, 3 (general will infallible).

36. Cf. his "Profession of Faith of the Savoyard Vicar" in *Emile, IV.*

37. Cf. Hegel's *Philosophy of Right* tr. by T. M. Knox (Oxford, 1953), 33 and 156 f. Cf. also Hegel's discussion of "absolute freedom and terror" in the *Phenomenology of Mind,* 599 ff., a critique of Rousseauism and the French revolutionary "reign of terror."

38. Philosophy of Right, 157. Cf. also Hegel's discussion of the "cunning of reason" in history in his *Philosophy of History,* 33, and what is said about it above in Chapter Three, Section 2.

39. Luther, *The Freedom of a Christian* in Pelikan and Lehman, *op. cit.,* 348 and 355.

40. Political power is defined by Marx as the "organized force of society" and force is said to be "itself an economic power" in *Capital* tr. by Edward Aveling and Samuel Moore (Chicago, 1906), 823 f.

41. The process by which the classless society comes into being is described dramatically in the *Communist Manifesto* but more soberly in *Capital,* 834 ff.

42. Social Contract, III, 11.

43. Cf. the debates of the Puritan army leaders on these ideas in A. S. P. Woodhouse, *Puritanism and Liberty* (London, 1938) where there are also included other documents reflecting Puritan views of liberty.

44. Eikon Basilike or *The King's Book* ed. by Edward Almack (London, 1903), especially chapter 10 (p. 46), also chapters 11 and 15. Cf. the corresponding chapters of Milton's *Eikonoklastes.*

45. For the history of this passage cf. Carl Becker, *The Declaration of Independence* (New York, 1933), 142 ff.

46. Cf. Locke's discussion of life and liberty in terms of the problem of slavery in *Second Treatise on Civil Government,* 4. Contrast Rousseau, *Social Contract,* II, 5.

47. Cf. J. H. Stewart, *A Documentary Survey of the French Revolution* (New York, 1951), 113 (Declaration of 1789); 234 (Constitution of 1791); 457 (Declaration of 1793).

48. Ibid., 115.

49. Robespierre's address to the National Convention on February 5, 1794, in *Choix de rapports, opinions et discours prononcés à la tribune nationale,* vol. XIV (Paris, 1821), 19.

50. Saint-Just's letter to Vilain d'Aubigny, July, 1792, in Geoffrey Bruun, *Saint-Just* (New York, 1932), 22 f. Cf. the discussion of the terror in Camus, *op. cit.,* 125 ff.

51. Cf. Camus, *op. cit.,* 149 ff.

52. Cf. Leon Trotsky, *Lenin* (New York, 1925), 133 f.

53. Karl Kautsky, *The Dictatorship of the Proletariat* tr. by H. J. Stenning (London, 1919), answered by Lenin, *The Proletarian Revolution and Kautsky the Renegade* (New York, 1920), and Kautsky, *Terrorism and Communism* tr. by W. H. Kerridge (London, 1920), answered by Trotsky, *Terrorism and Communism* (Ann Arbor, 1961).

54. *Op. cit.,* 166.

55. The doctrine of the eternal recurrence is the main theme of *Thus Spake Zarathustra,* III, especially 2; 3; 13; 15; 16; also IV, 9; 10; 19. Cf. Karl Löwith, "Nietzsche's Revival of the Doctrine of Eternal Recurrence" in his *Meaning in History* (Chicago, 1949), 214 ff.

56. *Critique of Pure Reason,* preface to the second edition, tr. by F. Max Müller (New York, 1961), 504.

57. Newton sets forth this idea in the "General Scholium" to his *Principia* (second edition), and in the "Queries" appended to his *Optiks.* Cf. Alexander Koyré, *From the Closed World to the Infinite Universe* (Baltimore, 1957), 208 f.; 219; 221 ff.; and especially 235 ff.

58. This is the thesis of the "Transcendental Aesthetic," the starting point of the *Critique of Pure Reason,* 37 ff.

59. In the preface to the second edition of the *Critique of Pure Reason,* 505, Kant after speaking of the Copernican Revolution says "a similar experiment may be tried in metaphysic so far as the *intuition* of objects is concerned." This passage indicates that Kant's own Copernican Revolution consisted, as he understood it, in the viewpoint on intuition adopted in the Transcendental Aesthetic and thus in the doctrine of the subjectivity of space and time. For the concordance of the subjectivity of time with the relativity of time cf. Kurt Gödel, "A Remark about the Relationship between Relativity Theory and Idealistic Philosophy" in P. A. Schilpp, *Albert Einstein,* vol. II (New York, 1959), 555 ff. The idea of relativity is an idea of intersubjectivity if by "intersubjectivity" one understands a unity of human experience such that one can extrapolate from one person's experience to any other person's experience. The theory of relativity is concerned, of course, only with external experience or observation not with internal experience or consciousness, but it is concerned with the possibility of extrapolating from one observer's external experience to that of another.

60. Freud, "A Difficulty in the Path of Psychoanalysis" (1917) in James Strachey, *The Complete Psychological Works of Sigmund Freud,* vol. XVII (London, 1957), 139 ff.

61. This conception appears in his discussion of immortality as a postulate of conscience in the *Critique of Practical Reason* tr. by L. W. Beck (New York, 1956), 126 ff.

62. This conception appears in his discussion of "radical evil" in human nature in *Religion within the Limits of Reason* tr. by T. M. Greene and H. H. Hudson (New York, 1960), 15 ff.

63. Compare the *Eikon Basilike* and Milton's *Eikonoklastes,* especially chapters 1; 2; 6; 11; 15; and 19 of both works.

64. *Social Contract,* I, 8.

65. Cf. Louis' proclamation of June 20, 1791 in J. H. Stewart, *op. cit.,* 210,

and also cf. Louis' testament in S. K. Padover, *The Life and Death of Louis XVI* (New York, 1939), 341.

66. *Eikonoklastes,* 2 and also 11 ("universal conscience").

67. Cf. Carl Becker's chapter on the "Uses of Posterity" in his *Heavenly City of the Eighteenth Century Philosophers* (New Haven, 1932), 119 ff.

68. Cf. Ernst Cassirer, *The Myth of the State* (New Haven, 1961), 249.

CHAPTER TEN

The City of the Gods

THE history of hitherto existing society is the history of a struggle for life. This struggle, though, has not been the struggle among races or among classes which it is supposed to have been according to the totalitarian ideologies. Rather it has been a struggle of all human beings against the common nemesis of every human life, a struggle to overcome death. The shadowed figure of Gilgamesh roaming over the wasteland in search of the means of indefinitely prolonging life is the figure of man himself wandering through these many centuries in quest of immortality.

The indefinite prolongation of life, it is true, though it has always remained the ideal, has never, at least by an entire society, been seriously considered feasible. The problem of death has ordinarily been cast instead into some such form as the following: "If I must some day die, what can I do to satisfy my desire to live?" To solve the problem of death even in this form, nevertheless, would be to solve all the fundamental problems of life. The three questions in which Kant believed the whole interest of human reason, whether speculative or practical, was concentrated, "What can I know?," "What should I do?," and "What may I hope?,"[1] would all be answered. What I can know, if I know what I can do to satisfy my desire to live, is the meaning of life and death, the "how" of life and the "why" of death. What I should do or try to do, knowing this, is what I can do to satisfy my desire to live and not what I cannot do if I must some day die. What I may hope, knowing this and doing this, is not indeed that I may escape death but that I may, notwithstanding death, satisfy my desire for life.

The oldest solution to the problem of death posed in this form would be the solution which is alluded to in Genesis 3:20 where it is said that Adam, after being excluded from the garden of paradise and the tree of life and thus from the possibility of actually prolonging his life indefinitely, began to call his wife Eve or Life because she was the mother of all the living, the substitute, we might say, for the inaccessible tree of life.[2] The many metamorphoses of the mother of the living from the figurines of the mother which date from Paleolithic times to the highly developed cult of the great mother goddess which existed in Neolithic times and lasted into early historical times are difficult to trace, but her aspect in early historical times in the cities of Mesopotamia, the first times for which there are written records, is somewhat sinister, like that of Eve offering to share with Adam the forbidden knowledge of good and evil. The first cities, being temple communities, were places where mortals were thought to consort with immortals, where human kings consorted with the divine mother, sharing not only the experience of life but also the experience of death, and where the generality of mankind, often by participating vicariously in the experience of a king, acquired the knowledge of life and death which was thought to belong to the gods.

The shared experience of life and death, cultivated as it was in these first cities, could well be considered a solution to the basic problems of life since it yielded an insight into the "how" of life and the "why" of death, a measure of what man could know, and since the knowledge of life and death was a knowledge of good and evil, a measure of what man should do, and since knowing life and death or knowing good and evil was consorting with the gods, a measure of what man might hope. By giving men a foretaste of death, on the other hand, this experience could provoke them as it did Gilgamesh to seek all the more urgently and desperately for a means of prolonging life. Gilgamesh, according to the ancient epic, witnessed and vicariously experienced the death of his best friend at the instance of the deadly mother goddess and this is what set him on his unsuccessful quest for immortality. What his quest expressed was the conscious longing for renewed youth and everlasting life which was generated in the first cities by the shared experience of death, but what his failure expressed was the realization generated by that same experience that this longing was vain.

The longing for bodily immortality met with something more nearly approaching gratification at this time or soon afterward in the kingdom of Egypt—not that mummies were thought literally to go on eating and drinking and making merry in their pyramids, but that identity was believed to consist in physical individuality and was thought therefore to be conserved as long as the body was preserved in the tomb. The spiritual essence of survival, according to this view, was the participation of the dead in the life of the living, a participation which was brought about by the living appropriating the experience which had belonged to the dead. The living king lived the life which had been lived by the dead king and the people shared vicariously in the experience of the king. Given such a unity of experience or of spirit, it was necessary only to preserve the bodily individuality of the dead or at any rate the bodily individuality of the dead king in order to compass the personal immortality of the king and the vicarious immortality of the people.

What a man could know, according to this philosophy of life and death, was what could be learned from the experience of those who had lived before him. What he had to do was repeat that past experience in the present experience of his life. And what he might hope was that his present experience would be repeated by those who were to come in the future. The weakness in the view was that the cycle of experience might be interrupted, that the experience of the past might not be repeated in the present or if it were, might yet not be repeated in the future. Such interruptions did occur in the three great interregna in the history of Egypt, the one between the Old Kingdom and the Middle Kingdom, the one between the Middle Kingdom and the New Kingdom or Empire, and the final one which followed upon the decline and fall of the Empire. The tombs were despoiled and a general spirit of disillusionment prevailed, especially in the first interregnum, and men felt themselves cut off from the past and the future, isolated in the present, and forced in their hopelessness to make the most of the passing moment.

The sense of man's mortality which thus arose in the Mesopotamian attempt to achieve intercourse between men and gods and in the Egyptian attempt to achieve intercourse between the living and the dead was paralleled elsewhere by positive doubt as to whether men could consort with gods at all and whether the dead could consort with the living at all. Cities which had once been conceived as cities of gods and men began to be conceived simply as cities of men, and kingdoms which had once been conceived as kingdoms of the living and the dead began to be conceived simply as kingdoms of the living. Wars which had been fought between cities over the presence of the great mother goddess, when the king ceased to be the human consort of the goddess and the city ceased to be a place where men consorted with gods and became simply a place where human beings consorted with one another, were succeeded by wars fought over purely human causes. The war described in the *Iliad*, for example, which had been a sacred war fought over a Helen who was a goddess became in Homer's account an essentially profane war fought over a Helen who was only a beautiful woman.

When the cause of war ceased to be divine and became purely human, ceased to be a goddess and became merely a woman, war ceased to make apparent sense and became, at least ostensibly, nothing better than a way of dying, became in fact an object of parody. The argument of the *Iliad* was not so much the Trojan War fought over Helen as the parody of the Trojan War fought over the slave girl Briseis which Homer actually narrated in detail. If the parody was deliberate, as there is every reason to suppose it was, then it reflected solutions to the problems of life somewhat different from those which had obtained until then in the civilized world. If men could not consort with gods, as indeed they could not in the Homeric view, then they might not reasonably hope for more than a mortal happiness. If they might not reasonably hope for more than this, then they had ought to make the most of their lives and, as the parody of the Trojan War implied, not squander them in foolish wars. And

if they had ought to do this, then they had to be able to recognize
their own blindness, as Homer's characters eventually did, to
the worthlessness of the causes for which they lived and died.

It might appear from this that in the Homeric philosophy of
life and in the society which it reflects the attempt to solve the
problem of death was actually abandoned. This impression could
be strengthened by comparing the *Epic of Gilgamesh* and the
Odyssey. Where Gilgamesh had wandered in search of everlasting
life and had returned home only because he failed to find what
he sought, Odysseus wandered in search of home and positively
rejected the offer of everlasting life when it was made to him by
the goddess Calypso. In rejecting the chance for immortality
Odysseus showed his discrimination between life and happiness,
between a blind desire to live and a rational desire to be happy.
To have remained with Calypso on her deserted island would
have meant the indefinite prolongation of his life but this, since
he was unhappy in her company and was pining for home and
the company of his own wife, Penelope, would have meant only
an indefinite prolongation of misery. He chose, therefore, to be
happy and die rather than to be unhappy and live forever.

If the choice made by Odysseus was the choice made by Homeric
society, however, what was really abandoned in that society was
not the effort to solve the problem of death so much as a particular solution to the problem. When happiness is defined as the
fulfillment of desire, its definition remains indeterminate until
desire is specified. But when desire is specified, whether it be the
desire to live with the gods or the desire to live with human
beings, it invariably turns out to be a form of the desire to live.
A desire to be happy, therefore, like that which led Odysseus
through all his wanderings and searchings cannot be set against
the desire to live except as another form of that same desire. The
problem of death, "If I must some day die, what can I do to
satisfy my desire to live?", was thus a problem in Homeric society
no less than it had been in the first civilized societies. Only the
solution to the problem in Homeric society was changed. Intercourse with the gods, the solution on which the first cities had
been founded, was exchanged for intercourse with human beings.

The city of men proved in the outcome to be as much a city of immortals as the city of gods and men had been, for as the human community came to be defined by a common past rather than by a common dwelling place what had at first been only immortal fame and survival in memory became the immortal past and unchangeable history. The immortality of the past meant that a man was his life, that his life was a series of deeds, that these deeds once done could never be undone. It meant that a city was its history, that its history was a series of events, that these events no matter what should become of the city in the future would never cease to have happened. Man, though mortal, was as immortal as his deeds, according to this, and the city, though destined to decline and fall, was as eternal as its history. The men whose lives were written by Plutarch were men who learned their values from the immortal deeds of those who had lived before them, who did noble deeds knowing that neither noble nor ignoble deeds can ever be undone, and who hoped by their deeds to create in their turn an immortal past for those who would live after them. The cities whose histories were narrated by Herodotus and Thucydides were urban republics in which the desire to live was the desire to be happy but in which men judged freedom to be happiness, as Pericles said, and courage to be freedom, and in which war therefore was no longer a mere way of dying but once again and in a new manner a way of winning immortality.

The tragedy of the immortal past was that man, while he could do noble deeds, could never undo ignoble deeds, that Oedipus, for example, no matter what he did could never undo the deed of killing his father and marrying his mother. Aeschylus, Sophocles, and especially Euripides, therefore, while deriving tragic effect from the immortality of the past, began to experiment in drama with the idea of the immortal deed, to allow the furies pursuing the parricide or the matricide to be placated, to allow the gods to intervene and do what even the gods were supposed to be unable to do, undo the deed which has been done. Socrates went further, maintaining that virtue consisted in knowledge rather than in deeds, in knowing what one was doing rather than in simply doing. Plato went still further, distinguishing between time and eternity, maintaining that time continually lapsed into nothingness, that time was only a changing image of eternity, a changing present the past of which no longer existed and the future of which did not yet exist. With Euripides it began to be doubtful whether the deeds constituting the immortal past could ever be undone, with Socrates it began to be doubtful whether it was important that they could or could not be undone, with Plato it began to be doubtful whether the past was immortal at all.

If the Homeric philosophy of life and death did not involve an abandonment of the attempt to solve the problem of death, the Socratic and Platonic philosophy did. The Socratic and Platonic answer to the question "If I must some day die, what can I do to satisfy my desire to live?" was in effect "Nothing," for in Socratism and Platonism man was called upon to renounce the will to live and to engage in what Plato had Socrates call the "practice of dying." There is a resemblance between this and the standpoint of Eastern mysticism, of Buddhism and Hinduism, according to which life is pervaded with suffering, the cause of suffering is the will to live, and the renunciation of the will to live can alone give release. Positions of this sort which are solutions to the problem of suffering or which involve at any rate the renunciation of the will to live might well be called forms of "mysticism," while positions which are solutions to the problem of death and which suppose therefore an unrenounced will to live might well be called forms of "myth." The problems of life have their solutions in mysticism no less than in myth, but the solutions, since the will to live is renounced, are somewhat disparate. What man could know, according to Socrates, was not the meaning of life and death or the nature of good and evil but only his own ignorance of that meaning and that nature. What he had ought to do, therefore, was not attempt to satisfy his blind will to live but engage in the practice of detaching himself from it. And what he might hope, according to Plato, was not to enjoy an earthly immortality but to enjoy the immortality of the spirit.

A serious attempt was made to found a society on mysticism during the age of savior kings initiated by Alexander the Great,

the Hellenistic kings who were Alexander's successors in the
portions of Europe, Asia, and Africa which he had conquered
being in theory and sometimes in practice approximations to the
ideal of the philosopher king which had developed out of the
thought of Socrates, Plato, and Aristotle and which was elaborated
by the Stoics during the Alexandrian age itself. The deification
of Alexander and his successors enacted by the Greek cities, a
piece of mythmaking by which mysticism was translated into
myth, was a recognition in law that they were above the law,
something which only gods could legally be, like the rulers described in Plato's *Statesman* and Aristotle's *Politics,* the law
being conceived as the immortal and normative past of the city
and the laws of other peoples under the sway of these kings being
conceived on the analogy of Greek law as the respective past
and traditions of each of those peoples. If the Hellenistic rulers
could have actually attained the mystical emancipation implied
in their condition of being above the law it might have been
possible for their subjects to participate in it vicariously and to
taste something like the immortality of the spirit, but as it was
the Hellenistic peoples were not really raised above the ways of
life embodied in their laws, ways of life which were essentially
solutions to the problem of death.

What change there was in ways of life was due largely to mixing
one way with another, a process which continued under Roman
rule and which resulted eventually in a new and common way of
life. In the Roman republic as in the Greek republics law had
been the immortal and normative past of the city, but in the
Roman Empire, though the empire was being built in the days
of the republic and its building was conceived to be a series of
immortal deeds, law gradually ceased to be the peculiar tradition
of Rome and more and more became an embodiment of the ways
common to all the various peoples living under Roman rule.
This was a process partly of Roman ways being imposed on other
peoples, partly of the ways of other peoples being adopted by
the Romans, partly of the ways of diverse non-Roman peoples
being mixed with one another. The uniformity of life, though
it was never actually perfect in the Roman Empire, became a

new solution to the problem of death according to which life was a series of experiences instead of a series of deeds, the series of experiences was a gamut which every man who lived a normal lifetime could run, and running the gamut of experience was the equivalent of living at any and every place and time.

After some centuries, however, the uniformity of human life began to seem purely conventional and the ubiquity and eternity of the Roman Empire which had been predicated upon it began to seem correspondingly fictitious. It became necessary ultimately to abandon the whole idea of a uniform way of life and to reorganize society on a highly differentiated and hierarchical pattern. It was thought possible nevertheless to preserve the idea of ubiquitous and eternal empire by construing the empire to be the rule of an ubiquitous and eternal God. Since this God, as Christ had argued against the Sadducees, was God of the living and not of the dead, a God to whom the dead were alive, he was not compatible as the gods of the living and the gods of the dead had been with human solutions to the problem of death. And no doubt it was partly for lack of a strictly human solution that Christianity was officially accepted. But the fateful step which was taken when the Roman Empire was construed to be the city of God made it necessary from then on to assimilate God either to the gods of the living or to the gods of the dead in order to make death seem a humanly soluble problem.

Initially God was made to replace the gods of the living and to ensure the continuity of society and eventually on this basis, too, late to save the Roman Empire but in time to build its medieval successor, an answer to death was found in the hierarchical structure of society. The answer was the immortality of status in a society in which every man had a special status, in which every man's identity consisted in his status, and in which every man's status or identity persisted after his death. What a man had been expected to know in the uniform society of the early Roman Empire was what could be learned from the whole range of human experience, but what he was expected to know in the hierarchical society of the late Roman Empire and the Middle Ages was what pertained to his special role. What a man had been called upon to do in the uniform society was to run the gamut of human experience, but what he was called upon to do in the hierarchical society was to play his special role in life. What a man had been permitted to hope in the uniform society was to have lived the equivalent of everywhere and always, but what he was permitted to hope in the hierarchical society, at least in that of the Middle Ages, was to survive death in his public person.

To be immortal in one's public person in the empire was to consort with God, the emperor being in his public person the vicar of God, and to be immortal in one's body public or body politic in the kingdom was to consort with Christ, the king being assimilated in his body politic to Christ in his risen body. The trouble was that God was a God to whom the dead were alive not merely in their public persons but in their private and individual persons, not merely in their bodies politic but in their bodies natural. What is more, if a man had some day to die in his private person or in his body natural, his desire to live was not fully satisfied by survival in his public person or his body politic. Views on the matter had ranged from that of Augustine who had been unwilling to allow that the Roman Empire was in any way the city of God to that of Dante who thought that in the empire man could find an earthly immortality while in the Church he found a heavenly immortality. What ultimately prevailed, though, was the sense of contrast between private mortality and public greatness which appeared in the dance of death, for example, or in the tragedies of Shakespeare, a contrast which made immortal status in the hierarchical society seem empty and futile.

Out of the contrast between greatness and mortality there arose the modern version of the problem of death according to which death, as Hegel said, is the sovereign master of the world. The sovereignty of death spelled the end of the hierarchical society because the great ones of the hierarchical society, if death was sovereign, were not the real masters of the world but the only master was the one to whom they and all other human beings were subject. It meant that God who had been assimilated to the gods of the living and whose vicars the great ones of the hierarchical society had been was now to be assimilated to the gods of the dead and was to become the God of those who were alienated to death. It required that solutions to the problem of death, since the problem was one of alienation to death, be forms of autonomy with respect to life and death, that society provide man with some sort of inalienable hold upon life, either an inalienable right to life which would deprive death of its sovereignty and reduce it simply to an occurrence or else an inalienable disposal over life which would place the power of life and death in the hands of all and give each a share in the exercise of death's sovereignty.

While the inalienable right to life has proved to be as successful a basis for society as any previous solution to the problem of death, inalienable sovereignty over life has proved to be a source of periodic reigns of terror. Terrorism is, in fact, the only way in which the desire to live can be fulfilled when it appears that there is no future but death and when man's desire to live becomes the desire to have life at his disposal. When it appears, on the contrary, that there is some future other than death, then it is possible to renounce or to mitigate the desire to have life at his disposal or to desire instead to enjoy simply the inalienable possession of his own life. What can be known if there is no future beyond the horizon of death is what is within the scope of an autonomous reason; what should be done is what is within the scope of an autonomous conscience; and what may be hoped is what is within the scope of a free and autonomous death. What can be known if there is a future beyond the horizon of death is not only what is within but what is beyond the scope of an autonomous reason, transcendent truth; what should be done is not only what is within but what is beyond the scope of an autonomous conscience, transcendent good; and what may be hoped is not only what is within but what is beyond the scope of a free and autonomous death, transcendent existence.

Of all the solutions to the problem of death which man has found in the course of his long quest for life, the shared experience of life and death, the appropriation of the dead by the living, immortal fame and the immortal past, the uniformity of life, immortal status, autonomous life and autonomous death, there is not one that has fully satisfied his desire to prolong his life indefinitely upon earth. This is why all but the latest ones have been abandoned and why the latest ones, autonomous life and autonomous death, will probably be abandoned in time to come. This is also the best argument for abandoning the will to live itself and for laying hold upon that immortality which has been discovered in the very experience of renouncing the desire to prolong life upon earth, the immortality of the spirit.

For all their shortcomings, nevertheless, man's solutions to the problem of death have not entirely disappointed his anticipations. The experience of life and death has actually been shared, the life of the dead has actually been appropriated by the living, fame has actually been remembered and deeds have been done which actually cannot be undone, the gamut of experience has actually been run, status has actually survived those who enjoyed it, autonomous lives have actually been lived and autonomous deaths have actually been died. Perhaps it would be unreasonable, then, for man to renounce his desire to live, seeing that it can be at least partially satisfied. Perhaps it would be more reasonable simply to recognize that if he must some day die there is nothing he can do that will fully satisfy his desire to live.

What man can know about the meaning of life and death can be measured by what he is able to do about prolonging life and overcoming death. He knows how to share the experience of life and death, how to appropriate the life experience of the dead, how to do deeds which will never be forgotten or which can never be undone, how to run the gamut of experience, how to attain a status which will outlive him, how to live an autonomous life or to die an autonomous death. He even knows how to renounce the will to live. What he does not know how to do is what Christ spoke of when he said "No one takes my life from me, but I lay it down of myself," or he would know how to do this, for he knows how to die an autonomous death, if it were not for what follows, "I have power to lay it down and I have power to take it up again" (John 10:18). Not having the power to lay down his life and take it up again, man cannot know about Christ's Resurrection the way he knows about facts which correspond to what

he himself knows how to do or to experience. He can know it
only as he knows the goal of the quest for life not as he knows his
own attainments on the way to the goal.[3] He can recognize the
goal in the tidings of the Resurrection and, while not living
when and where the Resurrection occurred, in the signs of the
continuing presence of the risen Christ, the Christ who promised
to be with his disciples all days unto the consummation of the
world.

What man should do if he must some day die is be willing to
lay down his life. He may be willing to do this because of what he
has done to satisfy his desire to live, because he has already run
the gamut of experience or because he has attained a status which
will last after him, or he may be willing to do it because laying
down his life satisfies his desire to live, because it means doing
an immortal deed or winning everlasting fame or sharing the
experience of death or allowing his life to be taken up by another, or because the willingness itself is an autonomy with
respect to life and death. Such willingness, though, would be
imperfect since in none of these instances would the will to live
be fully satisfied. He may be willing to lay down his life, on the
other hand, because he has renounced the will to live. But this
willingness would be imperfect too since in spite of being renounced the will to live would persist. He may be willing to lay
down his life, however, because he has renounced not the will to
live but the attempt to satisfy his will to live himself. This, implying as it does that death is not a humanly soluble problem, is
the willingness of which Christ spoke when he said "No one has
greater love than this that he lay down his life for his friends"
(John 15:13). And this greater willingness, more than the willingness of which Pericles spoke, would be the courage that is
freedom and the freedom that is happiness.

What man may hope is not that he may escape death but that
he may, notwithstanding death, satisfy his desire for life. He
may hope by sharing the experience of life and death to consort
with the gods or he may hope that his own experience of life will
be relived by posterity, or, if he despairs of mortals consorting
with immortals and of the dead consorting with the living, he

may at least hope to make the most of his own life and death. He may hope by his deeds to leave an immortal past to those who live after him, he may hope to live the equivalent of everywhere and always, he may hope to survive death in his public person, he may hope for everything within the scope of an autonomous life and an autonomous death. Seeing that life is subject to disease, decay, and death, and is lived in ignorance of its meaning, it is true, he may hope to escape from life and to enjoy instead the immortality of the spirit. If he relies not upon his own knowledge and power, though, but upon that of the God to whom the dead are alive, the God who reveals himself in the risen Christ, he may hope rather to lay down his life subject as it is to evil and to take it up again released from all evil, to do what Christ spoke of when he said "I lay down my life to take it up again" (John 10:17). This is man's last and best hope, the hope Christ has brought to him, the Christ who said "I am the resurrection and the life; he who believes in me, though he be dead, shall live; and whoever lives and believes in me shall never die" (John 11:25f.).

From the age of the gods to the age of God, from the gods of the living and the gods of the dead to the living God and the dead God, the city of man has remained the city of the gods. At first men sought to consort with the gods and hoped when dead to consort with the living. Then they despaired of mortals consorting with immortals and of the dead consorting with the living, but the distinction between the gods of the living and the gods of the dead still remained the framework of their views on life and death, some views entailing an immortality of fame or of the past or a universality of experience in the land of the living and others entailing an immortality of the spirit in the land of the dead. The immortality which consists in being alive to God has never really been at any time the foundation of society but, like mystical immortality which was translated into the mythical deification of kings, has become a basis of society only through a translation into myth, God playing in medieval society a role similar to that of the old gods of the living and in modern society a role similar to that of the old gods of the dead. If ever man should renounce his attempt to satisfy his own will to live, though, without thereby renouncing the will to live itself, if ever the courage that is freedom should become the willingness to lay down his life that is greater than all mortal love and the freedom that is happiness should become the power to lay down his life and the power to take it up again that is greater than all mortal power, then the city of man will have become in truth the city of God.

NOTES TO CHAPTER TEN

1. *Critique of Pure Reason*, 471.

2. The preceding nine chapters are recapitulated in order in this and the following paragraphs.

3. This, I believe, is the distinction to be made in answer to the question as to whether the Resurrection is an empirical fact. For a critique of Bultmann's position on this and for a general critique of his idea of "demythologizing" Christianity cf. my article "Two Contemporary Approaches to Theology" in *Theological Studies*, XXI (1960), 45 ff. and especially 54 ff.

Index